Ashes Taken for Fire

Ashes Taken for Fire

Aesthetic Modernism and the Critique of Identity

Kevin Bell

University of Minnesota Press
Minneapolis · London

Portions of chapter 5 previously appeared as "The Embrace of Entropy: Ralph Ellison and the Freedom Principle of Jazz Invisible," *boundary 2* 30, no. 2 (Summer 2003): 21–45; published by Duke University Press and reprinted with permission. Chapter 6 previously appeared as "Assuming the Position: Fugitivity and Futurity in the Work of Chester Himes," *Modern Fiction Studies* 51, no. 4 (Winter 2005): 846–72; published by The Johns Hopkins University Press and reprinted with permission.

Published by the University of Minnesota Press
111 Third Avenue South, Suite 290
Minneapolis, MN 55401-2520
http://www.upress.umn.edu

Library of Congress Cataloging-in-Publication Data
Bell, Kevin, 1966–
 Ashes taken for fire : aesthetic modernism and the critique of
identity / Kevin Bell.
  p. cm.
 Includes bibliographical references and index.
 ISBN-13: 978-0-8166-4900-6 (acid-free paper)
 ISBN-10: 0-8166-4900-6 (acid-free paper)
 ISBN-13: 978-0-8166-4901-3 (pbk. : acid-free paper)
 ISBN-10: 0-8166-4901-4 (pbk. : acid-free paper)
 1. American fiction—20th century—History and criticism.
2. Modernism (Literature)—United States. 3. English fiction—20th
century—History and criticism. 4. Modernism (Literature)—England.
I. Title.
 PS374.M535B45 2006
 823'.9109112—dc22
                                            2006016780

Printed in the United States of America on acid-free paper

The University of Minnesota is an equal-opportunity educator and employer.

12 11 10 09 08 07   10 9 8 7 6 5 4 3 2 1

Consume, consume: we take ashes for fire . . .
—Raoul Vaneigem
The Revolution of Everyday Life

Contents

Acknowledgments

It is necessary to thank several individuals without whose assistance this book would likely never have appeared.

Kelly Regan's unwavering encouragement of this book, and her imagining of other of our life-works, has for several years been an inexhaustible source of strength. Her many suggestions have been invaluable. There is music to this presence.

The generosity and wisdom of my mentor, Jennifer Wicke, must be recognized from the beginning as being unmatched in intensity, depth, or ingenuity. This is to say nothing of her inarguable style. Her contributions, as must be said of her gifts, are incalculable.

Ulrich Baer's spirited athleticism and tirelessness as a reader is an ongoing model of the ways in which intellectual commitment can also be powerfully poetic.

Phil Harper, Ronald A. T. Judy, Nathaniel Mackey, Perry Meisel, Fred Moten, Aldon L. Nielsen, Avital Ronell, and Hortense Spillers have, in different ways at different moments, provided both abundant intellectual inspiration and hands-on support. Each has offered something in its own way infinite.

Christine Froula has been an exemplary colleague, editor, and mentor at Northwestern University. The same is true of Jennifer Devere Brody, Regina Schwartz, and Julia Stern. In scholars Jorge Coronado, Hannah Feldman, Nasrin Qader, Alessia Ricciardi, and Christopher Yu, I've found perhaps the liveliest critical comradeship one could ask of university colleagues. In Ashley Byock, Paul Flaig, Justin Glick, Deana Greenfield, Brandon Gordon, Kevan Harris, Nicholas Johnson, John McGlothlin, Jarrett Neal, Emma Stapely, and indeed Alissa Tafti, I've found fiercely dedicated students and supremely talented thinkers who have also become friends.

Marianella Belliard, Jeremy Braddock, Jonathan Eburne, Kevin Everson, Tonya Foster, Jessie Labov, Rayna Kalas, Peter Kung, Laurie Monahan, and Joel Wanek are among those animating a conversation on imagistic gravitations and new social contours that I try to extend here.

I thank Richard Morrison, my editor at the University of Minnesota Press, for his sensitive shepherding of this book. His insights can proceed only from a true attunement to its various movements and undercurrents.

I thank Michael Tan for his painfully meticulous reading of the entire manuscript and Carol Lallier for her equally assiduous editing.

The everyday sorcery of the scholars and life-artists who once comprised New Orleans's brilliant Royal Street Circle presents certain ideas I've attempted to redirect or to give new critical shape in these pages. James Anderson Jr., Stephen Casmier, Lynn Casmier-Paz, Christopher Harris, John C. Hill, Joseph Razza III, and Keith Woods continue to create philosophical magic as a matter of routine and necessity. Parts of this work try to at least punctuate a conversation now more than fifteen years in the air.

Even longer ago, the Washington bassist Walter Cosby and the Philadelphia trumpeter Charles Kelly invited me into some of the more obscure dimensions of music and literature. Their friendship and guidance are acknowledged here in gratitude. Equally timeless is the supportive friendship of Mary Grecyzn, Sheala Durant, Suzann King, John A. Mathis, and Rudolph West.

I owe my brother, Christopher Bell, his wife, Faviola, and their children Vanessa, Christopher M., and Briana more than they will ever know, and it is to them, along with my aunt Barbara Jean Bell and my parents, Yvette L. and Michael D. Bell, that this book is dedicated entirely. Our parents tried for many years to show us, among other things, that the greatest truth is likely found in the work and energy by which our own possibilities are created. This book is no more than an opening exploration of some of these.

Introduction: Modernism under the Sign of Suicide

Opening in paradox and never leaving the scene, literary modernism is obsessed with the ways in which language supplants the nothingness that precedes it. More relentlessly than any other, this literature thematizes both the profound absence prior to language and the strategic concealment of that void by language. This book is concerned with how such aesthetic investigations undo the essential logic of cultural identity.

One example is found toward the conclusion of Ralph Ellison's *Invisible Man*. Speaking from within the pirated, artificial light of the Harlem basement that embodies his material inheritance of abandonment, the novel's nameless protagonist admonishes us to embrace the originary paradox that initiates all signification and all culture:

> And the mind that has conceived a plan of living must never lose
> sight of the chaos against which that plan was conceived. (580)

The very structure of this utterance performs the most exhaustive critique of its own history and its own expression available. For it is issued into space and silence by an anonymous unit of fugitivity who, at some point within the circularity of both his narration and his personal progression, has finally come to realize the impoverishment of every external source of authority and validation in which he had formerly been invested. Speaking from the abjected zone of a squatted,

1

slum hovel, his utterance solicits neither the auditors nor the approbation he once craved. Reflecting on what he now sees as the destitution of the legitimating authorities (such as the University or "The Brotherhood") that had once shaped him, he finds in his present isolation a new order of plenitude.

The Invisible Man's narration of his own "fall" out of culture sounds for us at once an acknowledgment and a return of the primary nothingness, the disorientation and nonidentity that he had previously disavowed in favor of the bright world of shining visibility, power and belonging. The stolen light illuminating his stolen apartment allegorizes the concealed instability and actual dispossession of the official, visible world. The 1,369 bulbs transmitting that light chase out the darkness, but they also suggest the proliferation of glittering images by which that world of power and light had so hypnotized him for so long, shutting out the "chaos" it had worked so tirelessly to displace.

This book follows the admonition of the Invisible Man's utterance. It pursues the dark movement of literary modernism's aesthetic inquiry into the nonknowledge, failure, or "chaos" that utilitarian or instrumental language necessarily suppresses. It argues that unlike its romantic or realist precursors, literary modernism, in its British and American contexts, elaborates an idiom for what is denied or lost at the very opening of ideology and instrumentality. This opening is the moment at which the foundational incomprehension that animates all questioning and all wonder is transformed into the fixed transparency of the representational and informational. This study foregrounds modernism's critique of the cultural pressures exerted on individual subjectivity to abandon the ongoing experimentality of its own experience and to abdicate its own potentiality.[1] Such sacrifices are made in exchange for preordained, everyday roles of cultural identity that pretend resolution to that opening by promising an illusory social constancy; by sustaining fictions of "belonging" within a self-securing hierarchy of fabricated categories, kinships, and routines.

This opening, as Ellison's protagonist suggests, is perpetually present, in the sense that no word ever escapes its origin. Its genesis is the anxiety, the hesitant questioning that impels language into existence as a way to name and secure control of experience. But language's connection to the negativity from which it issues is not severed in the moment that it asserts the truth of its references. "Though every term and relation" emerges from and is fused with "the dark night" of such entropy, writes J. Hillis Miller in discussion of T. S. Eliot, "that unity does not vanish in the entities which derive from it."[2] Werner Hamacher finds even more broadly, and just as negatively, that "The aporia incites understanding, but it remains incomprehensible— and with this abyss of understanding, so too does understanding itself."[3] The "blackness" of this zone, limned so customarily in terms of nonknowledge, is rethought in this study as a sphere of unbound improvisation and possibility.

The Ellisonian pronouncement upon the fusion of chaos to conception is here treated as a paradigmatic instance of a problem central to modernism. The question is tracked extensively throughout British texts I consider such as Joseph Conrad's *The Nigger of the "Narcissus"* (1897) and Virginia Woolf's *Jacob's Room* (1922). It drives American works such as William Faulkner's *Light in August* (1932) and Nathanael West's *Miss Lonelyhearts* (1933). It organizes African American texts such as Ellison's 1952 novel and many of the writings of Chester Himes. Tracing the workings of "chaos" and its cultural progeny, we find that few critical accounts offer any sustained analysis of literary modernism's unyielding inquiry into language's incapacity to secure the truth of its own propositions. Fewer still consider the implications of this failure for the logic of cultural identity, devastating as they are for such reductive rubrics as "race" or "gender." But this study takes as its point of departure modernism's embrace and exposition of that incapacity.

The Invisible Man's admonition to respect the chaos that accompanies every presumably untroubled expression of certitude eviscerates the oppositions of mind and reality, history and futurity, subject and object that structure so many works within the traditions of literary romanticism and realism that anticipate the modern. His utterance encapsulates modernism's imagining of subjectivity as an endless interstitiality rather than as any project of identity formation, however liberationist any such formation may be conceived. His words explode the notion of an autonomous perspective that would organize an objective, freestanding world, as if positioned on its outside.

Modernism necessitates instead the thinking of subjectivity as a liquid constellation of singularities of experimentation and experience. It is a constellation whose unfolding always gives the lie to imperatives and systems of social classification, revealing all strategies of definition and naming to be nothing more than discursive instruments of naked power and narcissism. The literature is concerned less with *what* is designated by the names "boss" or "employee," "prince" or "pauper," than it is with the genesis of the desire for each term's exclusivity and finality. It is concerned less with what might be summoned by the terms that ethnicize, sexualize, or gender the play and excess of subjectivity into the comfortable stasis of manageable category or subject positionality, than it is with the *urgency of the summons* itself. For the urgency of the call always exceeds the limit or boundary drawn by the name itself. In the same way, something within its respondent always fails to respond; always there is some stray remainder, some element of singularity that resists conversion from namelessness into identity; from alterity into fixity; from fugitivity into lockdown.

It is only within this sense, one in which the very idea of the subject's scattered opposite can somehow make itself heard, that any references to the term "subject" throughout this book can register meaningfully. For the kind of modernism I analyze here presents a structure of social identification in which there can be no idealized, anthropomorphic paradigm on which to model the fluid reality of self-becoming. Instead, these texts show that all true identification is with forces of motion, energy, and intensity, given tangible body in the concrete matter of personal idiom, affectivity, or *style*—itself the very *surfacing* of thought.

Each chapter in this book pursues the thinking by which British and American modernisms undermine such monumentalizing discourses of knowledge as are introduced by categorizations of cultural identity. For the novels considered here never sacrifice to the empty promises of eternity or belonging the materiality and opacity of language's surfaces. These surfaces are the field upon which movements of fluidity and mutation play themselves out fully in the course of modern literature's becoming.

These affective surfaces of modernist figurality perform in sound, rhythm, cadence, and color an ongoing, explicit, and irreducible politics. For through these attributes, entire ideological frameworks of social classification, positive explanation, and identity are continually exposed to their inherent artificiality and insubstantiality. In this way, literary modernism takes account beforehand of the frequent, authoritarian criticism that it is an essentially aestheticist retreat into unreality. An entire trajectory of critical work, extending from Georg Lukács to such scholars as Fredric Jameson and Hazel Carby presently, has justified the all-but-wholesale dismissal of aesthetic modernism on the grounds of its supposed flight from reality into formalistic ephemerality. While this study's thematic premise is itself an implicit challenge of traditional accounts from such figures as F. R. Leavis and Albert Guerard, who assess modernist works according to a humanist logic of personal alienation by forces of modernity—a logic that these literary texts actually deconstruct in vigorous manner—my attempt to counter the more recent historicist designations of modernism's alleged apoliticism and solipsism is made more overtly.

Such historicist imperatives as Jameson's miss the radical thrust of an art that abjures the presumed responsibility of articulating the world of "real" events through language. Instead, the texts I examine here convert that world momentarily into an instrument by which to foreground the *event* that is *the giving of language itself,* allowing its intonations and intervals to sound their own reality and to open other registers of signification by which those realities less visible or less audible to official history and representational writing might recognize something of their shape or voice. The historical effects that modernism takes as its immediate object are never abandoned by its expressivity. But it is only by way of such expressivity that these effects of official history and politics are made to confront the ongoing possibility of their own emptiness; by way of a literary language that, in refusing to reduce itself to the neutralized function of mere representation, reveals the tension between language and its themes and explodes the regulative authority that strict denotation would pretend to guarantee.

On the contrary, dying in its own commencement, violently shaping itself into a shimmering body of aesthetic difference—always

at the expense of revealing its own inessential and voided origins—
literary modernism, as Walter Benjamin writes in his study of Baudelaire, is an expression that discovers its infinite life in the understanding
that it cancels itself in the moment it is made; in the understanding
that its very utterance is at all times "under the sign of suicide."[4] In
other words, this art becomes art not merely in its thematic dismantling of the determinism and identifying logic of instrumental language's founding urgency, this being to somehow reconstitute the
objects for which it can substitute only at an impossible remove.
Modernist literature becomes literary by finding the value of such
dismantling, or deconstruction, *only in the particularity of its own
forms;* in the realization that it is an always experimental progression
whose transformative power is found only in the body and the tonality, the sight and the suggestiveness of its figuration and its gestures.

What is at stake politically for the works discussed in this book is
the material surfacing of a new testimony to the violence enacted
whenever language successfully conceals the aporia from which it
necessarily emerges. Literary modernism traces the steps of this verbal concealment, unraveling the procedures of an almost automatic,
everyday deception inhering in the very logic of speaking, and in any
labor of communication or representation. For if it is true that "the
function of language is not to inform, but to evoke,"[5] then no instance of communication is ever more than a momentary suture of
the ever-present opening, on its underside, toward a zone of nothingness; of nonknowledge or radical incomprehension. What language
sounds is its wanting for a responsiveness that will somehow address
and respect the anterior incomprehension, disorientation, and wonder that always compels the knowing reassurance of authoritative
speech. This wonder has never disappeared, despite its having been
hidden so deeply by the vocabulary of utility.

Foregrounding this originary zone of abandonment, modernist
literature discovers its aesthetic eternity in the abrogation of any pretense to solution. It finds its truth in its nuanced attunement to and
animation of the color, sound, and texture of the fragment of time
and experience, dislocated from its mythic continuity or its affirmative belonging in a flat linearity of order and meaning. It discovers its
afterlife in the knowledge that the tonal and idiomatic singularity of

its figuration cannot be abstracted into the finality of any one meaning. This figural irreducibility, which eludes every interpretive accounting, lies at the core of the literary modern, structuring its tightly *reflective* relation to the opacity at the opening of language itself.

Returning to this question incessantly throughout his writing, Joseph Conrad meditates in *Heart of Darkness* on the lived consequences of certitude's continual displacement of wonder. Firing blindly into a dark, immobile thicket of dense African vegetation, an anchored French warship off the continent's coastline opens what Conrad's Marlow designates as nothing less than a war on the incomprehensible; a full-scale, material attack on material's presumable opposite. The vertiginous progressions of anxiety identified by Marlow are sent into combat by the threat of nothingness, and are resolvable, it seems, only by openly rioting upon the void. Abandoned in confrontation with this aporetic brush is any inclination toward actual investigation or concrete questioning. Mandated in their place is the militaristic language of mastery and conquest, which in Conrad usually attends the elimination of doubt. At stake in the narration of the one-sided French war on the inscrutable coast are literary modernism's political investments in finding expression for the means by which terror and ignorance are able to convert themselves into domination and authority.

> In the empty immensity of earth, sky and water, there she was, incomprehensible, firing into a continent. Pop, would go one of the six inch guns; a small flame would dart and vanish, a little white smoke would disappear, a tiny projectile would give a feeble screech—and nothing happened. Nothing could happen. There was a touch of insanity in the proceeding, a sense of lugubrious drollery in the sight; and it was not dissipated by somebody on board assuring me earnestly there was a camp of natives—he called them, enemies—hidden out of sight somewhere. (17)

What is "enemy," then, is what is "hidden": that which is not readily accessed by the investigative machinery (or the materiality) of authority itself. What is "enemy" is designated as such on the basis of its

invisibility, or its withdrawal from any logic of untroubled identifia-
bility within an accepted order of valuations. Beyond this logic of
mastery is the unseen singularity that resists the demand for its conversion into an object of recognition, and is therefore outlaw. Outside
of Marlow's simultaneously authoritative and anxious recording of
the scene, its only historicizing agents are the sonic "pop" of the
French gunfire, the darting flames, and vanishing wisps of smoke
curling from the gun barrels in the field of vision. Disappearing into
the void they are supposed to combat, the shots' sound and image
provide the only testimony to the actual movement of imperial decision, power, and progress. What insists itself into reality during the
course of reading is the urgency with which images of nothingness,
silence, and ocular darkness are consistently evoked in terms of antagonistic dread:

> Land in a swamp, march through the woods, and in some in-
> land post feel the savagery. The utter savagery had closed round
> him. . . . There's no initiation either into such mysteries. He has
> to live in the midst of the incomprehensible which is also de-
> testable. And it has a fascination too, that goes to work on him.
> The fascination of the abomination—you know. Imagine the
> growing regrets, the longing to escape, the powerless disgust,
> the surrender—the hate. (10)

The fact of the journey's moving into an otherness—designated as
such by an organizing view (Marlow's) that never takes into account
its own status as merely a single projection among others—only begins to suggest what is at stake in the text's staging of the psychic
intolerance of nothingness and nonknowledge. For the irony structuring Marlow's representation of "horrific" incomprehension lies in
that very representation's complete absence of active substantiality.
For instance, there is "the utter savagery" that one might supposedly
"feel," whose only actual fabric is the dark stillness of the woods; or
the "inscrutable" African shipworkers, described so casually and frequently as "cannibals" by Marlow, without the novella's containing a
single instance of human flesh being consumed. Such characterization underscores the philosophical and figural negativity by which

the text's installation of empty incomprehension is made central to its interpretation. The entire narrative of movement from "Outer" Station to "Central" Station to "Inner" Station, culminating in arrival at the very "heart" of darkness—which itself consists only in the drone of Kurtz's "discoursing"—is saturated by the images of "detestable" abyss, always in terms of fear or "the horror." The very object of the journey, Kurtz himself, is described as being "hollow at the core" (55).

In this way, a principle of fissure emerges as the text's signature. For the relentless exposure of its characters to the nothingness at the center of culture produces a purity of terror that breaks away from the smooth rationality or consistency of its narrators' speech. In so splitting itself, such writing creates a dark poetry of the void's iconography.

In literary modernism, the flight out of affirmative, subjectivist economies of recognition and identification never leaves the scene of the everyday, instead generating itself from the banality of the pedestrian. It is the tonality of modernist prose such as Conrad's that summons the anonymous experience of social realities that unfold outside the connectivity of denotative discourse. Modernism is distinguished by this incessant thematization of its fundamental disengagement from strict designation—by its ongoing encounter with the presence of its own nothingness. This is announced (as that nothingness is also) at every moment of assertive speech. For to what prior demand does such speech respond? Whose doubts does such assertion hope to eliminate before its own? This book asks how these novels keep radically open this space of an inarticulate, yet absolutely essential demand prior to language. They do so, I argue, by working in affective modes that derail denotation, go astray, and in their errancy, reorient the project of reading.

At the same time, this art's very figuration in word leaves it totally powerless to escape the fundamental implication that it bears a solid meaning. Indeed, modernism's notoriously difficult figurality always generates a multiplicity of longing gestures toward gesture's opposite—substantiality. Such longing for the reassuring solidity of meaning relies upon categories of knowledge and identity that are themselves organized by the self-established protocols of a culture whose functions and images throughout modernity have been almost entirely determined by the drives of commercial power to install within culture new needs, and to extract mass obeisance to those needs. Such automatized systems of valuation and identity prop up a culture that ultimately bends our lives toward samenesses and satisfactions that we ourselves do not request or create.

The literature discussed in these pages, however, begins and ends within differentiality and dissatisfaction. Such art produces different avenues of duration that dissolve, expand, circle, split further, recombine, and allow for multitudes of interpretive and material effects unavailable within humanist frameworks of identitarian thinking. These spasmodic effects and experiences are undetectable within accepted orientations of history or politics—indeed, they are depreciated only by the idea of culture itself and are violently reified in the moment they are (mistakenly) codified in language. They are recognized in their truth only when the utter impossibility of rendering them in terms outside the opacity of their own is acknowledged. "There are no words for the sort of things I wanted to say," says Conrad's Lord Jim.

Or, in a passage from Avital Ronell on the emergence of the written modern:

> At about the same time as Romanticism turned it into the seriousness of *oeuvre*, literature initiated the experience of its own substance: organized by a concept of work, it soon came to know play's gravity. Such gravity exposed the work to experiences of peril and experimentation, obligating literature to map out a toxicogeography—an imaginary place where literature could crash against its abysses and float amid fragments of residual transcendency. The engagement with its essence threw literature off any predictably legible course but also created the mirage of a genuine autonomy.[6]

In literary modernism, not only is impression the fabric of the real; not only is sensation the living inversion of fantasy; but also style, intensity and tonality of movement, phrase, color, and sound are themselves the surfaces—and therefore the truest substances—of thought. In this art, language is no longer the transparent vehicle of the informational, but is always the living echo, or the mobile extension of a foundational abyss. Language is the always futile attempt to close an anterior void of knowledge and certitude, against which instrumental speech and all its localized lines of discourse are elaborated positively, as wishfully impenetrable mechanisms of defense. Silences and ellipses, fragments and cries do not merely punctuate but *saturate* the language of these texts, making plain the excess of meaning that overburdens every term by which any character or any idea might try to demonstrate the completeness of its self-mastery. In each work analyzed, the foundational incomprehension that Ellison and Eliot, Miller and Hamacher all acknowledge takes center stage, breaking incessantly into the world of power, action, and visibility; it is manifest in continual collapses of cognition and verbal breakdowns of self-articulation and representation.

Modernism stages the futility of culture's defensiveness against this collapsing, not in the form of an aggressive topical attack or a resentful stance of oppositionality, as if somehow perched outside ideology and language. Instead, it playfully deconstructs its own assemblage from within conventional systems of language and history. Working within language, the modern necessarily performs its complete indebtedness and even enslavement to the historical and cultural inscriptions of the systems that produce it.

But it also relentlessly tracks and illuminates the methods by which such systems muzzle the reality and force of competing idioms of affectivity, gesture, and silence. Conventional systems of history, politics, and language establish cultural dominance precisely by sustained repression of their own zones of passivity, doubt, and self-questioning. Modernism, however, inverts culture's disavowal of its own self-doubts by foregrounding the techné of communication. It draws attention to those irruptions of personal and verbal affectivity that are not managed or dominated by communication's intentionality.

Of Apaches and Ragmen

For Walter Benjamin, such an insistently negative logic of abandon and subverted referentiality openly pervades Baudelaire's cultural sphere, one in which thinking sensibilities must look to culture's discarded margins, to the impoverished "refuse of society," to disengage from the incessantly celebratory self-affirmations of market-driven sociality. Benjamin notes that in Baudelairean modernism, the abandoned figures of "the apache" and "the ragpicker" are elevated to the status of aesthetic icons by their very survival within a society that reveres only the "certified, official subjects, our victories and our political heroism."[7] "[T]he apache abjures virtue and laws" while the ragpicker, in his patience and discernment, embraces the social otherness of devalued things, reading and breathing into them new, hermeneutically singular life:

> Here we have a man who has to gather the day's refuse in the capital city. Everything that the big city threw away, everything it lost, everything it despised, everything it crushed underfoot, he catalogues and collects. He collates the annals of intemperance, the capharnaum (stockpile) of waste. He sorts things out and makes a wise choice; he collects, like a miser guarding a treasure, the refuse which will assume the shape of useful or gratifying objects between the jaws of the goddess of Industry.[8]

To the materials of waste discarded by utilitarian cultures of commerce and then reanimated via the negative dialectical practices of the wasted or marginalized themselves, this study adds but a single crucial one. This would be the very inchoate difference and multiplicity of the always *yet-to-be* subject of modernity.[9]

At no point divergent from the surface materiality of its phenomenal existence, the subject of modernism is most properly not any subject at all, at least not one of discrete, continuous social autonomy. It is hardly any self-contained, cohered being whose idiomatic habits of action and affect correspond neatly to its representations or private identifications. It is rather an anthropomorphic vessel of incessantly contravening material/cultural/historical inscriptions, a vessel of an ongoing *promise* of consistency. It is simultaneously structured and annihilated by a perpetual series of disconnected perceptual interventions or cuts—linguistic as well as visual, affective as well as ideological—inscribed at every moment of everyday life on the sensorium.

This perpetually deferred "subject" is written into the finality of determination and linear history only by its endurance and internal-izing of the psychic violence of these external markings and cuts. Only through the violence of experience and language, through the ideo-logical script that preordains its naming and symbolic mut(il)ation, does the body of this would-be subject claim "its" space of unique isolation, its own zone of alienated privation that, in truth, is not even its own.

Such cardboard distinction is achieved in the very moment when this would-be subject is paradoxically vaporized and vivified by its linguistic abstraction into the static life of representation and object-hood. The social reality of this subject appears only after the willed termination of radical subjectivity itself, by which I mean, after the abandonment of its own wonder, after its required acceptance of the very idea of its social positionality. Such self-establishment is never more than its total subjection to language, definition, and societal role-play. This administered identity is an endless double movement, toward and away from freedom, toward the inheritance of the aspira-tions and responsibilities defined and disseminated by official market culture, and away from the infinite "difference for the sense" by which the child first experiences the material world outside its body.[10] It is necessary, therefore, to follow modernism's conceptual flight out of the critical commonplaces of cultural identity and the subject-bound logic of identification in its received philosophical and psycho-analytic interpretive contexts.

Literary modernism disables the traditional notion of cultural identity, exposing it as nothing more than a walking, talking satellite of ideology, a projection of sovereignty that, in its being administered from elsewhere, performs a total repudiation of actual individuation. Instead, what passes for individuality becomes only another signa-ture of the completeness with which one has invested in the desires one has inherited from ideology's dissemination of images as ideals and values. What results is the total obliteration of any presumable distance or opposition between those who produce images and those who consume and repeat them. Social positionality becomes its own desire. It is the product purchased by the would-be subject who, in performing it, abrogates the differential processes of his or her own becoming. Content instead to accept his or her predesignated social role, he or she conflates the script of that objectified role with actual life, or what other modernists, such as Fernando Pessoa, term "true" or "radical" subjectivity.[11]

However, it is the resistant character of the modernist nonsubject's own figurality, its unique idioms of presentation, that never fail to betray the efficiency of the exchange of negativity for positivity, or of differentiality for the permanence of identity. This conversion into fixity is never finalized or perfected, its crystallization always deferred or blocked by that unruly remainder of figurality that eludes the logic of transparency and meaning. This remainder cuts or distorts the presumptive content of every utterance, every articulation, and every classification of discourse, disclosing the real immanence of surface affectivity in everyday life. At the level of figurality, every expression finds its liberator and its inescapable regulator at once, governed as that expression is by the necessity that it break, that it surface, that it show itself outwardly in shape, sound, or color by way of a texture, cutting its way into the differential field of the audible and the visible.

This book suggests nothing less than to read modernism as the inscription of this expressivity—before, beyond, and outside the inscriptions that lock authors, texts, and readers into comforting subject positions and allow texts to be disposed of as "conservative" or "revolutionary," as "minority discourse," "feminist," or "queer." The literature stages a violent confrontation between the multiplicity of fluid subjectivity and the cultural imperatives of positionality that conspire to lock that fluid vessel—that fugitivity—into a mythic unit of coherence and designation that might be named authoritatively, without risk of any stray, resistant remainder that would contravene or escape the project of its definition.

Another way to put this is to say that this work investigates the ways in which literary modernism animates the formative pivot between subjective aporia and subjective arrest. This is the space in which this yet-to-be subject resides uneasily prior to claiming itself as such in the ecstatic, agonistic moment of fracture during which it at once aggressively assumes and passively accepts public designation as one thing or another. For it is in this moment that the inchoate subject is simultaneously elevated to the status of "autonomous" agent in culture and diminished to the status of rank object in language.

Complying lovingly with its own interpellation into yet another object of social representation, identifying with a discursive force of power that will annihilate its idiomatic exceptionality, while at the same time granting it the powerful semblance of self-determination, this would-be subject turns its back on exactly that idiosyncratic mode of its own impressionistic blindness (and insight) that would actually guarantee its own radical differentiation within culture, if also its material consignment to culture's margins or gutters, alongside "the apache" and "the ragman."

Slaves without Masters

At the surfaces of the body rest and rage whatever potentialities exist for all historical, political, and cultural formation. These potentialities simultaneously explode and expire in the moment of their verbal articulation as an "I," for the utterance of this differentiating and at the same time profoundly mimetic "I" is addressed not only to its anthropomorphic other of everyday sociality and exchange but also to its *ontological* other and origin, the entropic space of the former absence of the "I"—the void against which its naming is only a reactive tactic of combat. Sounded as a defense against the frightful abyss that is its birthplace, the utterance of the "I" enacts a final self-arrest, even as it enunciates an always experimental release of self-expression— experimental not only in the sense that it has no control over how or even whether it will be received by its auditor but also in the sense that however compliantly, the utterance always emerges from the negated underside of a power whose centralization is already long-established. The "I" originates in exposure to its own dispossession; it issues from a zone of uncertainty that seeks resolution, recognition, and validation of its autonomy in the response of a source to which it is completely external.

In this way, modernist subjectivity is seen to be the paradoxical outcome of an anterior coercion. For it is never more than a forced exchange of one's unique diversity of inscriptions and impressions in return for the monoregistration of one metaphysically contrived and necessarily abstract rubric of social identity or another, such as "ethnicity," "religion," "sexual orientation," "race," "gender," or "class," to name only a few of the broader cultural classifications that are so pervasive and so unquestioned within culture as to appear by now completely naturalized.

In its subjection to language, the symbolic matrix in which the status of social positionality is conferred and confirmed via the recognition of another within the political grammar of cultural identity, the assumption of such an identity emerges as a self-protective and self-perpetuating strategy of foreclosing its own uncertainty—its own excess—of experience. In its claim of pure identity and autonomy under some unitary social code of masculinity or femininity, or of racialized "whiteness" or "blackness," or of professional or classed status, this being reassures itself of its own mythic agency only in the slavishly mimetic articulation of an absolute dependency. It is a dependency on what is gained by this subject when he or she internalizes the logic of social categoricity—a categoricity that is itself brought into existence as an ideological instrument of division and power.

And at the same time, what is required of this being is a complete forgetting of the disorientation that formerly opened the world to wonder, an abandonment of the irruptions of tonal experience that are nullified by the ideological ordering of world and life into classificatory regime. Such irruptions of texture, color, and tone are now designated under the rubric of excess, superfluous to any project of propriety and definition.

This abandonment of abandonment itself is central to the pursuit of any identity that unfolds within the boundaries of practical sociality. Everyday practices of communication necessarily keep themselves insensate not only to the phenomenality of the sonority and figure by which each term would take on singular contour, but also to the density of the nonlanguage that is all but obliterated by the emergence of utilitarian speech. Such are the daily practices of flattened or deintensified communication that by remaining deaf and blind to the diversely provocative velocities, rhythms, and intervals of language, they would deprive all subjects constructed therein of the very firmament of difference that the irreducibly idiosyncratic singularities of syntax and vocabulary actually help to install.

Whatever narcissism carries art, philosophy, speech, and their interpretations out of the abyss is not a negative trait of "personality" that alone should connote derogatory social valuations. The very narcissism that enables communication by allowing one the confidence that his or her thinking will be of value for someone else is one of the rewards of the Hegelian battle that makes masters of some and slaves of others who imagine themselves only within subjectivist zones of social recognition and identification. The mimetic recognition for which this battle is waged in Hegel's *The Phenomenology of Spirit* breaks from the habits of questioning already driving sensibility and thought by the time such conflict takes place. These habits negotiate the amorphous, transient world of images, sensations, and perceptions that already inscribe memory and subjectivity.

With the appearance of a "rival," however, this transient world is supplanted by the world of conception and the sharply vivid portrait of a knowing, masterful humanity. The imagery of sovereignty in relation to the other orients the fight among beings competing for the status of subjecthood's prestige, and is the only means by which they can elevate themselves above what Alexandre Kojève, following Hegel, calls "mere thingness." To enter into this scene of combat is, in one sense, to give up the entropic impressionism of T. S. Eliot's amorphous "immediate experience," so as to establish a differentiated position within a cultural matrix of "legitimacy" and "value."

In other words, to collect on the promise of affirmation from another, thinking life must identify paradoxically with an agency installed from outside it. It must perform another's idea of what sovereignty means. To fight is actually to implicate oneself passively within an economy of inherited values and desire. To kill, with the supposed aim of establishing the self as sovereign and as desirable in the eyes of another, one must live by a purely mimetic imperative that from the start undoes the very idea of sovereignty. The spirit of sheer violence and sacrifice to which the master submits himself fanatically to win, blinds him to the intensity of his own zeal and to the completeness of his dependency on the confirming gaze of another—even an eviscerated and beaten other. To fully enjoy his lordship, the master must simultaneously celebrate and repress that his sense of self-value necessarily derives from elsewhere, even from Marlow's jungle of so-called cannibals. The master dares not consider his own sovereign existence without affirmation from what is radically separate—and is, in that sense, no less a slave than his cowering opponent.[12]

But in the slave's total exclusion from the flattened prestige of such a circumscribed sovereignty, he discovers another order of life. Within the abjection of his toil, he *lives* the mobile experience of change, experiencing the transfiguring movement of radical nega- tion. The labor of his body transforms raw material into material of a unique functionality; the witnessing and enduring of the transfor- mation he has wrought transforms him.

The Metaphysics of "Materialism"

In its suggestion of liquefied referentiality and dissolved values, liter- ary modernism enacts its emancipation from the recognizability of writing itself. The totality of this emancipation is heard in the dis- junctive cut marked *by* its very writing—the cut that dispossesses any referent of its presumed place at the center of discourse and so dis- possesses the presumed self-mastery of its speaker and its auditor. "If language can become complete, as poetry asks it to," Maurice Blan- chot writes, "if it can be completely realised, either by becoming an ability to say or to hear previous to any sayer and any listener . . . it must overtake language and, each instant expressing itself as totality, each instant be completely outside of language."[13]

This means that the overtaking of the utilitarian function by the intensity and the sonority of the utterance disconnects language from the presumption of a purely informational functionalism and signals its "totality" or its fusion with an unadministered, always fugitive re- ality. This reality is the chaotic zone in which language's imperatives commence. Blanchot's poetry, as described above, announces its con- nection with this zone by preventing the reassurance of anything like the familiarity of form from establishing itself as such. It thereby dis- allows itself the claim of function, at least as any kind of guiding pat- tern or prescriptive frame.

What emerges is one of the "new idioms" so strikingly demanded by Jean-François Lyotard in *The Differend*.[14] It is an expressivity that need not find its shape within accepted language to be respected in the moment of its utterance. It is the articulation of an experience that would "be smothered right away" in the commerce of cognitive, denotative languages of exchange—and may retain its meaning only in such ruptures of denotation as the sounding of a scream, a sigh, or a laugh; in the rhythm of a jaunt or a limp; or in an impassive folding of the hands. This kind of expressivity bears mobile attributes of the affective life that is so casually and so completely obliterated by the official imperatives of the instrumental in daily sociality that our alienation from such affective life may no longer occur to us as being in the least bit alienating.

Modernist figurality, however, as viewed from certain other critical trajectories that themselves proceed from more narrowly schematic conceptions of the political and the historical, delegitimates itself in a solipsistic and effeminized egoism.

Such conceptions insist on the notion that literary modernism works in the service of a self-isolated "I" that, in the stupor of its endless self-contemplation, divorces itself from all "proper" sociopolitical commitment to the concrete interests of a denuded, collective "mass"—one necessarily reduced and deformed by the very naming of the concept into which its constituents are herded. What this disparagement of aesthetic modernism necessarily overlooks is its own originary destitution, a lack that motivates its own announcement of its being an effectively "oppositional" art and criticism. The violence of such a procedure depends on a silence central to its very articulation. For its reading of modernism reveals itself to be only another offspring of the modern-*ity* it believes itself to critique. By way of example, we witness certain moments in the work of Fredric Jameson, whose concern with modernism orients the political thrusts of certain generative, if often contradictory, critical responses.

While he does not subscribe to the antiexperimentalism of Georg Lukács (who by the time of his "The Ideology of Modernism" in 1957, is, to say it mildly, a more politically ossified and pontificatory Lukács than the author of the invaluable "Reification" essay of 1923), recognizing its "shrill and outrageous" crudity,[15] Jameson seems not much more impressed with the later arguments of Lyotard or Paul de Man, both of whom, in stressing the incommensurability of the utterance and the object of its reference, proceed, in Jameson's account, to "go all the way and affirm the ultimately scandalous position that language is inhuman."[16] In so doing, they fashion a philosophy of experimental figurality and linguistic materiality that undermines the imperatives of referential realism and historical periodization to

which Jameson is so attached conceptually.[17] This is evident when
Jameson writes that Lyotard is some sort of "closet" modernist whose
"ostensible postmodernism" keeps "hidden" an elitist "aesthetic modernism" that is somehow "embarrassing" for him; in Jameson's view,
only such a philosophical repression could account for the "outrageous position that postmodernism does not follow but actually
precedes, true modernism as such, whose return it prepares."[18]

   The Lyotard who insists repeatedly that philosophy must learn to
"bend itself" to the fluid demands of aesthetic thinking—thinking
that unfolds less in the prescriptive or descriptive discourse of an already given "humanity" than in the specific tonalities of art's color,
line, and pitch[19]—is adjudged by Jameson to be working "in the
spirit" of the "high modernism" of Theodor Adorno. In Jameson's
view, Lyotard's urging of aesthetic experiment is only an ornamental
means to an explicitly politicized thrust enabling Lyotard to claim "a
certain kind of revolutionary stance."[20]

   The problem here lies in Jameson's hesitance to see or hear that in
the critical sphere momentarily housing the fractiously conjoined Lyotard and Adorno, the utter abandonment of representationality in
modernism cannot be said at the same time to perform the utterly
representational task of situating itself as any substitutional stance
that would immediately accomplish something beyond the exercise
of its own form. No formal abandon theorized by either Lyotard or
Adorno could produce anything other than the experience—the
event—of a crucial epistemic vanishing, let alone posture as any self-
consciously rebellious or antagonistic "avant-garde" oppositionality.
The politics of these thinkers' (post)modernisms are addressed less to
the retrospectively conjured critical "stances" of modern artworks
than they are to the futuristic demand that these works come into
being. They are addressed to the ways in which the works' internal
specificities of color, line, and pitch necessarily disrupt whatever narratives of meaning in theme and coherence in design they might be
presumed to present. For Lyotard as well as for Adorno, this demand
is as deeply embedded in the historical circumstances of time and
place as it is sharply defined by its need to reveal the inadequacy of informational language to articulate the full reality of those circumstances. The demand, as each thinker hears it, is for the artwork to

evoke new modes of imagining such concepts as art itself, alongside accepted notions of history, tradition, and identity—so as to make us aware of the questions, forms, and practices of life that such given notions exclude. For each thinker, each artwork of this kind *enacts the impossibility of its success,* suspending figurally the final closure of meaning that would constitute such "success" and thereby opening an ongoing series of critical gestures toward the lie of culture's coerced consonances.

With this in mind, it becomes somewhat easier to see why Jameson, however defensively, aligns the "postmodern" figural thinking of Lyotard with the "high-modernism" of Adorno's aesthetic theory. In Lyotard's well-known thesis, "modernism" is shot through with an ultimately nostalgic reinscription of traditional ideological practices by which such pieties as the conventional notion of "art" are established and perpetuated in the first place. Individual works by such writers as Proust, however adventurously conceived, finally reinsert themselves into existing quarters of tradition by articulating even the most unpresentable thought within the reassuring tones of what Lyotard calls "good forms," themselves produced by "the consensus of a taste which would make it possible to share collectively the nostalgia for the unattainable."[21] He takes sharpest issue with what he sees as Adorno's Enlightenment-inspired notion of art as a zone in which critical thought can raise itself to its highest expression, and by which "Artists and writers must be brought back into the bosom of the community, or at least, if the latter is considered to be ill . . . must be assigned the task of healing it."[22] In Bill Readings's analysis, Lyotard dreams of an art that will "displace the rule of truth" altogether, instead of finding truth inside a grander, redemptive social paradigm served uniquely by a simultaneously innovative and subservient figurality.[23]

At the same time, the liberatory opacity in such works as those produced by Joyce, that for Lyotard shakes itself free of modernist pieties, must be acknowledged to correspond with important moments in the negative aesthetic procedures of Adorno. For to what else does Adorno refer when he deflates the criticism of Samuel Beckett's works as absurd, writing that "Beckett's plays are absurd not because of the absence of meaning, for then they would be simply irrelevant, but because they put meaning on trial; they unfold its history. . . . Artwork that rigorously negates meaning is by this very rigor bound to the same density and unity that was once requisite to the presence of meaning."[24] At stake here is nothing less than the displacement of "the rule of truth" or the abolishing of the position of legislative discourse at stake in Lyotard. In ways that must be seen as more incendiary precisely at the joints of their incompatibility, Lyotard and Adorno each advocate artworks that make us realize, in the incomprehensibilities they produce, the truth of the incomprehensibility that initiates their movement as artworks—that which induces the very demand for another idiom of expressivity. The more general argument of this book is that the gestural ineffability by which the signature of Beckett's plays is made so palpable must also be read as a strong reverberation of another interpretive impossibility, set into motion by the self-suspending gestures that so plainly characterize the works of the writers discussed in this book—figural gestures that have frequently been received in critical discourse as aestheticist elaborations, bereft of cultural critique or even investment, and that have been, in certain cases, read even as thematic defenses against such critique.

The trope of disparagement by which Jameson designates the "minority 'elite' modernism in which our thinking about aesthetics today is inevitably locked," a view expressed elsewhere in his writing, functions, however reluctantly, as a latent reinforcement of the Lukácsian theory of modernist detachment and solipsism that he disavows as vulgar.[25] What he rejects in fact, however, is the realization that such "solipsistic" art can materialize only in its necessarily *outward* "ignition" upon the very sociopolitical reality that, as art unbound from any presumptive obligation to represent anything, it is bound, finally, to turn away from later.[26] This necessary second part of the equation, the realm in which modernist art answers to no materiality other than that found in its own fabric and body, is what antagonizes the modes of historicism exemplified by Jameson and a host of critical allies.[27]

For instance, a frequently brilliant and incisive essay by Hazel Carby can be said to sacrifice some of its power by channeling a Jamesonian definition of modernism that for all its influence still seems uncharacteristically one-dimensional when compared to much of his other work. In a piece from her book *Race Men*, titled "The Body and Soul of Modernism," Carby accepts Jameson's notion of "the modernist aesthetic" being no more than the apolitical, solipsistic "strategy of inwardness" that he had announced it to be in 1979.[28] While arguing forcefully that Nickolas Muray's 1925 series of photographs of Paul Robeson imperiously appropriates and indeed invents racialist images of what is from its conception a "blackness" brutally reduced and reified in a manner completely consistent with the murderous gaze of the lynch mob, Carby ultimately ascribes Muray's project to a customarily subjectivist and solipsistic, or simply "inwardly" oriented aesthetic modernism.

Carby writes that Muray's photographs demonstrate that to "modernist imaginings, Paul Robeson offered the possibility of unity for a fractious age."[29] Her frequent use of the term "modernist imaginings" acknowledges the source of its unitary conception to be Jameson's formulation of modernism being primarily a genre made of various "strategies of inwardness" by which to combat "the tensions, anxieties and contradictions of the modern age." Not only in its vocabulary but also in its very accents, Carby's piece appears to recognize as "modernist" only the inherited image of modernism as the romanticized and detached art of alienation, repeating the premise of modernism being simply a frustrated and hungry, Eliotic/Leavisite art of those starved for the prelegislated values and icons of a now-disappeared premodernity, of tragically forgotten transcendent meanings and a unified, even "noble" consciousness. While the racialist reductiveness of Muray's project is not questioned here, its attribution to a modernism that is defined only in terms of subjectivist alienation and longing for unity falsifies the endlessly dispersive movements of an aesthetic language far more self-interrogative and self-suspending than such limited projects as Muray's.

This Jamesonian dismissal of modernism as being uncomplicatedly "bourgeois" and "elitist," depends not only on an avoidance of contravening theorizations of differentiality in modernist expression from the "Frankfurt School" through to Jacques Derrida, Paul de Man, and the trajectories of deconstructive critique proceeding from or orbiting around theirs—it relies also upon the complete noninterrogation of other tracks of Marxist thought whose relative "progressiveness" is seldom said to be fatally compromised by its ability to consider art and aesthetic questions without "bending" these to its own needs and who, indeed, appear able to accomplish quite the opposite, yielding their own habits of discourse to the tonal or gestural specificities, nondiscursive though they may be, of art and literature. These would include not only Benjamin, Adorno, and contemporaries such as Ernst Bloch, but would extend also to figures as disparate as Jean-Paul Sartre, Louis Althusser, Henri Lefebvre, Cornel West, and Stuart Hall.

Such criticism as Jameson's and, in these isolated moments, Carby's demands an art that replicates a tightly determined antagonistic "reality," in which the forces of political liberation are seen clearly to be locked in battle against equally obvious forces of oppression. The figurality of art—the materiality intrinsic to the flows and shudders, drives and hesitations of its thinking and its expressivity, in the works of such modernists as Woolf, Ellison, or Conrad—is not met or engaged by the binarism of this critical structure. Indeed, in the Carby essay, Robeson—who as an artist, is described essentially as the unwitting dupe of a uniformly and inherently elitist, politically indifferent modernism—is recuperated only by his subsequent political activism, by a lifelong "stand" in which his variously extraordinary artistic gifts are positively abandoned and his work is "wrenched . . . away from performative associations with modernist strategies of inwardness (in which he) acted in defiance of all cultural aesthetics that denied or disguise(d) their political implications."[30]

Criticism of this kind, at least in the instances referenced, appears impermeable to those dimensions of experience that disclose no readily apparent "political" utility. It signals a deep distrust of those experiences that cut or inscribe outside denotative language. Such is a criticism that in the imagining of its own transparency, actually finds the greatest point of commonality with the powers of ideological domination (state and capital) that are its preestablished objects of attack. Tailored to the patterns of established realist imperatives that insist on linguistic immediacy, transparency, and universality without acknowledging the absence of skepticism about the terms and values they inherit from the agencies of power they oppose, and with little provision at all for the independent errancy and ineffability of its figurality, this "materialist" analytic reduces itself to a dogmatic claim of right or truth whose investment in the fact of its own positionality, however antagonistic to those more dominant, locks itself into the tightest discursive kinship with those presumptive antagonists.

Edouard Glissant blazes a clear path for us when he writes:

> It is not certain that in the West materialism does not some-times appear as the metaphysical adjunct of idealism. Since it is the same view of history, it can support the most intolerant form of transcendentalism.[31]

Glissant is sensitive to the necessity of cutting loose those stances that claim to produce a certain political *effect* without respect to the inescapable questions of material *affect* that inform them and are then completely disavowed. By adopting the identificatory logic and vocabulary of domination, such materialism demonstrates a core mimeticism, only reversing the antagonistic tables of class and ideology that alone give it meaning. The values of the identitarian thinking necessary to the construction of any hierarchy of force, instead of being exploded by much materialist literary analysis, are there frequently repeated, reflected, and reinstalled. There is no transvaluation in such materialism.

The disparaging post-Lukácsian strain of historical materialism that today so easily dismisses aesthetic thinking within the various fields of cultural studies, converts its textual tone-deafness, its readerly color-blindness, its apparently complete foreclosure of sensory rupture and arrest, into a point of political honor.[32] Its rigid joylessness before a literature of percept and alterity *that is at all points material itself* becomes an insignia of political rectitude, commitment, and responsibility. The ineffability of the modern constitutes as much of a nuisance to this supposedly radicalized legislative body of critical thought as it does to the static cultural strata of ideological domination, convention, and propriety it so displaces and scandalizes when and wherever it surfaces. The irruptiveness of modernist inhumanism throws harsh light on the curiously conservative, Leavisite aspect of this presumably fiery "materialism."

For modernism's disengagement from the logic of unmediated identity and determination, from the flatness and one-dimensionality of the historical or anthropological fact, and from the self-centralizing

"I" of subjectivity and "we" of community, necessarily gives no answer to the Althusserian hailing of laws mandating determination or
positionality. After Ellison's protagonist in *Invisible Man* makes an
impassioned speech protesting the eviction of an elderly Harlem
couple and is then invited to work for "The Brotherhood," he resists,
explaining "I have no more interest in those old folks than I have in
your job. I wanted to make a speech. I like to make speeches" (293).
His intensifying recognition of self through the exercise and style of
his expression illustrates the political charge found within any insistence on stylization. In no way is such an insistence necessarily dependent on the work's content or its object. Its *charge* cannot be
ascribed to any imperative beyond its expressivity; its fascination
does not owe to anything other than its exposition.

A text such as Ellison's concerns itself with the plurality of forces
that first demand and install laws of social interpellation and the sociality it organizes. But it is just as occupied with those laws governing the verbal and significative relations between provocative surface
elements within language itself. In relinquishing the thinking of a
self-identical "self," a surrender hardly altruistic but, on the contrary,
even devastating, the strains of modernism discussed here reanimate
the dialectical brutalities of social interpellation imaginatively. These
texts create constellations of experience within which the notion of a
subject answerable to a rubric of identity is shown at all times to ex-
ceed, undermine, and even contradict the designations by which that
would-be subject is recognized socially. It is a subjectivity able to become, actively, only by ceasing to be, passively—in the restrictive
terms of its cultural recognition or identification. This is a continual
becoming within the movement of a modernism painting in sound,
writing in color, fighting for life, in narrative.

The Blackness of Modernism

Silently communicating a warrior's willingness to embrace his own
death and to suspend the self-affirming consolations of linguistic and
cultural referentiality (or rather, its incessant promise), both the
enigmatic art and black clothing of Baudelaire's Parisian poets and
conspirators of the mid- to late 1840s give testimony to a concentrated and violent strength in the face of hegemonic cultural impera-

tives toward finite designation and determinism.[33] This strength is found in the fluid materiality of textual modernism, a hardness within the porous molecularity of a warlike fictional, mobilized under a program of paradox that can be articulated only by the terms of its divorce from the very notion of the programmatic.

Surfaces of writing open for us the perspective within which modernist expression produces artworks that perform their own endless self-critique. Perspectives of literary modernism in English are formed by rhythms, textures, and images that extend alongside discourses of meaning that they cannot help but undercut. Affectivity, in all its apparent emptiness and banality, is the only point of entry for modern literature's philosophical critiques of domination. As Emmanuel Levinas writes in a different, yet resonant context, it is a zone in which:

> The face is the personality—but in its manifestation, its externalization and reception; in its original frankness. The face is of itself, and, if I may express it so, the mystery of all clarity, the secret of all openness.[34]

Modernism's faces, its stylized exteriors, are the material signatures of a fatigued endurance of explicitly politicized abjection, as these works from Conrad through Himes disclose. Simultaneously, they bear an impenetrability at the bare level of the surface that disallows any promise of a deeper meaning begging to be accessed—an opacity of texture at the level of interpretation that cannot be abstracted into an emblem of any kind. The surface's inability to be exchanged—to be recognized and rehabilitated into another's schematic of representation and value, is the negative transgression that inaugurates the aesthetic modern into a certain criminality, into a certain public imaging of illicitness having to do with its apparent departure from the social. *This has everything to do with what notions of blackness have meant in the modern world.*

Adorno posits a critical mantra for the stronger works of literary modernism when he writes:

> To survive reality at its most extreme and grim, artworks that do not want to sell themselves as consolation must equate

themselves with that reality. Radical art today is synonymous with dark art; its primary color is black. . . . The ideal of blackness with regard to content is one of the deepest impulses of abstraction . . . ever since Baudelaire the dark has also offered sensuous enticement as the antithesis of the fraudulent sensuality of culture's facade. There is more joy in dissonance than in consonance: this metes out justice, eye for eye, to hedonism. The caustic discordant moment, dynamically honed, is differentiated in itself as well as from the affirmative and becomes alluring; and this allure, scarcely less than revulsion for the imbecility of positive thinking draws modern art into a no-man's land that is the plenipotentiary of a livable world.[35]

The attitude of abyssal darkness and self-risk in this art, manifest in the art's very fabric and figure, demonstrates evidence of modernism's having ingested, endured, and overcome the banality, apathy, and cruelty of a vulgarly commercialized and reified cultural sphere. It bears evidence of its subjection thereto in its revisionistic materialization of textual bodies that confront and deconstruct the anterior modes of inscription that produce them, *even as* these bodies perform their indebtedness to such schemas of descriptive definition, referentiality, and simple disclosure. The blackness of modernism enunciates its indifferent attitude toward its inability to be countenanced socially or assimilated epistemologically, as it critiques the very will to understanding and untroubled reference that first anxiously identifies its blackness as such, in order to legitimate casting it out as menace, as hopelessly and abjectly "other."

For blackness, as circulated throughout traditional Western philosophical and critical aesthetic lexicons since antiquity, is the primary conceptual metaphor for the absence of information and thus of mental life, the imagistic (non)embodiment of the originary space that is filled (or obliterated) by the substitutional material of language. Speech converts the black void from which it issues into a calcified, dogmatic, and drearily mimetic representation of a self-instituted "reality" that conditions the very notions of history and subjectivity that organize the material field of sociality. These notions integrate to form a governing nexus of metanarrativity that perpetuates the retro-humanism undergirding it, a matrix of parallel lines of

cultural "truth," unbroken bars of unquestioned, subjectivist continuum. Regulating the categories of experience that they initiate, these
lines of discourse summon themselves into social life in the moment
they are articulated, as if the linguistic/acoustic materiality of their very
utterance is identical with the "substance" each rhetoric is presumed
to immediately access.

Such pretense confers on the disorienting specter of blackness visible, a new social reality of philosophical closure, a paradoxical posi-
tivizing of negativity. In other words, the absence or void presumably
communicated by the signifier of blackness amounts in humanist or
subjectivist critical practice to an all-too-facile link with death, now
brought into view as synonymous with epistemological abyss. Blackness visible, in the Baudelairean context, is the aestheticized figuration
and enactment of an aporia at once new and ancient, an intrusion of
the nonmimetic. It is the form of a nontruth that destabilizes a self-
designated cultural "real" by confronting it with the threatening
specter of a phantom, all the more horrifying for being, as Ellison so
casually puts it in *Invisible Man,* a phantom of that cultural sphere's
own making.[36]

At once nihilistic and passionately teleological, silently forbidding
the phantasmagorical brightness of fact, determinism, and identification, refusing to answer even to the call of its "own," modernism's
black intrusion of noncertitude is the transmission of an always already sharply historicized politics, a nonidentical figuration that in-
troduces a perpetual negativity and sudden blindness into the
ritualized glare and narcissism of what Lyotard identifies as the twin
antagonists of philosophical unbinding: the legislative, canonizing
discourse of mastery that characterizes the university and its shinier
counterpart, the capitalistic marketplace.[37] It is the underside, the
negative function, the (un)natural outcome of each locale's political
self-authorization by means of self-concealment.

Black is openly abjected by every logic and cultural practice of certitude, by every gesture in the cognitive wiring of the entire social field,
which is to say every wink, nod, and handclap that signals the acknowledgment and approval of knowledge's performance before a universal tribunal constituted only of knowledge's own. Black is excluded
from the ongoing installation of mechanisms that enable the knowing "I" as the human center from which all orders of understanding,

classification, and subjection issue. Black, as a universalist figuration
of void itself, is therefore niggered long before it is attached to its anthropomorphic nonsubject, Kant's "Negro," Hegel's "African," the an-
imalistic non-I, the rank, subhuman of Kant's "Observations on the
Feelings of the Beautiful and the Sublime," from his *Critique of Judgment*,[38] and Hegel's *Philosophy of History*.[39] Black, in other words,
is radical nothingness long before it finds its radically (sub)human
"referent"—a referent whose presumable distance from legitimating
Enlightenment and Idealist valuation is determined only by the suddenly defining tonality of its skin, this surface alone encoding all the
information necessary to sanction its banishment. This surface, in
racialist ideology, sediments the philosophic principle of nothingness, the abyssal terror of untruth or epistemological lack, within the
one people on earth (if we follow Kant and/or Hegel) with no cognitive access to any redemptive truth whatsoever, "marked" epidermally
by a foundational absence that is simultaneously read socially as absolute, unmediated, animal excess, and wantonness. Cedric Robinson
offers one of the more penetratingly lucid historicist assessments of
the nothingness at the foundation of the category called "Negro," cutting Hegel in the process:

> The "Negro," that is the color black, was both a negation of
> African and a unity of opposition to white. The construct of
> Negro, unlike the terms "African," "Moor," or "Ethiope" sug-
> gested no situatedness in time, that is history, or space, that is
> ethno- or politico-geography. The Negro had no civilization, no
> cultures, no religions, no history, no place and finally no hu-
> manity that might command consideration. . . . The Negro
> constituted a marginally human group, a collection of things of
> convenience for use and/or eradication. This was, of course, no
> idle exercise in racial or moral schemata since it directly applied
> in a most extraordinary way. Slave labor in the New World . . .
> was an inextricable element in the material, commercial, and
> capital development that took place.[40]

The anthropomorphic designation of "Blackness" offers therefore
perhaps the prime example in our time of what Judith Butler dis-

cusses in her introduction to *Bodies That Matter*, as the abject, which in her words:

> designates precisely those zones "unlivable" and "uninhabit-able" zones of social life which are nevertheless densely popu-lated by those who do not enjoy the status of the subject, but whose living under the sign of the "unlivable" is required to cir-cumscribe the domain of the subject.[41]

The practical politics of racialization, the deproblematizing of the conception and discourse of "the Negro," "the African," or most suc-cinctly, "the Nigger" depends in ways that are seldom addressed in the sphere of modern philosophy or critical theory on the racialized/abjected being's surviving, even thriving, within that putrid zone of nonsubjectification, on its living what would presumably be for "white-ness" exactly unlivable. The "nigger" depends upon internalization of his or her racialization out of the legislating zone of "normativity"; upon an engendering within the racialized nonsubject a specific in-vestment in his or her particular nonstatus.

In other words, the category disintegrates in the moment that the designation is applied to a being who does not answer to it. Such fail-ure results not from anything so determinate as a rejection or refusal of power's terms, but merely from a complete absence of need for recognition of any kind; from the absence of any inclination to iden-tify "properly" as one thing or another. The totality of such disen-gagement may seem impossible—until the cultural and political implications of Adorno's supposedly purely "aesthetic" problem of blackness are acknowledged and worked through. Without the want of recognition, the inclination to recognize outwardly is far from cer-tain; such passivity puts the entire hierarchy of cultural identifica-tions, and indeed the denotative, identificatory logic of language itself, into severe question. The crisis of nonidentity lies at the always fragmenting center of modernism, and it is embodied in the figure of nonrecognition, nonhumanity and nonsubjectivity that is "the Negro;" a "nonbeing," *who* at the same time *lives,* and in so living, ori-ents the imagination of the culture that so despises him. This figure of infinite nonidentity lays wide open for modernism the truest and most agile play of subjectivity as continual "free experiment in the field of abolished values."[42]

The potentially incendiary implications of the full internalization of one's own abjection are not lost on canonical modernist figures of social liminality such as Conrad's James Wait, the inscrutable "Nigger" of the *"Narcissus,"* Ellison's Rinehart, or Faulkner's Joe Christmas. Nor indeed are they lost on Baudelaire, who insists on an aesthetic of blackness not least because this percept tends to produce in its beholder a shattering nonreflection of his or her own values.

Blackness visible is an absorptive withholding of the return of the "I's" gaze. Blackness recognizes within itself the density of its own nothingness, feeding upon the contempt in which it is held for exactly this reason, its nonrecognizing, ineluctable thwarting of social narcissism and the categories of classification erected toward this end. As demonstrated in each of the works discussed here, blackness visible, aporia materialized and lived, is the freedom that results from the relinquishing of the very concept of subjectivity altogether, along with all the mythifying narratives of united "positionality" that keep it propped up, such as "race," "gender," "nation," "community," and "identity." Blackness is the social void into which one drops after abandoning the ideal of humanist centrality. To borrow from Ellison one more time, it is where one lands after falling headlong out of someone else's History.

When Virginia Woolf writes that life is shaped only by the relentless rain of "myriad impressions" constituting "the incessant shower of innumerable atoms" in the duration of the everyday, she accents this sense of life's formative abandonment to spheres outside the visible world of action and decision, outside the denotational or properly historical or political.[43] Woolf understands that the relentlessness of this impressionism disrupts the narrative historicizing of life even as its showering of sound, light, color, texture, and movement structures that life and organizes its ways of hearing, seeing, and perceiving—structuring, in other words, its ways of being and thinking. In modernism, the impenetrability of a poetic language that designates "no sayer and no listener," that lays no claim to saying anything outside the vocative boundaries of its own saying, animates a world that withdraws from positive naming.[44]

In other words, this book argues that the stakes of politics are never higher or more intensely personal than in the moment that they articulate themselves at the surfaces of affectivity in sound, color, and gesture; a moment that is worked out exhaustively, incessantly, within the literary precincts of the presumably irresponsible, the "purely aesthetic," the solipsistically bourgeois/apolitical sphere of the literary modern.

This inherent relationality between the visible and the invisible, which is sounded and silenced at the very moment of speech, unfolds within an agonistic scenography that literary modernism stages and restages incessantly as a theater of paradox that its texts theorize and dismantle relentlessly as the supremely ecstatic and shattering moment of narcissism and sacrifice, of sovereignty and enslavement, of self-actualization and self-relinquishing. A cataclysmic scene in which the presumptively dialectical turns out to be dazzlingly errant and multiple; in which the subject turns out to be nothing more than its endlessly dispersed opposite; a scene in which questions of style, impression, and sensation materialize in such a way as to demonstrate that the stakes of the political are never separable from the modes of their expression, and that, therefore, nothing about expressivity can be said to be in any way nonpolitical.

Part I

Mimetic Elusives

1

Holographic Ensemble: The Death of Doubt Itself in The Nigger of the "Narcissus"

*Music can engender images which will only ever be
schemata, instances of its authentic and universal
content, so to speak. But how could the image, the
representation—let alone the concept, "the poetic idea,"
as it is called—engender music?*
—Friedrich Nietzsche, "Uber Musik und Wort"

Borrowing unashamedly from a critical theory of art that will soon find its most powerful expression in the practice of his own fiction, Joseph Conrad, in the famous Preface to his 1897 novella *The Nigger of the "Narcissus,"* posits a fluid model for aesthetic thinking that inherits both its conception and its figuration from an aggressively perspectivist Walter Pater.

In Pater's essay "The School of Giorgione," we find the striking formulation "All art aspires to the condition of music." In music, Pater discerns an art obsessed only with finding its own contours, in this way sounding its liberation from all ideological burden. Provided such a model of experimentality, every other art now has to

become a matter of pure perception, to get rid of its responsibilities to its subject or material . . . It is the art of music which

most completely realises this artistic ideal, this perfect identification of form and matter . . . although each art has its incom-
municable element, its untranslatable order of impressions, its
unique mode of reaching the "imaginative reason," yet the arts
may be represented as continually struggling after the law or
principle of music, to a condition which music alone completely realises. . . .[1]

Meanwhile Conrad, in his Preface, addressing more directly "the art
of fiction," repeats Pater's beckoning to aesthetic identification with
the ideal of music:

Fiction—if it at all aspires to be art—appeals to temperament.
And in truth it must be, like painting, like music, like all art the
appeal of one temperament to all the other innumerable tem-
peraments whose subtle and resistless power endows passing
events with their true meaning and creates the moral, the emotional atmosphere of the place and time. Such an appeal must
be an impression conveyed through the senses; and in fact cannot be made in any other way, because temperament whether
individual or collective is not amenable to persuasion. All art,
therefore, appeals to the senses, and the artistic aim when expressing itself in written words must also make its appeal
through the senses, if its high desire is to reach the secret spring
of responsive emotions. It must strenuously aspire to the plasticity of sculpture, to the color of painting, and to the magic
suggestiveness of music—which is the art of arts. (707)

Here the timeless is a function of the momentary; the lasting "moral
and emotional atmosphere" of the work is a consequence of the differentiated sensations and sequential impressions it produces. For
both Pater and Conrad, the impressionistic pattern alone is able to
provide entry to the invisible realm of the imaginative reason; the secret spring of responsive emotions is the hidden world of impassioned essence that itself turns out to be nothing more than a
function of "the senses" that are only activated by exposure to the
surfaces of sounds and images external to them, links in the chain of

dialogic communication between affectively and semiotically constituted beings.

In Conrad, the artistic aspiration is to "plasticity," to "color," to
"suggestiveness." His vocabulary is not one of access, retrieval, or destination but of tracing the vibratory play between the signifying links
of the chain; of opening and following new patterns of imagining,
writing, and sounding. It is the movement of such play alone that determines the "character" of the object as envisioned in Pater's "deep
places of the imagination."

What is usually overlooked in critical approaches to the theories of
art that we glimpse from Pater and Conrad is the central issue of art's
necessary distance from itself, though in both, this distance is the
fundamental condition of art's viability. In order for art to become a
form to which other forms would "aspire," it must first, itself, aspire
elsewhere. It must assume the place of another: in this case, the idealized form of music. It begins not with any originary sense of its own
self-totality, but within a context of relational identification. This
identification would not be with any fixed social or historical proto-
type but with the elements of affect that alone enable art to shape and
deepen itself—texture, tonality, color, and rhythm. In other words,
the identificatory turn of art is not toward any immediately assimilable object *but is only with the freeing movement of becoming.* For art
to become art, it has to assume the qualities of something other than
itself, usurping the place of that other by transforming itself into a
form outside the accepted boundaries of all given form.

Pater unravels the customary oppositions by which art is split conceptually, either into a phenomenal object of pleasure and confirmation of existing values or into a noumenal practice of critique and
radical revision. His fascination is with the simultaneously rebellious
and reverential character of an artwork that is at once retrospective
homage and futuristic defacement of the formal traditions that inform it. Ever mindful of the artwork's endlessly complex relation to
the real content upon which it feeds—and which its imagination
simultaneously obliterates—Pater emphasizes the dialogism inhering
in art's production and interpretation. He foregrounds the self-
liberating and self-abolishing oscillation by which the absolute unique-
ness of the artwork initiates its own obsolescence by the forward and

transformative historical movement made possible by its own visionary expression.

In *The Renaissance,* Pater discerns an irreducible foreignness central to any experience of art: an opacity produced by a visual, aural, or textural materiality alien to any explanatory logic or system of accountability—a singularity that outdistances theoretical reflection and eludes total absorption into a system of specific signification. This mute inability to grasp or represent the event of aesthetic fascination is addressed by Freud as "an unsolved riddle": an intensely personal exposure to aporia that leaves us powerless to put its experience into words.[2] For Pater, the problem lies in the attempt of the human to establish mastery over an event that is resolutely inhuman; it inheres in the human's failure to think as the poem, painting, or song thinks through its own procedures and the attempt instead to account for the singularities of a work by a logic that has nothing to do with the work's own. The movement that distinguishes artworks cannot remain irruptive once relocated into a project of knowing.

Doubly bound to its immediate object and to a more ephemeral aesthetic ideal of music, Conrad's art of fiction is thus divided at its formation. This fiction is impelled not only by the necessity of "igniting" itself upon the "raw," nonaesthetic materials of everyday life but also by the impossibility of its autogenesis as an aesthetic form with its own mechanisms for generating its own "magic suggestiveness."

What it takes from music is the silence within and against which music shapes itself. Attuned to the nothingness sounded by the intervals that separate one chord from the next, thus animating the song's structuring tension, Conrad's art can be said to take its signature hollowness at the core from another form, for neither the "plasticity," the "color," the "magic suggestiveness," nor the "secret spring of emotions" that he idealizes exists in terms of any tangible substance. They cannot be addressed or felt except by idiosyncratic sensibility. Each is an enigmatic reality of aesthetic experience whose power over us corresponds forcefully to our own internal enigma, to our own inability to articulate ourselves fully. The novella that follows Conrad's Preface exemplifies his fascination with the void that is always at the center of our experience and our strategies of living.

Conrad essentially gives away the ironic structure of *The Nigger of* the *"Narcissus"* elsewhere in the Preface, saying of the titular "nigger," James Wait, that "in the book, he is nothing; he is merely the centre of the ship's collective psychology and the pivot of the action" (292).[3] In so ironically assessing Wait's status in the narrative, Conrad also obliterates the ontological status of the rest of the crew. If Wait "is nothing," and is yet the pivotal figure around whom the others revolve, then "what" exactly must they be? Throughout the text, the inscrutability ascribed to the character of Wait emerges as the echo of a prior enigma—as the repetition of an encounter with the indecipherable that somehow must be accounted for representationally.

Before Wait's arrival, Conrad stages the chaotic rhythm of labored lives at sea, for which the motion of the sea itself can be seen as a strong metaphor. In so doing, he articulates the anxious insistence upon signification that follows from personal exposure to meaninglessness. In the following passage, taken from the novella's opening, textuality itself provides the means of familiarity that momentarily relieves the anarchic negativity of life distant from solid ground:

> The group swayed, reeled, turning upon itself with the motion of a scrimmage, in a haze of tobacco smoke. All were speaking together, swearing at every second word. A Russian Finn, wearing a yellow shirt with pink stripes, stared upwards, dreamy-eyed, from under a mop of tumbled hair. Two young giants with smooth baby faces—two Scandinavians—helped each other to spread their bedding, silent, and smiling placidly at the tempest of good-humoured and meaningless curses. Old Singleton, the oldest able seaman in the ship, sat apart on the deck right under the lamps, stripped to the waist, tattooed like a cannibal chief all over his powerful chest and enormous biceps. Between the blue and red patterns his white skin gleamed like satin; his bare back was propped against the heel of the bowsprit, and he held a book at arm's length before his big sunburnt face. With his spectacles and a venerable white beard, he resembled a learned and savage patriarch, the incarnation of barbarian wisdom serene in the blasphemous turmoil of the world. He was intensely absorbed and as he turned the pages an expression of grave surprise would pass over his rugged features. He was reading

"Pelham." The popularity of Bulwer-Lytton in the forecastles of
Southern-going ships is a wonderful and bizarre phenomenon.
What ideas do his polished and so curiously insincere sentences
awaken in the simple minds of the big children who people
those dark and wandering places of the earth? What meaning
can their rough inexperienced souls find in the elegant verbiage
of his pages? What excitement—what forgetfulness—what ap-
peasement? Mystery! Is it the fascination of the incomprehensible—is it the charm of the impossible? (296–97)

Providing a recontaining boundary to the open spillage of disconnected discourses, Singleton's excursion into the literary momentarily smooths over the disquieting babble surrounding him, offering an
escape into an ordered structure of meaning and value. In the scene,
Singleton's engagement with the text itself compels its own reading
independently of the narrative his book contains. His beard becomes
"venerable" only when it hovers above the pages; he takes on his
"learned" aspect only in the seeming incongruity of his "savage" absorption with the text. In the figure of Singleton, the reader is seamlessly refigured as the read.

By having his narrator juxtapose the notion of the popular novel's
impenetrability with the image of the old man who is utterly trans-
fixed by its "charm," a move that underscores the sharply reflexive
characterization of art's distance from amusement, Conrad implicates the knowing voice of his narrator in the analysis it delivers. The
opposition of "high art" to "low" is usually made by one who presumes to know the difference and what the difference means—and
who presumes also that his view bears universal legitimacy. The
"serene" dedication with which the at once "learned and barbaric"
Singleton reads his book carries him from a scene of cacophonous
differentiality into the event of its literary opposite; but the question
of *how* one reads (wisely, venerably) is plainly derailed by the question of *what* one reads (a "popular," "insincere" page-turner). This
narrative disruption intensifies the structuring tremble of the passage—
a trembling that joins and divides the images of Singleton's simplicity
and his profundity, each of which is sounded simultaneously by the
confident tonality of the narration. Audacious in its quietude is the

affective cut of Singleton's enraptured study, by way of which the text deconstructs the "high/low" economy its narrator deploys in dismissing Bulwer-Lytton. This dismissal is made to reflect upon itself by the intensity of Singleton's fascination. The totality of the old man's arrest by textuality shifts the narrator's comportment, however briefly, away from the complacency of the "subject of knowledge" he presumes himself to be and into the voicing of open wonder. As the scene ends, this shift is manifest by his narration's slip from reportorial description into a series of open-ended questions on textuality's ineffable allure.

Ideology against Itself

With the appearance on the ship of the vagabond Donkin, the text foregrounds the silences that secretly organize the dynamics of polarization attending any intrusion of the foreign. Throughout Conrad's fiction, these dynamics break along trajectories of either isolation or assimilation of the alien body. While Donkin's abject appearance communicates only evidence of severe misfortune, it is the inexplicably defiant irruptivity of his cry—"I can look after my rights"—that discloses all that the crew of the *Narcissus* needs to know about him:

> He looked as if he had known all the degradations and all the furies. He looked as if he had been cuffed, kicked, rolled in the mud; he looked as if he had been scratched, spat upon, pelted with unmentionable filth . . . and smiled with a sense of security at the faces around. . . . They all knew him. (300)

How, exactly, do they know him? What does Donkin's smile signify, if not his knowing absorption of the symbolic functions of abjection and how to replay these publicly to his material advantage? The social space he enters upon joining the *Narcissus* is a hierarchy of position and meaning into which Donkin's strangely "poetic" or "artistic" vocative difference cannot hope to integrate. As Martin Ray notes, Donkin's shattered utterances and the unusual tonalities of his pleas and insults are themselves the sounds of the submerged and alien breaking into the field of ideological consensus, a field which itself is denoted by the collective silence of the crew. Quoting Conrad's narrator, Ray writes:

> "We could not but listen with interest to that consummate artist," (100) as the narrator remarks, acknowledging reluctantly that Donkin's "impassioned orations" have come to replace the "impenetrable silence" of Singleton's generation: "his picturesque and filthy loquacity flowed like a troubled stream from a poisoned source." (101) . . . Donkin's demonic fluency . . . has its source far below the surface, and he utters his mutinous denunciations of the crew in a "bored, far-away voice, as though he had been talking from the bottom of a hole." (110)[4]

Donkin's cry sounds the nondialectical wound of his suffering, giving voice to his filth and insolence in the *completely* dialectical eliciting of direct recognition. This is accomplished not so much by the imposing of its message onto its audience but rather by its absolutely *passive* function as a text itself, by its manipulation of the crew's uncertainty into a unified task of collective decipherment. Exposing them to a reality that cannot be addressed in the professional language of hardened sea laborers, his words also expose each man to his limitation: to his own inadequacy before the task of response to the sounding of a different order of truth. It is the tone and the unlettered energy of Donkin's utterance that accounts for the depth of its incision; it is a sonic cut whose meaning escapes the boundary of the word that would bear it, its value split away in the aural fugitivity of that which is rasped, cried, sputtered, or screamed and never simply or cleanly "spoken." It is this signification in reverse, this communication that, following Lacan, *does not inform* but *evokes* interpretation and response, which reveals both the spectacle and the spectator as being all but entirely ideologically constituted. It is the remainder of affective singularity that so transfixes the crew, something that remains outside language but inside the grain of Donkin's voice, outside the professionally seasoned logic of each sailor on board but inside his ability to hear the naked expressivity of need.

To furnish a more detailed understanding of what the crew sees in the image of Donkin, Conrad intervenes momentarily, as his narrator shifts into what sounds like a more collectively authoritarian or official voice of judgment:

> He was the man that cannot steer, that cannot splice, that dodges the work on dark nights . . . the man who curses the sea while others work. . . . The sympathetic and deserving creature that knows all about his rights, but knows nothing of courage, of endurance, and of the unexpressed faith, of the unspoken loyalty that knits together a ship's company. (301)

Conrad's appeal to an unseen noumenal ethic or meta-agency of universal ship protocols operates on two levels in this passage. The "unexpressed faith," the "unspoken loyalty" of those who labor anonymously, reinforces itself silently as an instrument of unity and cohesion in the midst of the wild sea, though this silent unity cannot point with certainty to any single bonding element of which it might actually consist. At the same time, this inexplicable cohesion presents a potentially totalizing machine of mindless self-preservation that must either neutralize or assimilate all sources of negative dissent, such as Donkin's disruptive appearance and sound. It is his manipulation of this invisible ideological presence against itself that at once enables his acceptance onto the ship and perpetuates the monadic structure that might have excluded him.

Resorting to the performance of his poverty, Donkin asserts his coherence as a "subject" in the open proclamation of his nothingness, demanding acknowledgment of his abjection (resulting from a supposed losing encounter with American sailors while working on another ship). He thus thwarts linguistically the enigma he represents imagistically, more firmly establishing his status as one who "belongs to the ship" with the verbal cut of his impunity and the strange precision of his opaquely accusatory utterances than with any actual work he might perform:

> "The bloody Yankees been tryin' to jump my guts out 'cos I stood up for my rights like a good 'un. I am an Englishman, I am. They sat upon me an' I had to run. That's why. A'n't yer never seed a man 'ard up? Yah! What kind of blamed ship is

this? I'm dead broke. I 'avent got nothink. No bag, no bed, no blanket, no shirt—not a bloomin' rag but what I stand in. But I 'd the 'art to stand up agin' them Yankees. 'As any of you 'art enough to spare a pair of old pants for a chum?" . . . (302)

And in another passage from the same scene:

"What are you?" asked another voice—"Why a sailor like you, old man," he (Donkin) replied, in a tone that meant to be hearty but was impudent. . . . Charley lifted his head and piped in a cheeky voice: "He is a man and a sailor"—then wiping his nose with the back of his hand bent down industriously over his bit of rope. A few laughed. Others stared doubtfully. (302)

The brokenness of Donkin's speech gives testimony to a lived experience of shattering that is augmented by the *content* of his speech—and not the other way around. He makes audible the sound of destitution, the tonality of need, the phonic cut of abjection that the word or phrase itself would conceal. Declaring himself somehow "a sailor," his appeal to actual sailors fails almost completely, undone largely by the physical picture of personal disaster that the irruption of his gnarled speech completes. But his indignant plea registers with the crew by way of an ethical (and narcissistic) feature of ideology that keeps its members narrowly and comfortably defined.

Donkin strategically insinuates himself into the unity that he knows to bind the crew by making his otherness something abjectly familiar. He succeeds by imperiously asserting nationalistic and professional solidarity with those who see him as a disgrace to both social codes and who are yet bound by those same codes to do his bidding. It is in the name of these ideological codes, by which the men recognize themselves as "solid" countrymen and sailors, that they sacrifice to Donkin the clothing and material they then throw at his feet, thereby eliminating the lack that scandalizes them so and issuing him the uniform that confirms him a member of "the team."[5] If "Sacrifice is a guarantee that the Other exists,"[6] then it also reassures the Same of its own agency. In this case, the act of giving reaffirms to the crewmen the sense of mastery and propriety that the shattered pleas of Donkin had so shaken previously.

The sailors know that in accepting him, they also initiate him into their own network of valuation, but they do not yet grasp that they have also been had as the unwitting servants of the social code that Donkin has just manipulated. This relation is made discernible by the knowingness of Donkin's smile; as the narrator informs his reader, "He knew how to conquer the naive instincts of that crowd" (302). Those "naive instincts," Donkin knows, are not nearly so altruistic as they are narcissistic. By accepting a stranger who appeals to the social metanarrative by which they keep themselves defined, the crewmen affirm the substantiality of the code and thus confirm their own. But from Donkin's standpoint, they are only dupes of ideology.[7]

Donkin's appeal is not to each man's individual sense of generosity but to the tropes of kinship that he knows to constitute any British trade ship's code of professional solidarity. The crew's acceptance of Donkin into its ranks is based not upon any singular attribute of his but upon each sailor's own internal adherence to this code. The subjective specificity of each man is erased, to some degree, in the name of a broader cultural acceptance; in this way, the fact of misrecognition discloses itself as a precondition of public recognition *as* one thing or another, of *joining* one recognized community or another.[8]

The Sounds of Whiteness

The inevitable fact of this effacement is performed famously by the "smudge" that once spelled out the name of the sailor James Wait but that now, as he frantically attempts to board the departing ship, only spells his symbolic nonexistence:

> There was a moment of silence while the mate peered at his list.—"Sixteen, seventeen," he muttered. "I am one hand short, bo'sun," he said aloud. The big west-countryman at his elbow, swarthy and bearded like a gigantic Spaniard, said in a rumbling bass:—"There's no one left forward, sir. I had a look round. He ain't aboard, but he may turn up before daylight."—"Ay. He may or he may not," commented the mate, "can't make out that last name. It's all a smudge . . ." The distinct and motionless group stirred, broke up, began to move forward.
>
> "Wait!" cried a deep, ringing voice.

> All stood still. Mr. Baker, who had turned away yawning,
> spun round open-mouthed. At last, furious, he blurted out:—
> "What's this? Who said 'Wait?' What. . . ." (307)

Wait's inability to register himself as a member of the ship, represented first by his actual absence during the roll call for the new crew,
again in the erasure of his name from the roll, and finally by the unfa-
miliar character of his surname itself—the phonic substance of
which comes across only as the imperative command to hold the
ship—demonstrates the essential paradox (or failure) of all identifying signification. The signifier functions as the corrective substitute
by which to fill a primary absence, but its articulation is still necessary *even in the presence of the actual substance it is supposed to represent.* The signifier addresses an absence that is indifferent to the
signified itself; in other words, this absence is a void that only the signifier can fill. Wait's name on the roll promises his full participation
within the social; it is the promise of a substance with which to fill a
formerly vacant space. But when the written promise itself is undone
by the black smudging of his name on the roll, not only does *he* disappear as an agent with no means by which to articulate himself as
such, *but so does the originary absence itself.* Abolished is the empty
space that once demanded a presence to fill it. It appears that only
with the *promise* of substance does absence make itself felt. When
Wait actually appears to claim his position, he finds that he must
write himself into what has become a nonexistent vacancy. This brief
episode seems a negative variation on the Hegelian dictum that the
symbolic concept of the thing murders the thing itself; in this case,
the live body and voice of the person itself cannot immediately animate the dead concept presented by the smudge of the erased name.

Once he has secured his place on the voyage, Wait is apparently
untroubled by the crisis of identity that so persistently emerges as the
organizing problem of literary modernism. The low but steady hum
of "Nigger" that vibrates so mechanically on the deck as he emerges,
tall, erect, and clear-voiced, leaves him unfazed and indifferent as he
asserts his position on the ship. It is as if he ascribes the origin of the
machinic monotone's collective epithet to some inanimate source.
He silently resists not only vulgar racialization but the vulgarization

of any definitive identification, as if the epithet and the surrounding babble of speculation about him must be directed at someone else. "The nigger seemed not to hear . . . he stood in a swagger that marked time" (308). His indifference to the imposition of "identity" reveals the insubstantiality of that social narrative, and his nonresponsiveness disorients the crewmen, who now begin to lose their "composure." Standing implacably before the officers and crew, waiting to be confirmed a member of the expedition, Wait maintains a cool self-possession while the others, in their efforts to fix him socially, begin to fragment. Baker, the chief mate, thrown by Wait's impassive posture, barks questions at him in disjointed bursts:

> "Oh. . . . Ah! Your name is Wait. What of that? What do you want? What do you mean, coming shouting here?"
>
> The nigger was calm, cool, towering, superb. The men had approached and stood behind him in a body. He overtopped the tallest by half a head. He said: "I belong to the ship." He enunciated distinctly, with soft precision. The deep, rolling tones of his voice filled the deck without effort. He was naturally scornful, unaffectedly condescending, as if from his height of six foot three he had surveyed all the vastness of human folly and had made up his mind not to be too hard on it. He went on—"The captain shipped me this morning. I couldn't get aboard sooner. I saw you all aft as I came up the ladder, and could see directly you were mustering the crew. Naturally I called out my name. I thought you had it on your list and would understand. You misapprehended." He stopped short. The folly around him was confounded. He was right as ever, and as ever ready to forgive." (308)

The "confounded folly" of the crew is a scene of social incoherence that embodies the utter absence of meaning that structures so completely the invisible bond of unity between shipmates turned against itself by Donkin earlier.[9] Donkin's manipulation is dependent upon a certain performance of adherence to that ideological formation. But Wait's blithe unresponsiveness to every topically applied designation by which he would be interpellated effaces the self-installed authority of all ship protocol and undermines the ultimate appeal to the mythic superego upon which it premises itself. His implacable verbal expressivity presents the disruptive break of difference that triggers explanatory signification.

The smooth tonality and untroubled delivery of his explanation creates even a greater scandal than the wailing of Donkin during his introduction to the ship. Wait is evidently indifferent to the crew's bewilderment, and its members themselves are not equipped with suitable instruments for the kind of intellectual reconciliation necessary to heal it. In the radical "nothingness" of their cacophony is heard the nonlanguage that obtains outside of semiotically arranged culture; such internal dissension is *the realization of the void within the system of meaning by which the men define themselves.* In this cacophony, a mass of unending noise that is only the sound of a frustrated and denied determinism, Wait hears the announcement of a specter (the nigger) that has nothing to do with him.

Sounding the totality of its actual distance from Wait's realization of his own worth, the hum of "Nigger" performs the radical helplessness and isolation of life disconnected from itself by official ideological shaping, a force that demands of its individual satellites not the movement of thinking through its premises but only the immediacy of their unthinking, total compliance. What is heard from the men is the hollow echo, in search of a validating response, of domination finding the approbation of its slaves.

It marks something close to a complete inversion, along lines of social hierarchy, of Edouard Glissant's "conspiracy" of cacophony that may mark certain practices in Creole speech. This conspiracy actuates within the apparent sound of "gibberish" the utterance of brutalized and submerged thinking and experience issued by kidnapped and enslaved Africans bound in the dungeons of ships destined for America and Europe. This sound bears a muscular, signifying functionality, which is hidden to the masters of those ships by its very expression, to those ears no more than nonsense.[10] In Conrad, however, the gibberish of the "white" shipmates is the contrasting expression of a pathetic dysfunctionality. It is the sound of an entire system of racialist domination being hollowed out and demolished from the inside. *It is the sound of the law being made to realize its essential base-*

lessness, and it functions communicatively in its confirmation of the independence of Wait's casual eloquence therefrom.[11]

Uniquely sensitive to Conrad's attunement to things that cannot be heard, or at least heard to immediately signify or to mean, is much of the work of Edward Said, who writes:

> Nevertheless the utterance is spoken, if not only to, then before another. Words convey the presence to each other of speaker and hearer but not a mutual comprehension. Each sentence drives a sharper wedge between intention (wanting-to-speak) and communication. Finally wanting-to-speak, a specifically verbal intention, is forced to confront the insufficiency, and indeed, the absence, of words for that intention. It is not too extreme, I think, to say that in a very complex way Conrad is dramatizing the disparity between verbal intention apprehendable and possible, grammatically and formally, and verbality itself . . . Conrad's excruciatingly detailed understanding of this predicament makes utterance something far more urgent than a comfortable aesthetic choice. . . .
>
> Hence, for example, Conrad's penchant for repeating phrases like "he was one of us" together with reminders of how unique each individual and his experiences were. Moreover the text Conrad worked at ceased simply to be a written document and became instead a distribution of utterances around both sides of the rift.[12]

What Said hears is an internal gravitation toward the silences and silencings that organize so many of Conrad's works. This gravitation toward the unsayable, the inarticulate, announces much of what is singular about these texts. This broken underside of eloquence and articulation is the jabbering repetitiveness, "the murmuring," "the gibberish" by which instrumental language falters, hesitates, and finally disintegrates.[13] It is the abyssal Other before which language finds itself hopelessly and ultimately accountable in Conrad.

Wait's attribution to the ship's leadership of a misreading that he must correct personally in order to sign himself into the social amounts to a symbolic nullification of the ship itself. With the words

"I belong to the ship," he identifies himself with its governing agency and thereby provides the still-speechless crew with some signifier other than "Nigger" by which to recognize him. But when he concludes his explanation saying, "I thought you . . . would understand," and finally, "You misapprehended," he impassively asserts his own agency independently of the ship's authority. He strips Baker, and by implication, the entire crew, of their own logocentric substance, the presumptive natural and inherent ability to understand, by which they are so able to organize themselves into a silent, machinelike unity possessed of mythic powers of decision and deliberation, inclusion and exclusion. In a vocabulary of knowledge more perfectly refined than their own, the sailors' ability to know or to comprehend is challenged by a being whose very skin color is supposed to guarantee his total incapacity for comprehension.

Embodying at once the Enlightenment ideal of reason and the purely inhuman "black" void of absolute Otherness, Wait's elegant language and style contrast the crudities, grunts, and broken speech patterns of the crewmen. But for all his social "magnificence," there is something about Wait that provides the missing narrative by which to isolate and then exclude him, a narrative by which the ship may restore to itself its "lost" unity. This narrative is driven by "something" in the darkness of his face that not only equalizes the crew with this otherwise "superb" nigger but sends him outside the field of humanity altogether.

> He held his head up in the glare of the lamp—a head vigorously modelled into deep shadows and shining lights—a head powerful and misshapen with a tormented and flattened face—a face pathetic and brutal: the tragic, the mysterious, the repulsive mask of a nigger's soul. (309)

The category of race, functioning here at its crudest as a cultural code of subhumanity for which pigmentation provides all necessary signification, offers a stage for Conrad's deconstructive thematizing of Western understanding and its desperate elimination of cultural voids or blank spaces. The gap between Wait's eloquence and the "mysterious" marker of animalness that is his skin is a vacuum that can be closed only by "racial" fabrications of radical, inhuman otherness. The blank surface presented by the impossibility of a "nigger," Wait, who doesn't speak, behave, or evidently think "like a nigger," is a screen onto which resolving fictions of brutishness, based entirely upon physical characteristics, are projected in an effort to close the aporia opened by his spoken and affective disruptions of authorized ideological understanding.

In short, Wait eventually steps into the already prefigured role of the "nigger" not by opening his mouth and demonstrating the animalness that the term is supposed to connote but by simply stepping into the brightness of light and allowing others to see the darkness of his skin and the flatness of his nose. That he is incapable of performing the animal presumably immanent to the idea of the "nigger" does not matter in the least; in the ideological field of vision and meaning, in the inverted world of pure aggression untroubled by reflection, the animal is pre-inscribed in his physiognomy, presumed to be always already "there" even if somehow repressed behaviorally.

The physiognomic relegation of Wait to the primal opens an unclosable wound upon his presentation of knowledge and self-mastery. It restores to the crew justification of the idea of essential "racial" difference, which is no more than the execution of domination by, and the material privileging of, a self-anointed "whiteness." This category emerges in the text only after its designated "other," since no crewmember is identified as "white" by the narrator until after Wait makes his appearance. The fact that individual agency is addressed in all its heterogeneity until the arrival of Wait, at which point the signifier of "race" subsumes all other signifiers, wiping out all particularities of individual character and subjectivity, demonstrates the self-negation that inheres in the logic of the presumably benign or neutral "fact" of "race" itself. Wait *is* racial difference in this context, interpellated as the embodiment of absolute otherness that silently defines the interpellating subject—who now moves into the elevated new position of "whiteness."

This would seem to oppose the powerful formulations of Frantz Fanon and later Diana Fuss, who argue lucidly that the dialectics of racialization actually work in only one direction, upon the now "black," or more precisely, "niggered" body—which is to say that the "white" man never defines himself negatively as the "nonblack."

However, the fabrication of "race" as a social classification must at some point depend upon at least the superficial participation of its pure beneficiaries, who in naming (if not defining) themselves racially, perpetuate the logic of "racial" discourse itself in the symbolic pronouncement of their bodily and presumably essential difference from those they isolate and cast out. The thrust of Fanon's and later Fuss's work on this topic is that the driving point of "race" discourse is to expel the racialized being from subjectivity. Indeed, Hegel's thesis that "want of self-control distinguishes the character of the Negroes, who can therefore be capable of no development or Culture" is reflexively played back by Conrad,[14] for in this novel, as well as in *Heart of Darkness*, the inverse appears to obtain. This is seen not merely in that it is the "Negro" who appears to embody the ideals of self-control and culture and the "white" subjects who appear most in want thereof, but that even under these circumstances of apparently "relocated" subjectivity, Wait is still somehow the embodied nothingness that is "nigger" and the crew still maintains this power of designation.

This is why it is significant that the text's narrator does not racialize the crew until confronted by the "nigger." It is not any predicate or discourse of "Culture," "self-control," or "subjectivity" that designates "whiteness," but rather it is the defining power of "whiteness" that designates and establishes these predicates as ideological pillars of social life. It is "whiteness" that establishes itself as the irreducible guarantor or signature of thought, work, truth, history, and belonging. It is a bodily inscription of self-recognition and difference in the Western world that will always be absent from its fantasy of the nonhuman, nonthinking, bestial "black" body.

While the "white" subject, in its interpellating position of power is always presumed to be more than simply "white," "blackness" is the single measure by which to determine the social function and presence of the "black" object—the one without which "whiteness" loses all practical meaning. In being interpellated as "nigger," the "nigger" forfeits any claim to thoughtful, discerning activity or any intrinsic diversity, this remaining the domain of the determining "white" agent. This agent alone, unlike the "nigger," is presumed to have encountered his own negativity at the point of what Lacan terms "the mirror stage" and lodged himself into his cultural place of distinction. However, the racialized subject is not endowed the same capacity of intellectual self-realization.

Indeed the very fact of this unique interpellation or racialization it-self would suggest the contrary: that this nonsubject is rather a being who needs to be kept in a permanent location not only of exile but of subjugation. Conrad's narrator metonymically reduces Wait to the physiognomy of his "misshapen" head and abstracts this singularity it-self to a generalized function of facade, "the repulsive mask of a nigger's soul." But Conrad figuratively maintains the paralyzing uncertainty of identity in the presumed distance between the mask and the soul. Is the narrator to relegate Wait to the simple object status of "nigger" or to confer upon him at least the promise of subjectivity implied by the "mask" that would presumably conceal the essence or substance of an "other" being that would double or reflect the "white" man?

Conrad's rendering of the potential of "niggered" subjectivity seems to complicate Fuss's powerful characterization of the profound foreclosure that is racialism:

> Forced to occupy, in a white racial phantasm, the static ontolog-ical space of the timeless "primitive," the black man is disen-franchised of his very subjectivity. Denied entry into the alterity that underwrites subjectivity, the black man, Fanon implies, is sealed instead into a "crushing objecthood." Black may be a pro-tean imaginary other for white, but for itself it is a stationary object; objecthood, substituting for true alterity, blocks the mi-gration through the Other necessary for subjectivity to take place. Through the violence of racial interpellation—"Dirty nigger!" or simply, "Look, a Negro!"—Fanon finds himself be-coming neither an "I" nor a "not-I" but simply an object in the midst of other objects. . . .[15]

The near-total absence of Wait's point of view in the novel, which on one level would seem a prime example of the literary rendering of flattening "racial" objectification, should actually not be conflated with the issue of his personal agency, which registers throughout, though never in the forms of assertion. This distinction makes prob-lematic Conrad's characterization of Wait in the preface: that "he is nothing," and at the same time, the psychological "center" of the book. Wait's "nothingness," his denial of multiple dimensionality, is manifest in the relative absence of his voice, his continual relegation to the offstage. He is realized narratologically by the construction of a vacancy where he is "supposed" to be, by the systematic "framing" of his absence, upon which is superimposed an opaque character. In this sense, his silencing should be read as a technique enabling his symbolic perpetuation instead of a symbolic murder by which his *very place* would be eliminated. It is this place of absence to and about whom the shipmates and the narrator speak so obsessively. Wait is summoned to the "center" by the collective perspective of the crew and is heard in his own voice only intermittently, functioning as a "silent idol," rendered most often as the inscrutable aporia that compels some attempt at stable interpretation or solution. In short, Wait is the "antinarrative," the object of a collective narrative of foreignness against and through which the aptly named *Narcissus* can recognize itself.[16]

As the crewmen figure themselves primarily against Wait's constructed difference, they perform and embody their central lack, which, ironically is all they see in him—and yet of course, not all. "Forgetting their toil . . . forgetting themselves," as the voyage sets out, the men laugh and joke loosely outside Wait's cabin, setting themselves up for a confrontation with the presence of an absence they themselves have constructed:

Then James Wait's head protruding, became visible, as if suspended between the two hands that grasped a doorpost on each side of the face. . . . He stepped out in a tottering stride. He looked powerful as ever, but showed a strange and affected unsteadiness in his gait; his face was perhaps a trifle thinner, and his eyes appeared rather startlingly prominent. He seemed to hasten the retreat of departing light by his very presence; the setting sun dipped sharply, as though fleeing before our nigger; a black mist emanated from him; a subtle and dismal influence; a something cold and gloomy that floated out and settled on all the faces like a mourning veil. . . . Many turned their heads, trying to look unconcerned; others, with averted heads, sent half-reluctant glances out of the corners of their eyes. They resembled criminals conscious of misdeeds more than honest men distracted by doubt; only two or three stared frankly, but stupidly, with lips slightly open. All expected James Wait to say something, and, at the same time, had the air of knowing beforehand what he would say. He leaned his back against the doorpost, and with heavy eyes swept over them a glance domineering and pained, like a sick tyrant overawing a crowd of abject but untrustworthy slaves. (324)

The disembodied head, lodged between the doorposts that Wait grasps with both hands, performs two allegorical functions at once, representing the ideologically fragmented subjectivity that the individual tries and fails to hold together as a unified whole and also the "pure" metonymic object of depersonalizing reduction that Fuss locates as the true project of racialization. The "departing light" that greets Wait as even the sun hides itself from his dark visage announces the relational structure in which "the subject" protectively guarantees its self-possession by avoiding its negative. The presumptive purity of the force of light behaves as if endangered by its dark other, as if the invisible, yet somehow "black," mist is a toxic vehicle of "dismal" contamination or infection.[17] The expectation of Wait's speech and the return of the voice and discourse that had sonorously overwhelmed all others and thus signified his regal "magnificence" are grounded in the sovereignty accorded the speech of Lacan's radical Other, from whom the would-be subject itself (in this case, any shipmate) seeks acknowledgement of his difference. The effortless perfection of his grammar and the apparently easy appearance of his subjective coherence ironically position Wait, for the shipmates, as the agent of this inhuman, Absolute Other that is the symbolic network itself.

In this sense he is the figure of authenticity who alone sits in position to confer upon the speaking (or in this case, listening) subject confirmation of its reality as a subject, since his emanating, inhuman "mist" allegorizes the limitless implicatory power of language and interpellation. The self-negating internalization of "criminality," of the "abject, untrustworthy" slavishness of the mates who avert his interpellating gaze, would seem to substantiate his status as "the Other witness . . . for the Speech that it (the Symbolic order) supports, to be capable of lying, that is to say, of presenting itself as Truth."[18] The

violence of the law of identity turns upon itself as the shipmates refigure themselves into abjection, into criminals who *must* be guilty of
something to be so reduced by Wait's gaze, rather than contend with
the absolute blank of information he presents them.

The liminal space that Wait occupies is the vast distance between
sovereign, authenticating Other and abject, niggered nonsubjectivity.
The passivity of his shipmates' prostration before him, of their waiting upon his every syllable, of their collective sense of being "beneath" him, of being "slaves" to whom he can freely "condescend,"
reflects the belief that he possesses a knowledge of them that they
themselves are without. This is seen in the guilt produced in them
simply by his blank gaze. Their shattering of self-agency results from
the understanding that while they must look to him for such truth, he
has no such need for them. His presence brings into sharp relief the
fiction that he possesses some pivotal, essential information that
might be accessed by his speech. In this sense, the relation might be
likened to Slavoj Žižek's accounting of the psychoanalytic transfer-
ence in which the analysand tells the analyst that s/he doesn't know
what s/he wants, in the assumption that the analyst *does* know:

> [T]he truth about his desire already exists, it is registered some-
> where in the big Other (represented by the analyst), one only has
> to bring it to light and his desiring will run smoothly. . . . The
> end of the psychoanalysis, the dissolution of transference, occurs
> when this "epistemological" incapacity shifts into "ontological"
> *impossibility*: the analysand has to experience how the big Other
> does not possess the truth about his desire either, how his desire
> is without guarantee, groundless, authorized only in itself.[19]

The gaze by which the shipmates are reduced to "slaves" is itself
strangely positioned between the two polarities of Wait's otherness.
While customarily located as an instrument by which to exercise
power, the gaze is at the same time necessarily a position of paralysis,
of mere "impotent" observation. The negative underside of Wait's
power is not only the fact of his niggering out of sociality but also the
strange palpability of his physical illness.

The impressiveness of his entry onto the ship is immediately complicated by the "tremendously loud" cough that sends his eyes rolling wildly and metaphorically rings "the dome of the sky" as the image of his majesty is, inhumanly, coughed into that of infirmity.

When he warns Belfast, "Leave me alone. It won't be for long. I'll soon die. . . . It's coming right enough," his presence is inscribed with the threat of something more vast than personal death. The inscription of death lends only further auratic credence to the notion of Wait's absolute power; the threat of death now marks him with weakness and fear while at the same time underwriting the dread and finality of his gaze. As executor of the radical otherness against which all other signification must register itself, Wait is now also a shadow of death, the final validation of the premise of his absolute cultural authority, which sits juxtaposed from his social status as some subhuman "nigger." In this paradoxical location of animallike nigger *and* absolute arbiter of subjectivity, Wait assumes the impossible position of Hegel's slave in the idealist master–slave struggle for identity and recognition that propels subjectivity and history. The slave, who exists only to do the master's bidding, recognizes the singular trace of its labor within the object produced, knowing its responsibility for its creation.

Wait, of course, performs little labor of any kind in the text and yet has come to possess the slave's multiplicity of experience embodied— at least, as far as his shipmates can tell. They assume the space claimed by Hegel's "master" but see in Wait a multiple threat of the transcendent alterity that bears greater understanding of their minds than they do themselves.

In foregrounding the mechanisms of understanding and determination that sustain the "unseen" coherence of the *Narcissus,* we are careful to retrace the framing of Wait's absence. This is the process by which the silent voice is made the "pivotal" one in the novel. In the specter of the "stalking death" that becomes Wait's double, Conrad shifts the locus of presence from Wait to the shaded figure of death he bears, as if it constitutes a stronger justification for the speculative accounts of his "presence":

> Men stood around very still and with exasperated eyes. It was
> just what they had expected, and hated to hear, that idea of a

stalking death, thrust at them many times a day like a boast and like a menace by this obnoxious nigger. He seemed to take a pride in that death which so far, had attended only upon the ease of his life; he was overbearing about it, as if no one else in the world had ever been intimate with such a companion. . . . Was he a reality—or was he a sham—this ever-expected visitor of Jimmy's? We hesitated between pity and mistrust, while, on the slightest provocation, he shook before our eyes the bones of his bothersome and infamous skeleton. He was forever trotting him out. He would talk of that coming death as though it had been already there, as if it had been walking the deck outside, as if it would presently come in to sleep in the only empty bunk; as if it had sat by his side at every meal. It interfered daily with our occupations, with our leisure, with our amusements. We had no songs and no music in the evening, because Jimmy (we all lovingly called him Jimmy, to conceal our hate of his accomplice) had managed, with that prospective disease of his, to disturb even Archie's mental balance. Archie was the owner of the concertina; but after a couple of stinging lectures from Jimmy he refused to play any more. (326)

Wait can be likened to a walking photographic negative whose sedimented layers of presence at once contain, exclude, and define each other. Since he represents the epitome of the "complete" subject whose apparent self-possession commands recognition across various cultural registers, and at the same time, is thought to bear the mystical essence of the subhuman "nigger" whose face or "repulsive mask" is only a window onto the monstrosity of his asymbolic soul, the addition of this new specter to his gallery of identities collapses his prior multiplicity into an even more disorienting compound of life and death forces, an opposition of the energetic, self-sufficient subject and the dead shell of an alinguistic, "timeless primitive." His diversity is now reduced to a "mere" doubling; but since this doubling is with the infinite force of death, the question surfaces whether it is possible for the death of a subhuman nonsubject to signify elsewhere. *In other words, can a "nigger" die, in any sense beyond the immediate and biological, given the "nigger's" relegation by culture to an unreflec-*

tive position outside subjectivity? And if not, why does the mere mention of the possibility of his death so terrorize the ship? Strangely, a moment of doubled identification emerges, as his shipmates form paradoxical relations both with the object of their fascination and with the shadow that threatens its very life.

Given James Wait's figuration as the representative of Symbolic determination before whom the others obsequiously supplicate, we must consider the implications of the death of Symbolic judgment or authority itself. Remembering that the name "Jimmy" is itself only a wishful metaphor for comradeship, a strategy of retaining the "incomprehensible" Wait within the fictive bond of a collegial "family" and thereby of subsuming his singular, disruptive difference, it is somewhat unclear whether the authority to which the men appeal with this scheme is Wait as arbiter of the Symbolic or Wait as the abstracted figure of death.

Death does not appear on the ship prior to Wait's invocation, banished as it is from discursive exchange, but is forcefully repressed until Wait's admonition to Belfast resuscitates it, sending his shipmates into a paralysis of indecision, trepidation, and rage. The purely verbal "return" of death from which they recoil, however, is not simply the resurfacing of an unpleasant notion or memory long buried; it is rather a return to the Hegelian violence *of subjective genesis itself,* in which the mere possibility of Symbolic death, or public nonrecognition, compels the subject to fight "to the death" upon encountering a being similar to himself who must now be reduced to the status of a thing. Only violence will ensure the subject's own unrivaled, unquestioned right to exist as a free, differentiated being and not as a slavish, nonsubjective vessel of unmediated servility and mere subsistence. Such freedom is dependent upon this risk of life, according to Herbert Marcuse, "not because it involves liberation from servitude, but because the very content of human freedom is defined by the mutual 'negative relation' to the other."[20]

Orchestrating the hegemony of inscrutability as a strategy by which to master those who seek the meaningful essences supposedly within, the essences for which only discursive "evidence" is ever available, the text plays upon the necessarily narcissistic, reassuring function of the metaphor: to impose the subject's reflection upon the unknown and to therefore be able to identify it safely within language and comprehension.[21] Death's resurfacing as Wait's double generates for the crew a terror of the return to the negative and violent genesis of desire (or self-recognition) that humbles them and leaves them the choice of slavishness before this figure who, in rejecting their very idiom of communication, also refuses compliance with his own reification into a mere object of an abstract, abjected otherness. For Conrad, as before for Hegel and later for Kojève and Lacan, the promise of death is necessary to the emergence of selfhood. It instigates the temporal sensibility of each moment's disappearance into pastness as well as the egoistic struggle for pure prestige and social mastery in the first place: the fight for the right to name, to designate; in other words, to solve the anterior enigma of how to identify the self for the self and how to translate that self to another. It is the other who is paradoxically vanquished in the "fight" for recognition and is yet the one upon whom the victor is absolutely dependent for that same recognition.

The novella's foregrounding of this narrative logic is observed in the reflexive title of the work, *The Nigger of the "Narcissus,"* which locates Wait not simply as a member of the ship but, more subtly, as its very invention, as the outcome of a fictional movement that is at its base profoundly narcissistic. This resolution erases the uncertainty that his skin and bearing embody for the crew and replaces it with a firm designation that reaffirms primarily the fixity of the position of domination from which it is issued. Wait is not only arrested symbolically by way of "Nigger;" he is assigned a nonstatus that, in its difference, confirms the solidity of the ship. His "mystical" inscrutability is temporarily resolved for the crew by its imagining of his "true" identity as "that casual St. Kitts nigger."

In its refusal to confirm itself as fact or presence, the purely conjectural status of Wait's eternally stalking death seems only to augment its suggestive force, as if its very absence were in fact a statement of death and its nonsubstantiation were actually a source of otherworldly credence. Death, it seems, would hardly lower itself into language in order to demonstrate its veracity to its subordinates, and though it intrudes upon the social incessantly, thereby coming to occupy a central place therein, the fact that its verification can take place only at a remove from experience, at a distance from the living that can be shortened only by way of a psychic identification, means that for all its "presence," death is always imaginary.

This only means that death is also always Symbolic, and perhaps more purely so than any other category of experience, as its ubiquitous power is never made tangible for thought until its actual expiration. "This explains," writes Blanchot, "why no one is linked to death by real certitude. No one is sure of dying. No one doubts death, but no one can think of certain death except doubtfully. For to think of death is to introduce into thought the supremely doubtful, the brittleness of the unsure."[22] For Giorgio Agamben, the experience of death can only be recognized and spoken as an " 'anticipation' of its own possibility, although this possibility boasts no factual content."[23] Deepening the thrust of this point, Georges Bataille's observation that "Knowledge of death cannot do without a subterfuge—the spectacle" demonstrates the absolute necessity of language to the social functioning, indeed the conceptual framing of death in the first place. "In order for man finally to reveal himself," Bataille writes, "he would have to die, but he would have to do it by living, by seeing himself cease to be . . . it is a question of identifying with some character who dies and of believing that we ourselves die while we are still alive."[24]

However, as Conrad's narrator states, the death of James Wait would also be the death of doubt itself; the death of the alterity that contains all "other" possibility for the self; the death of the other within, the other by whom one is able to recognize oneself; the one against whom to measure oneself. Death of this other would thus constitute the death of self. For Wait's terrified and disoriented shipmates, Conrad inverts the usually designated outcome of identification, that being the narcissistic reassurance and affirmation of self in the imperious adaptation of another's desired "position" or the incorporation of some significant marker of that other's identity and desire itself, the desire of another's desire. He reverses this into a specular, fearful, and equally narcissistic identification with the terror and rot of death, resembling the identification theorized by Blanchot, Bataille, and Agamben.

This fear is multiplied by the threat of the symbolic death that would result from Wait's removal, the elimination of the difference against and within which his mates determine themselves as independent agents. His occupation of the space of Otherness, in both modes, allows the crew a negative recognition of self-differentiation (albeit collectively, for only Belfast, Singleton, and Donkin emerge clearly as individuals) that is literally "whited out" with his demise. This is witnessed in the concluding pages of the novel, as the shipmates return scattershot to social anonymity, following Wait's burial at sea and the return of the ship to England. Since the meaning of death can be realized for the living only by witnessing its decay work upon another, its linguistic signification functions only negatively as something to keep exterior to the self. Clearly, the crew's fear that follows Wait's invocation of death is in no way an altruistic fear for his singular life but a narcissistic fear that his death will liquidate them also. Reflexively, Conrad stages this death-by-identification in darkly comic tones ironizing the fact that on its surface, the identification is with nothing; there is no specular death or decay, for Wait is still quite alive, at this point without visible symptoms of illness, and is able to torment the crew by constantly keeping the specter of death alive as well in his speech. "He would say—'Can't you find a better slice of meat for a sick man who's trying to get home to be cured—or buried?'" (326), or, later, "can't you see I'm a dying man?" (333), all the while refusing to relocate this death from the discursive to the concrete and physical.

Though rampantly speculated upon, Wait's death is not specularized at this point. Sickness and death are rather woven about him linguistically like a cloak so that his very image suggests the presence of death without in any way displaying or demonstrating its physical ravages. However, this absence of visible evidence seems not to matter, since he is marked with death anyway; as the narrator blithely recalls, "You couldn't see anything was wrong with him: a nigger does not show." (333)

In this instance, the fact of Wait's unchanged appearance is stripped of its power to signify at all. The "nigger" becomes the point of erasure of all normative standards of empirical judgment; the narrator does not call for a new method of measurement but rather does away with the idea of measurement altogether, leaving the "nigger's" condition a space of nonintervention, only logical since "nigger," here, operates in its most customary register, as a term of nonexistence or exclusion from symbolic participation. For "niggers," it is not that different rules apply but that no rules apply. Left unresolved is the question of whether this abandonment owes more to the idea that the "nigger" is somehow outside measure or that the "nigger" is simply not worth the labor of investigation and possibly cure. A profoundly ironic Conrad allows his narrator the easy, unmediated facticity of the flat statement "a nigger does not show," without regard for the possibility of disease rampaging inside Wait's body, while elsewhere frequently having the narrator tie himself in contradictory knots of explication and speculation concerning the precise nature of *what it is exactly* that this "nigger does not show" *epistemologically.*

Of course, it is Wait who reverses this logic of "white voodoo," exploiting its racism by playing up the deathly possibility of what his skin momentarily "does not show" and making it impossible for the mates to contradict his claim without risking the validity of their own increasingly unstable positions. "He would not let doubt die," the narrator reminds us.

Feeding blindly upon the strangeness of the "spectacle" of this already exoticized site of scandal, his shipmates work harder and harder for a recognition that is never forthcoming, and indeed they develop a certain libidinal interest in its continued denial and in their continued degradation at the hands of this otherworldly "nigger." The pure "entertainment" value of a character who "would not let doubt die" is the dialectical undoing of their narcissism; the attraction is rewarded only in the incessant refusal of its acknowledgment, one that feeds continually upon the empty promise of a return or an exchange.

> We served him in his bed with rage and with humility, as though we had been the base courtiers of a hated prince; and he rewarded us by his unconciliating criticism. He had found the secret of keeping forever on the run the fundamental imbecility of mankind; he had the secret of life, that confounded dying man, and made himself master of every moment of our existence. We grew desperate and remained submissive. . . . Such was the infernal spell which that casual St. Kitts nigger had cast upon our guileless manhood. (326)

Wait is presumed to possess the same mastery of the codes of cultural ideology that Donkin demonstrates earlier, and like Donkin, he appears to manipulate those codes to his own ends. Unlike Donkin, however, he does not beg for his exalted place. He simply accepts it, "casually," when it presents itself:

> It was a nice little cabin opening on deck, and with two berths. Jimmy's belongings were transported there, and then—notwithstanding his protests—Jimmy himself. He said he couldn't walk. Four men carried him on a blanket. He complained that he would have to die there alone, like a dog. We grieved for him, and were delighted to have him removed from the forecastle. We attended him as before. . . . He fascinated us. He would never let doubt die. He overshadowed the ship. Invulnerable in his promise of speedy corruption he trampled on our self-respect, he demonstrated to us daily our want of moral courage; he tainted our lives. Had we been a miserable gang of wretched immortals, unhallowed alike by hope and fear, he could not have lorded it over us with a more pitiless assertion of his sublime privilege. (336)

Abdicated in the accounts of the narrator is all pretense to independent agency on the part of the shipmates, bound as they are under the singularly "infernal spell" of Wait; however, this silent and unseen "spell" may be manifest. The narration continually foregrounds the "object" rather than the idiom of its defining "subject," keeping Wait speechless. Yet, this very speechlessness *does* signify and is narrated as a profoundly alien idiom that in lifting, or more precisely, dropping itself affectively out of the lockdown of mere instrumentality and recognition makes plain the baselessness of the crew's fascination. Wait's dominance is never asserted but is always assumed, as the novel's quiet deconstruction of cultural understanding and convention enacts a narrative retrieval of silence as perhaps the strongest substance of symbolic judgment.[25]

Conrad's refusal to have Wait himself speak maintains this "nothingness at the center," allowing the character instead to be spoken by the other sailors and therefore to have them enunciate the speculative terms of his "sovereignty." Were Wait to attempt to give voice to his symbolic self-mastery, it would implode upon itself in its very vocalization, evidenced simply by its need for the validation of another auditor—but instead, his silence enables his pure construction from the outside; the question of whether he knows his own desire is never addressed to him and never answered.

The blind completeness of the crew's identification with him, enacted most dramatically in the collective fury with which they rescue him from his flooded cabin, demonstrates the patterns of paradox and futility that constitute Conrad's deconstruction of identificatory structure and movement within the novel. Having risked their lives to save Wait from drowning, the sailors finally extricate him from the makeshift cabin that was transformed into a deathtrap during a bad squall. The reward is a momentary oceanic oneness with the figure of their fascination, a moment at once self-validating and self-alienating, gratifying and thankless:

> We stood up surrounding Jimmy. We begged him to hold up, to hold on, at least. He glared with his bulging eyes, mute as a fish, and with all the stiffening knocked out of him. He wouldn't stand; he was only a cold black skin loosely stuffed with soft cotton wool. His arms and legs swung jointless and pliable; his head rolled about; the lower lip hung down, enormous and heavy. We pressed round him, bothered and dismayed; sheltering him we swung here and there in a body; and on the very brink of eternity we tottered all together with concealing and absurd gestures, like a lot of drunken men embarrassed with a stolen corpse. (358)

As Conrad fragments Wait into the "jointless" disjunction of his limbs, his statuelike self-possession finally at the point of dissolution, his shipmates finally achieve the unified sense of "eternity," of being "all together," for which Wait's composure itself had provided the supreme model. But upon reaching this "oneness," they can only celebrate in "concealing and absurd gestures" that are more feigned than genuine, and which, immediately undermined by the impossibly obstinate Wait, not only explode all dialectical presuppositions of self, other, and the illusory fusion of recognition but also expose the complete instability to which they long ago gave way:

> [H]e groaned slightly, and with a great effort whispered a few words. We listened eagerly. He was reproaching us with our carelessness in letting him run such risks: "now, after I got myself out of there," he breathed out weakly. "There" was his cabin. And he got himself out. We had nothing to do with it apparently! . . . No matter. . . . We went on and let him take his chances, simply because we could not help it; for though at that time we hated him more than ever—more than anything under heaven—we did not want to lose him. We had so far saved him; and it had become a personal matter between us and the sea. We meant to stick to him. Had we (by an incredible hypothesis) undergone similar toil and trouble for an empty cask, that cask would have become as precious to us as Jimmy was. More precious, in fact because we would have had no reason to hate the cask. And we hated James Wait. We could not get rid of the monstrous suspicion that this astounding black-man was shamming sick, had been malingering heartlessly in the face of our toil, of our scorn, of our patience—and now was malingering in the face of our devotion—in the face of death. Our vague and imperfect morality rose with disgust at his unmanly lie. But he stuck to it manfully—amazingly. No! It couldn't be. He was at all extremity. His cantankerous temper was only the result of the provoking invincibleness of that death he felt by his side. Any man may be angry with such a masterful chum. But, then, what kind of men were we—with our thoughts! Indignation and doubt grappled within us in a scuffle that trampled the finest of our feelings. And we hated him because of the suspicion; we detested him because of the doubt. We could not scorn him safely—neither could we pity him without risk to our dignity. So we hated him and passed him carefully from hand to hand. (359–60)

Alienated from their own hatred by the necessity of a final cognition that would smooth over the contradiction of their tormented servitude before Wait, the narrator and his mates gently pass along the presumably "full" cask that he represents, apparently not discerning that they take such care with him precisely because they alone are the creators of its ineffable "contents." The innocence that the narrator ascribes to the analogical "empty cask" is rather its inanimate self-evidence, its very inability to be filled with a true "innocence" that would consciously acknowledge the identity of its saviors. For this reason, the narrator's analogy rings falsely. Whatever value the empty cask might have would likely be fetishistic, utilitarian, or sentimental but strictly *not* intersubjective. The narrator's notion that the cask would actually be "more precious" than Wait to the crew because "we had no reason to hate the cask" suggests also that there would be no reason to lovingly save that cask either, at least not at the expense of the hardship that Wait's rescue costs.

It is only through Wait's hostility toward them that his shipmates see themselves in some substantial form, and it is within this peculiar economy of narcissism that the labor of love of self translates into self-negation or risk for another. The crew's rescue of Wait is the narcissistic validation of their hatred of him and also of the strangled hatred of their own self-doubts. It reverses the execution of the master–slave antagonism, staging not a deathly fight for subjective superiority but rather the risking of life for the sake of the other's life, this time for recognition of self through negation of self. Painfully laboring to extract Wait from his cabin, his shipmates see in his continued existence a perpetuation of the negativity necessary to their own formation. It is a force of ideological and epidermal alterity that appears to exist outside of their social and ideological codes of meaning or identity and that therefore threatens the solidity of those codes. It is also against this negativity, however, that these codes institute themselves and give themselves shape and life.

The social cohesion of the crew, made stronger by its very unspokenness at sea, falls apart on land, as the mates appear now not even to recognize each other, splintering in all directions, no longer bound by a common context of labor and anxiety. Before then, the crew's "vague and imperfect morality," appalled by Wait's apparent feigning of illness, discloses its own inconsistency in its recognition of his "manfully" sticking to his "unmanly" deceit, seeing in his commitment to self and self-narrative a model of stability and coherence that is sorely missing from its own "tottering" representations of itself and its subservience to him. In other words, the integrity of Wait's lie, its steady refusal to disintegrate under public pressure, is stronger than all the tissues of "truth" by which the crew re-projects him—and itself. The absence embodied by the actual presence of James Wait is testimony to what Blanchot means when he writes:

> The renunciation of the first-person subject is not a voluntary renunciation, nor, thus, is it an involuntary abdication. When the subject becomes absence, then the absence of a subject . . . subverts the whole sequence of existence, causes time to take leave of its order, opens life to its passivity, exposing it to the unknown, to the stranger—to the friendship that is never declared.[26]

By its positive movement toward the visible world of action and power, instrumental language and identitarian logic conceals its abyssal origin, only to resurrect that origin with every utterance it issues. James Wait's insistent withdrawal from this economy, in the forms of silence and of speech that seems addressed to no particular auditor, exposes to this world its own fictivity. His utter indifference to domination is the stabilization, indeed, the centralization, of the marginal.

2

Something Savage, Something Pedantic: Imaginary Portraits of Certitude in Jacob's Room

*Missing is the truth of promising. If something
promises—and thus promises language—it is missing.*
—Werner Hamacher, *Premises*

*As frequent as street corners in Holborn are these
chasms in the continuity of our ways. Yet we keep
straight on . . . Every face, every shop, bedroom window,
public house and dark square is a picture feverishly
turned—in search of what? It is the same with books.
What do we seek through millions of pages?*
—Virginia Woolf, *Jacob's Room*

The "chasms in the continuity of our ways" that form the point of Virginia Woolf's literary departure expand the Conradian inquiry into the void at the center of all expression. This is true in the sense that the fracture, multiplicity, and groundlessness of meaning thematized by both writers at the level of plot is now extended by Woolf to the dimension of figure.

For Woolf, the modern artwork must install, and not merely implicate, the experience of nonlocatability into its own aesthetic machinery as a necessary procedure of the work's communication—a practice of both art's disclosure and its subsequent interpretation.[1] This is to say that by following a writerly nonpath of grammatical collapses and metamorphic narrators, Woolf restores to the experience of reading an originary dispossession, which is at the same time embedded as a narrative problem of story.

The visual plane on which this aspect of her writing so often seems to play out can be said, in its function as an aesthetic discontinuum rather than as a novelistic promise of consistency, to anticipate certain experimental conceptions of cinema. In such film, the singularity of the image's texture disrupts or even abolishes the contextual framework of the narrative. The film is no longer oriented around theme or plot, but on the trajectories and durations of its movement, on intensities of sound and immersions in color or grain. Siegfried Kracauer suggests this kind of engagement in his critical work on black-and-white photography and film, arguing that such filming heightens a hyperrealistic effect of individual image that would be obliterated by the actual color saturating everyday reality.[2] Woolf's disfigurations of conventional notions of time and conversational logic make textually prominent those moments of subjective excess and ineffability that are rendered to devastating effect in black-and-white film by the distortive techniques of artifice that Kracauer discusses. Such effects tend to disappear in the color film, often excised in favor of direct, explanatory speech that advances the story, indifferently to the scenic affects of texture and tone that constitute the story's body.

In the essay "Modern Fiction," Woolf discusses the singularizing of these arresting events/images/sounds, finding in these the secret life of any actual story:

> The mind receives myriad impressions—trivial, fantastic, evanescent, or engraved with the sharpness of steel. From all sides they come, an incessant shower of innumerable atoms. . . . They [the moderns] attempt to come closer to life, and to preserve more sincerely and exactly what interests and moves

them, even if to do so they must discard most of the conventions which are commonly observed by the novelist. Let us record the atoms as they fall upon the mind in the order in which they fall, let us trace the pattern, however disconnected and incoherent in appearance, which each sight or incident scores upon the consciousness. Let us not take it for granted that life exists more fully in what is commonly thought big than in what is commonly thought small.[3]

Rendering this multiplicity is simply beyond any representation's capacity if quantity is the sole measure of its value. Modernist literature takes shape instead within a language of economical substitutions, foregoing the attempts at a taxonomic capturing of such an overwhelming shower of information. With Joyce's *Ulysses* providing at once the massive exception to, and the most poignant evidence of this tendency, this modernism works instead within a paradoxically exclusionary mode, allowing the isolated portrait to imply the possibility of a greater, more "oceanic" experience while at the same time foregrounding the irreducible singularity of its event. Kracauer again succinctly posits a cinematic analogue to High Modernist narrative:

And since any medium is partial to the things it is uniquely equipped to render, the cinema is conceivably animated by a desire to picture transient material life, life at its most ephemeral. Street crowds, involuntary gestures, and other fleeting impressions are its very meat. Significantly, the contemporaries of Lumiere praised his films—the first ever to be made—for showing "the ripple of the leaves stirred by the wind."[4]

Animated by exactly such an impressionistic materiality, the project of *Jacob's Room* is to shatter and isolate into countless vibrant and significative fragments the silently institutionalized identities, values, and energies of the apparently naturalized social events and spaces within which identities are produced. In so doing, the text critiques the logic of discursive stability and understanding while submitting to it by deforming the novelistic idiom it inherits and transfiguring the language within which it is bound to think and speak. In

Nietzschean terms, the value of Woolfian modernism is that "the word becomes sovereign and leaps out of the sentence, the sentence reaches out and obscures the meaning of the page, the page gains life at the expense of the whole—the whole is no longer a whole."[5]

Written during the maelstrom of "High Modernism" in 1922, this text establishes its difference by repeating formalistically the abyssal failures of meaning and presence by which its thematic truth—its loss, its discontinuity, its transience—forges itself. Where both *The Nigger of the "Narcissus"* and *Heart of Darkness* initiate a literature of thematic anxiety about the necessary and perpetual otherness of all understanding, each of these texts addresses this unpresentable absence as a problem to engage from within the rhythms of a presentable idiom of language (this being the idiom of consonance). But *Jacob's Room* institutes the logic of semiotic failure as a paradoxically liberating and frustrating condition of expression. This illuminates the ways in which language is always exposed to its own limitations by its very function of reference. The danger, as E. M. Forster describes it, that inheres in Woolf's novels lies not simply in their willingness to "draw moustaches" on somberly and strictly representational portraits; rather, the radical otherness of Woolf's art lies in the nexus between its prismatic attunement to transitory sensation and its necessary inability to respect unreflectively *any* discursive claim of truth. The text's insistence upon this atomization of experience and sensation is, in itself, a pathless, writerly counterviolence to the normative, dogmatic violence of domination's metanarratives of canon, category, and meaning.

The "inhumanity" of *Jacob's Room,* as both Adorno and Lyotard might recognize it, obtains in the text's denial of its own explanatory closure, in the inconclusiveness that refuses to allow any signified in the narrative to emerge from behind the force of its signifier. The novel's subversion of consensual idioms lies precisely in this equation of presence with absence, in its refusal to narrate determinate meaning or identity into its terms, in its refusal to allow its characters to finish their very sentences. These linguistic voids compel the attempt of critical understanding and positive communication, including, of course, the institution of cultural identity as a category of final definition.[6] Since the essentially "plotless" *Jacob's Room* is about nothing if not the impossibility of language's complete identification with the reality it is presumed to represent, the failure of signification is redoubled at the level of the anxious reader. The novel's "plotlessness," however, hardly amounts to its nothingness, since the singular perversity of the work's form is only its rendering of an anterior perversity within social reality. This would be the perversity by which individual and cultural uncertainties are converted by social habituations of speech into the frozenness of determinate objectifications.[7]

Jacob's absence, unlike James Wait's in our first chapter, is total, although, like Wait's, his is a laboriously constructed and authoritative *presence* of absence. He takes shape as an accumulation of constructions that speak to one another through an ironically liminal narrator who shuffles without announcement among the identities of various informants, all of whom report on their separate encounters with and impressions of Jacob throughout the text. This may be the sharpest narrative device the text employs to dislodge the cultural dogmas of identity and position, for the narrator shifts from regulatory conductor of the text's unitary coherence to its most subversive source of disruption precisely by morphing frequently from the consciousness of one character to the next, sometimes speaking one sentence in the character's voice, and the next in wicked dismissal of that same figure. It is a commentary voice that, while independent, also remains amorphous, a textually institutionalized agent of textual antisystemicity. The narrator's boundless movement from one of Jacob's interlocutors to the next creates the final effect of leaving the title character perpetually "lost at the center."[8]

What emerges from this loose gallery of fragmentary impressions is an opaque, distant portrait of confidence, satisfaction, and judgment, in which a young man's signature gesture of smoking a pipe communicates such a complete sense of knowing and self-assurance that, for his "audience," the actual body of his knowledge need not ever substantiate itself. His very mode of idiomatic self-expression seems to constitute in itself a separate form of social mastery:

Insolent he was and inexperienced, but sure enough the cities which the elderly of the race have built upon the skyline showed like brick suburbs, barracks, and places of discipline against a red and yellow flame. He was impressionable; but the word is contradicted by the composure with which he hollowed his hand to screen a match. He was a young man of substance. (36)

Or:

"Distinction"—Mrs. Durrant said that Jacob Flanders was "distinguished-looking." "Extremely awkward," she said, "but so distinguished looking." Seeing him for the first time, that no doubt is the word for him. Lying back in his chair, taking his pipe from his lips, and saying to Bonamy: "About this opera now" (for they had done with indecency.) "This fellow Wagner" . . . distinction was one of the words to use naturally, though, from looking at him, one would have found it difficult to say which seat in the opera house was his, stalls, gallery, or dress circle. A writer? He lacked self-consciousness. A painter? There was something in the shape of his hands (he was descended on his mother's side from a family of the greatest antiquity and deepest obscurity) which indicated taste. Then his mouth—but surely, of all futile occupations this of cataloguing features is the worst. One word is sufficient. But if one cannot find it?

"I like Jacob Flanders," wrote Clara Durrant in her diary. "He is so unworldly. He gives himself no airs and one can say what one likes to him, though he's frightening because . . ." But Mr. Letts allows little space in his shilling diaries. Clara was not the one to encroach upon Wednesday. Humblest, most candid of women! "No, no, no," she sighed, standing at the greenhouse door, "don't break, don't spoil—what?" (71)

As do those "places of discipline against a red and yellow flame," so too does Jacob's "composure" emerge solidly only before an oppositional transience; his "impressionable" cast of mind is a ready contradiction of Paterian "flame" to the staid, brick "suburbanism" that surrounds him and that he rejects. But this means only that his "substance" is in urgent need of its insubstantial, unstable, and momentary other, against which it may take shape as a solidly distinct body. As yet, the "substance" of this substance is still not reported upon, its body supported by no anchoring sinew of textual evidence other than Woolf's outrageously reflexive staging of Jacob's "hollowed" cupping of a match's flame while lighting up.

The silent cupping of Jacob's hand around the live flame suggests not only a local emptiness within a larger void, as his apparent lack of position or discourse might suggest; it also connotes an allegorical antagonism toward the transitory and dynamic, demonstrated by his controlling enclosure of the flame. Woolf's staging of this composure calls attention to it as a quality of self-possession necessarily opposed to loss and fragmentation; one that would customarily go unmentioned, unless its terms of quietude are made to stand out radically within a context of chaos and disruption. Mrs. Durrant observes Jacob not with an eye to his actual difference (which is likely only an understated mode of stylization in his outward appearance) but rather with an aim toward a certain interpretive mastery or knowingness.

This inclination toward mastery is reinscribed subsequently when the narrator, in description of "the world of the elderly" and its "disagreeable relation to youth," says that any agonistic break that Jacob makes will issue from the conviction—"I am what I am, and intend to be it" (71). "Youth," instead of deconstructing the entrenched logic of its forebears, actually repeats the same anxiety of those precursors, only reversing it in warlike antagonism. It here undoes the cliché of its customarily presumed subversiveness and radicalism, grounding itself instead, barrackslike, in a concrete claim of absolute solidity that forgoes the fleeting dynamism of red and yellow flame for the permanence and stability of brick suburbs and personal ontologization.

In the second passage a metonymic reading of Jacob attains the representational status of completeness and certitude, or, as the narrator laughs, "the real thing." Jacob's "distinction" is proven conclusively somehow by the signifying manner in which he removes his pipe and authoritatively intones his commentary on "this fellow Wagner," a commentary whose actual content itself is never disclosed. Equally invisible is that mysterious "something in the shape of his hands" that traces to its unseen origins both "the greatest Antiquity and deepest obscurity." From these fragmentary, isolated moments without elaboration arises a resultant composite that is nothing more than a sustained reading of a series of gestures.

While the smoke from Jacob's pipe, the heaviness of his step and the timbre of his infrequently exercised voice create an idiomatic distinction on the seemingly "mere" plane of affectivity in his actual presence; in his absence, they become metonymic markers of his greater totality. At the same time, each gesture enacts a memorializing cut onto the verbal commentary of the one who narrates it. This greater abstraction of "Jacob" is one for which each of these indicators, if isolated, would be insufficient to account. But within the impressionistic imaginary of the conventional social sphere for which he has so little taste, the isolated details of his appearance are gathered and come to constitute a unitary image of ambition and authority, of aspiration and advancement. They become a signature of knowing and possession, even as materialized nonverbally. In this way they provide testimony to the completeness with which surface contours of style establish the permanence of "character" in social reality.

Each attempt by Mrs. Durrant to fashion an authoritative Jacob is either frustrated or enabled by an individual remainder of opacity that either undermines or invites its incorporation into a larger definitional whole. His evident lack of "self-consciousness" punctures the taxonomic criteria Woolf ironizes as specifically appropriate to the "official" idea of "the writer," while that evanescent, undisclosed quality in the appearance of his hands is in itself enough to suggest seriously that he might be "a painter." Suddenly grasping the impossibility of such unproblematic classification, Mrs. Durrant suspends as futile and silly the search for proper placement, but only because such an exercise is unlikely to actually *"find it"* finally. She fails still to locate within herself the chasm of desire or need that demands the closure of this elusive, explanatory "it" in the first place.

This type of failed investigation on Mrs. Durrant's part however, is not specifically what Woolf has in mind with the recurrence of feminine "fault" in the novel. Instead, the habit of fault is a masculinist projection by which to legitimate the official exclusion of female participation within art and academia. This is consistent with the function of Mr. Letts's corrective margin line in the pages of Clara's notebook—the line she does not allow herself to overstep, choosing instead to leave her thought unfinished, its possibilities defused and discarded. It is as a function of restraint that Woolf narrates all enunciation of feminine fault from already *within* the defensive verbal stance of the "offending" woman, rather than in the harsh words of an accusatory male, compelling a deconstructive, rather than an aggressively antinomic investigation.

This strategy enables critical analysis of feminine fault as a sedimented social residue of misogyny that has to be navigated *only* by women. Woolf posits it not as an individuated attack, punishment, or series thereof by isolated men of entitlement, but rather as an internalized, phenomenological, and social invariant endured by women generally. This relation establishes something deeper than a simple antagonistic structure of male accusation and female denial, for in completely removing the accusatory masculine voice, the narration suggests a ready naturalization of female fault in culture, in which presumably organically incompetent or inadequate women are always already interpreted to have absorbed anterior judgment from elsewhere. "It was none of *her* fault that this was not a smoking carriage" (30), says the narrator of Mrs. Norman, the matronly woman who shares a compartment with the sullen nineteen-year-old Jacob on the train to Cambridge. She asks him at one point not to smoke in the car, earning his complete and inscrutable silence. And again, "It was none of her fault," the narrator says of neighboring Mrs. Plumer,

> since how could she control her father begetting her forty years ago in the suburbs of Manchester? And once begotten, how could she do other than grow up cheese-paring, ambitious, with an instinctively accurate notion of the rungs in the ladder and an ant-like assiduity in pushing George Plumer ahead of her to the top of the ladder. What was at the top of the ladder? A sense that all the rungs were beneath one apparently; since by the time that George Plumer became Professor of Physics, or whatever it might be, Mrs. Plumer could only be in a condition to cling tight to her eminence, peer down at the ground, and goad her two daughters to climb the rungs of the ladder. [. . .] It was none of *their* fault either. (35)

Clearly the fault is organic, unique to the very concept of woman, for how could Mrs. Plumer "do other" than be born and grow up an acquisitive status-hound, genetically bound to reproduce more women in her own image who in their turn would not be able to help repeating the pattern? Even her "assiduity" is ascribed to a nonsubjective habit of animal instinct and not to thoughtful decision, a negating function of the larger ontological concept of "woman" that flattens out any possible particularity of an actual woman's thinking and living differently.[9]

By locating femininity within such an abstracted, and yet hermeticized space of spiritual and intellectual limitation, forbidding even the slightest unruliness or alterity, this masculinist discourse also seals off from itself any question of its own validity as a positing of knowledge. Left apoplectic at his exposure to the scene of domestic provinciality at the Plumers', Jacob can only sputter his hatred of this common and peculiarly feminine banality:

In they came to the drawing-room, in white frocks and blue sashes. They handed the cigarettes. Rhoda had inherited her father's cold grey eyes. Cold grey eyes George Plumer had, but in them was an abstract light. He could talk about Persia and the Trade winds, the Reform Bill and the cycle of the harvests. Books were on his shelves by Wells and Shaw; on the table serious sixpenny weeklies written by pale men in muddy boots— the weekly creak and screech of brains rinsed in cold water and wrung dry—melancholy papers.

"I don't feel that I know the truth about anything till I've read them both!" said Mrs. Plumer brightly, tapping the table of contents with her bare red hand, upon which the ring looked so incongruous.

"Oh God, oh God, oh God!" exclaimed Jacob, as the four undergraduates left the house. "Oh, my God!"

"Bloody beastly!" he said, scanning the street for lilac or bicycle—anything to restore his sense of freedom.

"Bloody beastly," he said to Timmy Durrant, summing up his discomfort at the world shown him at lunch-time, a world capable of existing—there was no doubt about that—but so unnecessary, such a thing to believe in—Shaw and Wells and the serious sixpenny weeklies! What were they after, scrubbing and demolishing, these elderly people? Had they never read Homer, Shakespeare, the Elizabethans? He saw it clearly outlined against the feelings he drew from youth and natural inclination. The poor devils had rigged up this meagre object. Yet something of pity was in him. Those wretched little girls—. (35)

Jacob's unharnessed contempt for this suburban stratum reveals the completeness and the violence of his subscription to the cold light of abstraction, typifying a mimetically rigid elitism. It is complete with its rehearsed, official litany of canonical figures who function here *not* as specific artists and thinkers, but as symbolic means of exclusion, as reified objects of snobbish representation. Absent is the innocence and attunement to figurality and its dangers and accidents that would induce the "blasting" of official history and canon described by Benjamin in his "Theses on the Philosophy of History"; the very sort of attunement possessed and actuated by Shakespeare, the Elizabethans, and those others who are canonized only *following* their irruptive cuts of figure and energy into "tradition"; the very breaks and ruptures that establish the movement *of* any tradition. In Jacob's hands, these figures are stripped of all singularity of production or style, and are reduced to rank signifiers of an academic snobbery that requires less a critical engagement with these figures' actual works and ideas than it does a convincing familiarity with their mere names.

Of such works and ideas, Jacob provides little actual knowledge throughout the text, but we will soon return to this issue of fractional or even false reference. His description of the events at the Plumer home as "beastly" evinces a tendency to remove minds less accomplished than his (by his measure) from the field of subjectivity altogether and is consistent with his practice, elsewhere in the text, of likening women to dogs and ants. Such exclusionary practice is possible, Woolf argues, only with the presumably "knowing" subject's refusal to investigate or question its own legitimacy as an arbiter of judgment, or to scrutinize the self-prescribed categories of knowledge by which it validates itself and converts its dogmatism into cultural truth.[10]

Culture's naturalization of feminine inadequacy and helplessness is extended in passages depicting Jacob's relationship with Florinda.

She represents for Jacob both the very embodiment of debased feminine otherness and, at the same time, the practical impossibility of
the ideal of spiritual, bodily, and intellectual unity to which he aspires. What fails to register with him is that she does have a system of
values uniquely her own, and that its private embeddedness, its withdrawal from cheap disclosure and assertion, signals strongly its independence of need for his or any other external authorization:

> As for Florinda's story, her name had been bestowed upon her
> by a painter who had wished it to signify that the flower of her
> maidenhood was still unplucked. Be that as it may, she was
> without a surname, and for parents had only the photograph of
> a tombstone beneath which, she said, her father lay buried.
> Sometimes she would dwell on the size of it, and rumour had it
> that Florinda's father had died from the growth of his bones
> which nothing could stop; just as her mother enjoyed the confi-
> dence of a Royal master, and now and again Florinda herself
> was a Princess, but chiefly when drunk. Thus deserted, pretty
> into the bargain, with tragic eyes and the lips of a child, she
> talked more about virginity than women mostly do; and had
> lost it only the night before, or cherished it beyond the heart in
> her breast, according to the man she talked to. (77)

Bereft of all belonging, absent even any institutionally certifiable narrative of biographical origin, Florinda improvises several of her own
fashion, experimenting with a different identity narrative to suit the
particular occasion. She embraces that untethered existence elasti-
cally. In so doing, she demonstrates not only the porousness of the
membrane separating the presumptive reliability of sober speech
from the content of drunken expression; she also makes plain that
every cultural and epistemological category of determinate identity is
a relation of wishful substantiality to dreaded nothingness, in which
even the justificatory lie is deemed preferable to the anxiety and wonder opened by the absence of narrative solution. Not even the actual
tombstone, but its photograph, connects the movement of her thinking and living to that of some long-dead "father," creating no fusion
with any specific progenitor, but dramatically implicating her within

a history, a past, to which she could never have access. The absence of an anchoring surname augments the freedom of this choice, by which Florinda so easily multiplies herself, proliferating the positions of an "I" that is seen now as more of an individual possession or property than as an ontologically defining expression or category of being. These multiple "I's must compete with rivaling narratives from the outside, such as this one from an idealizing Jacob:

> Wild and frail and beautiful she looked, and thus the women of the Greeks were, Jacob thought; and this was life; and himself a man and Florinda chaste. (78)

Florinda's "I" remains an object of possession, but one no longer her own, as she is dispropriated by Jacob, imported into his ongoing identification with the Greeks of antiquity. Her quality of "wildness," following a street education that itself is as necessarily ordered and as differentiated as any other, resonates for Jacob as a possible entry into meaning or "substance" that at the same time, given her comparative illiteracy, is a pivot out of the textuality that he so reveres. What remains at issue is whether this escape route is an inherent, organic property of "the feminine," or whether it is crafted by an individual-ized, thinking female subjectivity, and if the latter, how then to justify his general contempt of woman:

> Marvellous are the innocent. To believe that the girl herself transcends all lies (for Jacob was not such a fool as to believe implicitly), to wonder enviously at the unanchored life—his own seeming petted and even cloistered in comparison—to have at hand as sovereign specifics for all disorders of the soul Adonais and the plays of Shakespeare; to figure out a comrade-ship all spirited on her side, protective on his, yet equal on both, for women, thought Jacob, are just the same as men—innocence such as this is marvellous enough, and perhaps not so foolish after all.
>
> For when Florinda got home that night she first washed her head; then ate chocolate creams; then opened Shelley. True, she was horribly bored. What on earth was it *about*? She had to

wager with herself that she would turn the page before she ate another. In fact she slept. But then her day had been a long one, Mother Stuart had thrown the tea-cosy;—there are formidable sights in the streets, and though Florinda was ignorant as an owl, and would never learn to read even her love letters correctly, still she had her feelings, liked some men better than others, and was entirely at the beck and call of life. (78–79)

In briefly acknowledging, however condescendingly, the possibility of another legitimacy, another, separate substance of truth "equal" to his "own," (which, again, emerges only in the modes of citation and pos-session, in the works of Adonais and Shakespeare), Jacob momentar-ily risks himself, astonished at the "innocence" by which Florinda appears to "transcend all lies"; meanwhile, she dupes him with her own fiction of chastity. For Jacob, her "unanchored" life represents a naturalistic, innocent freedom from culture, but is still subsumed as only a "feminized" category of knowledge that takes its place along-side his own "petted and cloistered" formal education. It is certainly not for him a means by which to undo those foundational academic moorings.[11]

His revelation that "women are just the same as men" does not wonder at how this can be so despite woman's complete exclusion from the domains of art and academia that he so reveres. Indeed, he reduces this freshly discovered order of "wisdom" to an intuitive, or-ganic state of being, as involuntary a condition as the female shallow-ness that so horrifies him elsewhere in the text. The "wildness" and chaos implicit in the notion of the unanchored is, from Jacob's perch of certitude, exclusive of all reflectivity, an unmediated experience of raw "spirit" that automatically accesses the very "truth" that for him, necessitates the mediative labor of study and reading. This suggests, rather paradoxically from the perspective of Jacob's own determin-ism, that "wild and frail" female is "by nature" better suited to some-how reach and withstand absolute truth than learned, "petted and cloistered" male.

But we observe in the next paragraph that Florinda enjoys a life structured as much by the Nietzschean/Paterian transformative modes of reading, interpretation, and discernment as Jacob pretends to enjoy. Her indolence is in no way a static, self-satisfied ignorance, as is demonstrated by her constant inventions of self-narrative, her attunement to the movement of "the formidable sights in the streets," and her systematic choosing of companions. While their objects of investigation are clearly disparate, the pair's practices of reading and judgment are not dissimilar. Florinda's readings are likely more revelatory than Jacob's own shallow speculations, imprecise recitations, and name-droppings. No matter—for ultimately, she is not the one to judge; that privilege is reserved, as Woolf's narrator reminds us, for men. Like Jacob himself:

> If Florinda had had a mind, she might have read with clearer eyes than we can.
>
> She and her sort have solved the question by turning it to a trifle of washing the hands nightly before going to bed, the only difficulty being whether you prefer your water hot or cold, which being settled, the mind can go about its business unassailed.
>
> But it did occur to Jacob, halfway through dinner, to wonder whether she had a mind. (79)

He reverts to the positivist binaries that ground her insistent heterogeneity into a simplistic and convenient myth of female empty-headedness that must necessarily complement female beauty. However, he quickly realizes that the intensity of his feeling for her is something for which his scholarship has not prepared him. His simplistic oppositions of male knowledge to female stupidity, of feminine beauty to its companion brainlessness, of generalized metaphysical unity to chaotic discord, become for him knotty dialectics of agency and surrender, of metatranscendence and the Heraclitean flames of corporeality, all of which are "insoluble" to a mind insistent on the "inherited dichotomies" of identitarian culture. These are dichotomies that Woolf allows to emerge only as a willful misreading of what Pater before her recognizes not as any oppositionality between these experiences, but as their necessary continuance:[12]

> Jacob observed Florinda. In her face there seemed to him something horribly brainless—as she sat staring. . . .

The problem is insoluble. The body is harnessed to a brain. Beauty goes hand in hand with stupidity. There she sat staring at the fire as she had stared at the broken mustard pot. In spite of defending indecency, Jacob doubted whether he liked it in the raw. He had a violent reversion towards male society, cloistered rooms, and the works of the classics; and was ready to turn with wrath upon whoever it was who had fashioned life thus.

Then Florinda laid her hand upon his knee.

After all, it was none of her fault. But the thought saddened him. It's not catastrophes, murders, deaths, diseases that age and kill us; it's the way people look and laugh, and run up the steps of omnibuses.

Any excuse though, serves a stupid woman. He told her his head ached.

But when she looked at him, dumbly, half-guessing, half-understanding, apologizing perhaps, anyhow saying as he had said, "It's none of my fault," straight and beautiful in body, her face like a shell within its cap, then he knew that cloisters and classics are no use whatever. The problem is insoluble. (82)

Again, all attempts at proper classification fail abjectly, as canonical "knowledge" can in no way account for "stupidity" that refuses to be stupid—and can therefore not be a complete knowledge. Jacob's momentary rage at his now impotent texts and their surrounding cloak of now-perforated authority stems from his acute sense of betrayal, as the notion of formal knowledge in which he is so heavily invested reveals itself as powerless to address the incomprehensibility of the "woman" it invents, to say nothing of the abundantly contradictory sensations and emotions that surge within him during his relationship with Florinda. It is as if Jacob's beloved texts had never incorporated into themselves the contingency of uncertainty.

It is rather as if the revered, canonical order of philosophical and literary "great fathers" had instead, in their own works, refused the risks of opacity and radical noncomprehension that accompany any utterance, any writing—therefore denying the possibility of their own fault or untruth, and in so doing, had bound themselves to strictly mimetic rehearsals of social typology. In this sense, their

works would amount to nondialogical celebrations of automatic understanding and amusement. But considering the complexities of
even the progenitor of essences, Plato, to say nothing of ineffability in
Shakespeare or Marlowe, it would perhaps be more prudent to presume some very serious misreading on Jacob's part.

When Lyotard writes that "in Joyce, it is the identity of writing
which is the victim of an excess of the book (*au trop de livre*) or of literature,"[13] he is saying that Joyce displaces the logic of the "identity of
consciousness" at work in Proust (or, say, in the English situation,
Conrad), replacing problems of subjectivity with those of the character of figuration itself. But Joyce accomplishes far more than the
simple relocation of modernist literary practice within a false binary,
lifting its project from the presumption of modernism's somehow
"pure" interiority of subjectivity to the "exteriority" of language or
more precisely, of *figure*. Joyce's work in, and more patently, after
Dubliners replays the subjective character of language itself, staging
the temporary autonomy of figure by not only detaching it radically
from its referent, but also momentarily blacking out its speaking
subject.

Joyce foregrounds the figural dimension of language that is customarily absented during the seemingly transparent communication
of its practical content, the content for which language supposedly
serves only as vehicle and not *instigator*. It is this same negative character in Virginia Woolf's writing that demonstrates the constitutive
lack within the movement of subjectivity that speech is supposed to
at least camouflage, if not fill. In what Blanchot terms "the infinite
passivity," the opposite of the assertively "garrulous prose" of the
wishful "man of power"—the passivity that alone is capable of the
most deeply penetrating incisiveness—the language of withdrawal
that characterizes this novel holds up to explicitly political critique
and sharpest ridicule the explanatory, reassuring function that instrumental speech is culturally presumed to implement, as Woolf's
aesthetic of negativity throws sharp light on the Hegelian/Kojevian/
Lacanian notion that every instance of speech necessarily disappears
the position from which it is issued.[14]

At the same time paradoxically, it is the unique *figure* of the verbal
cut that speech provides, what Lyotard terms elsewhere "the mute

perseverance of the voice," the cut that reinscribes the absolutely irreducible difference or singularity of the speaking subject, with true indifference toward its actual discourse. The alterity of the figure, which is sometimes no more than "a hesitation or a stutter," only *disfigures* the intended order of its communicative content. In *Jacob's Room* we observe that while the failure of speech to close the anxious distance of recognition is staged as an unavoidable and painful condition of subjective emergence, this failure is not total. The spoken "I" is not a discursive space of absolute absence, but is instead its representational, and therefore, hopelessly incomplete access to the dream of "whole" selfhood and social recognition inherited from elsewhere.

This partiality is the very emblem of the processuality of identity formation, all the more resonant because it is so deeply concealed by the very terms of representation during their utterance. The incompleteness of the spoken "I," the anxious need for the confirmation of one's symbolic differentiation from another, bespeaks the constitutively fractional character of subjectivity and is the very condition that necessitates articulated self-assertion to begin with. Woolf's aestheticization of the partiality of all engagement requires that any returned recognition of that spoken "I" must be incomplete as well, if for no other reason than the space of originary fragmentation from which it sends itself into circulation.[15]

Thus, the defiant "I am what I am, and intend to be it" that typifies the agonistic spirit of "youth" embodied by Jacob. His declarative "I" is uttered in the hope that its very enunciation will institute it as a separate category of concrete distinctiveness and will be enough to place unbridgeable distance between itself and the stifling, contemptible world of provincial, unread women and other inferiors who surround him. What escapes his unrelenting identitarianism is the urgency with which he attempts to represent it, failing to understand that representation itself liquidates whatever "purity" its object might claim. He premises his individual difference, rather ironically, on the completeness of his absorption into the dominant literary and intellectual tradition. Bonnie Kime Scott notes that in this novel, "Woolf was actually ahead of Joyce in deconstructing the male plan that determines both Jacob and Stephen Dedalus."[16] This view is complicated somewhat, however, by the Dedalus of Joyce's *Portrait of the Artist as a Young Man* (1916), who, I would argue, is decidedly more "Jacob-like" than the Dedalus of the later *Ulysses*, (1922) and by the more general question of whether one agrees, as I do, that Joyce's project in *Portrait* is also a sharply deconstructive one. In any case, Woolf locates the exclusively male bastion of the academy as a dominant center of ideological determination, one within and against which Jacob attempts to forge individual identity. This process is necessarily blocked by the utter totality of his identification with the academy's icons:

> But what brought Jacob Flanders to read Marlowe in the British Museum?
>
> Youth, youth—something savage—something pedantic. For example, there is Mr. Masefield, there is Mr. Bennett. Stuff them into the flame of Marlowe and burn them to cinders. Let not a shred remain. Don't palter with the second rate. Detest your own age. Build a better one. And to set that on foot read incredibly dull essays upon Marlowe to your friends. For which purpose one must collate editions in the British Museum. One must do the thing oneself. Useless to trust the Victorians, who disembowel, or to the living, who are mere publicists. The flesh and blood of the future depends entirely upon six young men. And as Jacob was one of them, no doubt he looked a little regal and pompous as he turned his page, and Julia Hedge disliked him naturally enough. (107)

Forgetting completely the vehement, youthful spirit that drives his "savage" desire to obliterate, in thoroughly Eliotic fashion, the "wasteful" mediocrity of his "own age," Jacob plunges himself totally into the slavish recovery of an anterior moment on which to construct a renewed version of the ideal. In this paradoxically agonistic and yet profoundly mimetic pursuit, Jacob remains blissfully ignorant of his own alterity. He stays unaware, on the one hand, of the inherent contradiction between his violent need to affirm a unique public status, and on the other hand, his desire of a personal selfhood that can be located only through identification with another, in this case the abstract and masculinist iconization of Marlowe as a literary and intellectual "master." Jacob remains blind to the primary opening or wound of self-doubt that can be closed only with the institution of a firmly recognized grounding in a certifiable identity that is always necessarily derived from elsewhere. His intellectual aspiration is driven completely by a narcissistic anxiety to which he is oblivious, and which is safely concealed once the sense of solid identity is appropriated, since its mere signification structures the totality of its social truth. The fact of its necessary derivation, as Mikkel Borch-Jacobsen suggests, is absolutely consistent with the savagery and pedantry that Woolf lucidly ascribes to renegade, yet strangely obsequious youth:

> Since the subject has no relation to self except as relation to the other, the question of narcissism, as question of oneself, cannot be separated from the question of the social or homosocial bond, as question of the "other myself. . . ." Narcissism is in profound collusion with power—by which we mean tyrannical power or, put another way, political madness—by virtue of its mimetic, rivalrous, (a)social origin.[17]

The rule of the institutionally anointed six will be a rule of madness masquerading as its self-unified opposite, as sober, rational authority that in ignoring the epistemological vacuum that precedes its political self-birth, demonstrates its hopeless inaccessibility to itself and, therefore, following thinkers from Freud and Nietzsche to Lacan and Shoshana Felman, articulates the extent of its madness. This madness is not merely epistemological, but is also sharply egoistic, since it institutionalizes itself as part of a tradition to which it cannot have been witness, one within which it claims unquestioned membership by identificatory right, in an act of megalomanic entitlement and aggression. This violence accounts for the erasure of "minor" figures such as Masefield who obscure for the "true inheritors" the path toward absolute truth blazed by Marlowe, or Shakespeare, Virgil or some other now-atrophied idol. Liquidated also in the carnage of young Cambridge's intellectual becoming by way of inheritance is the entire category of "woman," barred from rivalry for the same inheritance of knowledge by a tautologically misogynist exclusion of woman's supposed nonsubjectivity.

> But this service in King's College Chapel—why allow women to take part in it? . . . No one would think of bringing a dog into church. For though a dog is all very well on a gravel path and shows no disrespect to flowers, the way he wanders down an aisle, looking, lifting a paw, and approaching a pillar with a purpose that makes the blood run cold with horror (should you be one of a congregation—alone, shyness is out of the question), a dog destroys the service completely. So do these women— though separately devout, distinguished, and vouched for by the theology, mathematics, Latin and Greek of their husbands. Heaven knows why it is. For one thing, thought Jacob, they're ugly as sin. (33)

Female "intrusion" upon the "proper" sanctity of the church service is the disruptive horror that removes the foundation of truth from beneath the patriarchal traditions of worship and scholarship. The critical logic by which such decisions of inclusion and exclusion are carried out does not bother at any point to manifest itself and, in so doing, give itself over to the scrutiny of another order of critical practice, such as psychoanalysis, or, in this case, narrative art. Such a giving over of self would constitute for the sanctified spheres of knowledge ("theology, mathematics, Latin and Greek") a risk of evisceration, not only for the individual canonized thinkers and artists who would then be subject to a new and different gaze, but also for the notions of knowledge and canonicity themselves, circulated as such by a self-designated, male body of critical legislation. Hence the palpable contempt and intolerance in Jacob's rivalrous conception of womanhood. As Woolf reveals, the privilege of self-concealment is perhaps the single most crucial advantage to the perpetuation of any legislative body of domination.

In the cited passage, the madness of identitarianism extends to the hostile gaze of crudely one-dimensional "gender" identification. Woolf's relentlessly deconstructive approach offers in the feminist ideologue Julia Hedge not a corrective to the narcissistic logic of male dynasty embodied by the pompous figure of Jacob, but only an equally egoistic repetition of Jacob's sense of entitlement. Julia's gaze fails to locate in the patriarchy that forbids female intellectualism, the symbolic determinism and insistence on solidity and conformity that is patriarchy's driving engine; her anger is directed instead only at the dynastic exclusion of women from the inheritance of public/academic agency. Julia's reductively "phallic" feminism jealously covets the specular position of academic prestige for itself, imagining the library not as an ideological center of metaphysical humanism to be dismantled through a dispersive logic of ceaseless difference and intertextual play, but only as a rivalrous obstacle to a substitutive female power.

Silently reading "the names of great men" inscribed into the very walls of the library, Julia mutters "Oh damn . . . why didn't they leave room for an Eliot or a Bronte?" articulating not only a righteous anger at patriarchal myopia but also, and more symptomatically, her own effacing of singularities in the name of the faceless ideological imperative; George Eliot and the Brontës would join the library dome not as particular writers of distinct novels, but as representatives of an undifferentiated, amorphous body of "women." Julia's frustration at the literal erasure of women from cultural memory and the concretization of masculinist self-monument at the same time demonstrates her stumble into the exact kind of transcendental trap of signifying practices that Woolf aims to deconstruct. Julia's wish to have women take up an equally visible role in the will to eternity and presence, symbolized by the concrete inscription of canon into the dome of the British Library, suggests no criticism on her part of the logic of canonicity, monument, or memorial, but only the strongest identification with such narcissistic gestures of self-perpetuation.

Woolf insists on the textual characterization of such self-identical foundationalism not as a critically deconstructive feminism, but only as yet another hopelessly incomplete and self-serving defense against epistemological doubt.[18] It is significant that Julia is not recognized by Jacob during this passage, but is instead sounded by the narrator, who renders the entire scene from within a set of shifting subjective vantage points. It sounds more like Julia's voice, for instance, that designates Jacob as "one of them," while certainly it appears to be Jacob's voice that advises not to "palter with the second rate." This narration, by which a definite presence emerges just long enough to suggest itself as such, only then to morph imperceptibly into a new and distinct one, constitutes the unstable structural system of the novel, and is itself a stylistic remedy for the logocentric foundationalism that Woolf situates and undermines in each of these two characters. In *Jacob's Room*, epistemological language enables elitist patriarchy to disguise itself as a necessary mode of cultural and intellectual mastery, hermeticizing itself into an impenetrable order of knowledge. The positing of truth, in other words, becomes truth. It is crucial to Woolf's project to distinguish the will to mastery as an acceptable, even desirable cultural norm to isolate the reflexive irony by which the text then stridently deconstructs it.

Just as the novel's knowing subjects legitimate themselves simply by self-proclamation and excessive identification with their distant objects of idealization, Jacob's informants so claim the validity of their interpretations, unwittingly narrating their own vulnerability to the originary blankness of what is unknown and what always exceeds them. That their constructions vary and yet produce truth value in the rendering of a necessarily makeshift and piecemeal Jacob only underscores the nonidentical, fractional nature of truth staged within Woolf's modernism. For Woolf, the quickly forgotten fact is that any wishfully authoritative concept of Jacob is only as strong as any tissue of its constituent percepts, that all reportage about him consists only of description of his gesturality and can go no "deeper."

The Image of the Taught

Jacob's fellow Cambridge men are never seen to trouble themselves with wonder of how they came to be there. The myth of Cambridge's self-evident substance, its "thereness," effaces the obligation to understand its cultural significance as anything other than a naturally ordered entitlement, although, of course, the self-evidence of such significance is for Woolf the very point at which such interrogation must commence. For such scrutiny would expose the various tissues of myth holding the concept firmly in place. This particularly violent dialectic between the timeless notion and the fleeting figurality of the enunciation on which it depends for self-actualization, is exemplified in the following passages. We observe that venerable scholarship is able to establish itself as truth only by denying its own alterity and then silently excluding any differing interpretation or even style of presentation. For Woolf, the cost of silently self-established cultural truth is difference within culture; it is culture's own brutal denial of its heterogeneity:

> Cowan, Erasmus Cowan, sipped his port alone, or with one rosy little man, whose memory held precisely the same span of time; sipped his port, and told his stories, and without book before him intoned Latin, Virgil and Catullus, as if language were wine upon his lips. Only—sometimes it will come over one—what if the poet strode in? "This my image?" he might ask, pointing to the chubby man, whose brain is, after all, Virgil's representative among us, though the body gluttonize, and as for arms, bees, or even the plough, Cowan takes his trips abroad with a French novel in his pocket, a rug about his knees, and is thankful to be home again in his place, in his line, holding up in his snug little mirror the image of Virgil, all rayed round with good stories of the dons of Trinity and red beams of port. (41–42)

Cowan's will to masterful autonomy is undone by its very object, before which he reveals himself a weak copy. Quickly banished is the specter of Virgil, whose presence would automatically render null that of the parasitic Cambridge scholar. His own image in the mirror displaced by Virgil and a long-dead past that he can only hope to approximate in his own way, Cowan sacrifices the living spirit of Virgil's work in return for a (non)selfhood defined by its complete identification with the original. Finalizing judgment is literally sent forth in this instance, from a nonposition, from a space of critical nothingness that has willfully supplanted itself with the image of a transcendent ideal by which Cowan denies himself all corporeality and his work all temporality. Cowan has no aspirations to art, creativity, or even to a dynamic scholarship that would move beyond antihermeneutic repetitions of ancient poems. He has devoted his life to little more than a fawning curatorship of distant art, devoid of any radical revisionism or interpretative newness. What is so devastating that it cannot be borne longer than the moment of its enunciation is the reverse possibility—that of Virgil actually looking for representation of himself on earth and finding only the useless discipleship of Cowan.

Such is Cowan's scholarly sense of genuine mastery, however, that he immediately papers over this gaping void with the reassurance that his singing of Virgil's poems ("language is wine upon his lips") would be more than satisfactory to the poet himself. "Nowhere else would Virgil hear the like," muses the narrator. Self-doubt is quickly transformed into self-glorification. This luxury is denied Cowan's female colleagues at the women's college, however:

> And though, as she goes sauntering along the Backs, old Miss Umphelby sings him melodiously enough, accurately too, she is always brought up by this question as she reaches Clare Bridge: "But if I met him, what should I wear?"—and then taking her way up the avenue towards Newnham, she lets her fancy play upon other details of men's meeting with women which have never got into print. (42)

Miss Umphelby is not paralyzed by the possibility of encountering Virgil, because in her work she has not sacrificed herself intellectually or professionally to any adolescent idealization of him or of (dis)covering herself in *his* ancient glory. The "I" that wonders only what it would wear on the occasion is not crowded out of its own mirror by a self-abrogating, total identification with an idol of antiquity. She takes on the contingency of the meeting in present time and space and *asserts* herself as a singular subject in the face of Virgil, whose mere image is enough to send Cowan into hysterical pretensions. But Umphelby's very assertion of self and temporality, and the possibilities it suggests, is deemed a vulgar debasement:

> Her lectures, therefore, are not half so well attended as those of Cowan, and the thing she might have said in elucidation of the text for ever left out. In short, face a teacher with the image of the taught, and the mirror breaks. (42)

It is crucial to note that the breaking of the mirror in each respective confrontation does not signify the same idea. Cowan's very aspiration to be no more than a mirror reflecting the genius of Virgil is hardly a generous or altruistic scholarly bent, but an acutely narcissistic drive toward professional distinction enabled by the cloaking of oneself in the work of another. Cowan's method is not to *renew* the original through sharp, agonistic revision, the spirit in which the original work establishes itself, but rather to rehearse it by rote, through a simplistic immersion in the work resulting in his ability to automatically parrot its verse. The mirror breaks under the strain of reflecting both the original and its copy, the master and his voluntary slave. What breaks the mirror held up before Miss Umphelby however, is not the image of Virgil himself, but the popular *conception* of Virgil that would remove him from "vulgar," sexualized dialogue with Miss Umphelby about her mode of dress, as if he weren't concerned in his own art with sex and appearance. This public view is suggested by Woolf's inclusion of the disparity in the two instructors' class sizes and the apparent explanation for the difference—one instructor's resistant ability to sustain a singular selfhood that is not liquidated in identification with a mythologically transcendent model, and the other's sycophantic capitulation before that model.

Jacob's Cambridge enjoys the loftiness of its self-instituted centrality to the well-being of cultural understanding in general largely because its "truth" never needs to announce itself. This is an atmosphere of austere repressiveness, as is made clear by the repeated sense of the imperative that characterizes the movement of each student the narrator follows. For Woolf, this urgency signifies a differentiality born not of a spirit of discovery, but of a deeper *ressentiment* that covets not so much the actual learning of a particular discourse or designated order of knowledge as it does the public recognition of, and deference toward, its pontificatory mastery. This kind of intellectual satisfaction realizes itself not in new discovery or theoretical accomplishment, but only in the mode of conquest, as in this scene from a Cambridge reading room:

> Although young men still went in and out, they walked as if keeping engagements. . . . There were young men who read,

lying in shallow arm-chairs, holding their books as if they had hold in their hands of something that would see them through; they being all in a torment, coming from midland towns, clergymen's sons. Others read Keats. And those long histories in many volumes—surely some one was now beginning to understand the Holy Roman Empire, as one must. That was part of the concentration, though perhaps it would be dangerous on a hot spring night—dangerous, perhaps, to concentrate too much upon single books, actual chapters, when at any moment the door opened and Jacob appeared; or Richard Bonamy, reading Keats no longer, began making long pink spills from an old newspaper, bending forward, and looking eager and contented no more, but almost fierce. Why? Only perhaps that Keats died young—one wants to write poetry too and to love—oh, the brutes! It's damnably difficult. But, after all, not so difficult if on the next staircase, in the large room, there are two, three, five young men all convinced of this—of brutality, that is, and the clear division between right and wrong. There was a sofa, chairs, a square table, and the window being open, one could see how they sat—legs issuing here, one there crumpled in a corner of the sofa; and, presumably, for you could not see him, somebody stood by the fender, talking. Anyhow, Jacob, who sat astride a chair and ate dates from a long box, burst out laughing. The answer came from the sofa corner; for his pipe was held in the air, then replaced. Jacob wheeled round. He had something to say to *that*, though the sturdy red-haired boy at the table seemed to deny it, wagging his head slowly from side to side; and then, taking out his penknife, he dug the point of it again and again into a knot in the table, as if affirming that the voice from the fender spoke the truth—which Jacob could not deny. Possibly, when he had done arranging the date-stones, he might find something to say to it—indeed his lips opened—only then there broke out a roar of laughter. The laughter died in the air . . . the laughter died out, and only gestures of arms, movements of bodies, could be seen shaping something in the room. Was it an argument? A bet on the boat races? Was it nothing of the sort? What was shaped by the arms and bodies moving in the twilight room? (43–44)

"Something savage, something pedantic" structures this excruciating tension, in which the price of knowing is made plain, since nothing less than "the truth" is at stake. The sound of the ominous stabbing of the penknife into the dead, dull knot of wood speaks the absolute finality of "truth" that is only implied by this fatalistic, alinguistic gesture. The silence shrouding the holder of the knife is the void of knowledge powerless to speak itself; its jabbing into the wood a null, resentfully repetitive expelling of that void from nothingness into public circulation, nonverbal and noncontrolled as it may be, in this way similar to Jacob's disgusted sputtering earlier as he leaves the Plumer residence. As forcefully as the blade itself, the student's senseless death-grip and repetitive stabbing articulates the ever-implicit violence that conditions, indeed propels, any self-assertion of knowledge and mastery. Woolf's narratorial prop of the digging knife makes murderously concrete that at Cambridge, the stakes of identity, determination, and truth are indeed high for those who pursue them unironically.[19]

Indicative of these students' mission is their solemn countenance; the imaginary engagements that the narrator conjures for them as they darkly march their books across the chamber do not appear happy ones. Their apparent neutrality toward the objects of their scholarly investigations bespeaks the complete absence of a libidinal component to their work. They study and read joylessly and defensively in the anxious, cautionary mode of Plato and his terror of wild poetry. In trusting their books to "see them through," they grimly place a sacral faith in texts that also amounts to an aesthetic sacrifice. They instead seek the timeless "truth" content that will "see them through" this period of unknowing or uncertainty, promising on the other side of completed study a point of mastery over the formerly incomprehensible and impenetrable, their locking down of the singular difference of individual texts into the conceptual sameness of their understanding, the abstraction of reading into the objectification of accomplishment.

For these students, the texts exist not as individual irruptions of vision but only as objects of general conception and representation that function as signifying pieces of currency to be accumulated and counted as intellectual property or as private conquests. Richard

Bonamy typifies this habit of reading *against* color, vibration and impression, preferring instead *substance*. In this remarkable passage, Woolf also underscores the narcissistic economy of taste, the mirroring operation that enables the formation of "schools" of art or thought, individuals drawn together by the sense of themselves apparent within the other:

> I like books whose virtue is all drawn together in a page or two. I like sentences that don't budge though armies cross them. I like words to be hard—such were Bonamy's views, and they won him the hostility of those whose taste is all for the fresh growths of the morning, who throw up the window, and find the poppies spread in the sun, and can't forbear a shout of jubilation at the astonishing fertility of English literature. That was not Bonamy's way at all. That his taste in literature affected his friendships, and made him silent, secretive, fastidious, and only quite at his ease with one or two men of his way of thinking, was the charge against him. (140)

Bonamy's repudiation by his more hermeneutically adventurous classmates is telling, for Woolf cannot resist alluding to the "perilous" practices of rigidly schematic reading that always involve some personal relation to the language of the text and thus invite, on some bare level, a sacrifice of the knowing self in pursuit of "senseless," sensory pleasure. This is the razor's edge of the "dangerous" threatened by the narrator—the premise that as long as one is reading, there exists the possibility of realizing the anarchic promise of fascination and the random irruptivity of language's internal gestures. Thus the necessity, in the library scene of viciously eliminating "the single book," "the actual chapter," the purely accidental figurality, the materiality of a localized sound, rhythm or color instantiated by word or phrase that arrests readerly sensibility and so derails an otherwise teleological, piloted reading from its narrow, content-oriented objectives of solid determination and truth value.

The text plays ironically on the self-established traditions of Western philosophical discourse by referring repeatedly to the significative *functions* of names like Plato, Virgil, Shakespeare and Mozart. But

it contains no contextual space in which these names, once introduced, are able to demonstrate the processes of thought, knowledge
or truth that their names are invoked to represent. These names are
sacralized and extolled not only within the canons of the academy
but also by Jacob and his young friends Timothy Durrant and
Richard Bonamy; but the "presence" communicated by the gesture of
invocation, or fragmentary quotation, is never actually *made present*
by any of these characters, by their actually engaging any formulation
from any of the ancestral masters. Woolf deflates the collective wind-
bag of uncritical, intellectual posturing throughout the text, as in this
hybridized, dandified interior ramble:

> ("I'm twenty-two. It's nearly the end of October. Life is thor-
> oughly pleasant, although unfortunately there are a great num-
> ber of fools about. One must apply oneself to something or
> other—God knows what. Everything is really very jolly—except
> getting up in the morning and wearing a tailcoat.")
> "I say, Bonamy, what about Beethoven?"
> ("Bonamy is an amazing fellow. He knows practically every-
> thing—not more about English literature than I do—but then
> he's read all those Frenchmen.")
> "I rather suspect you're talking rot, Bonamy. In spite of what
> you say, poor old Tennyson . . ."
> ("The truth is one ought to have been taught French . . .") (72)

Edward Bishop catches the charm and the attractively disjunctive
rhythm of Jacob's flittish cast of mind, noting how "his thoughts (run)
in obvious counterpoint to his utterances," and he juxtaposes its discontinuity against Jacob's inclinations toward the "statuesque."[20]
Beethoven and Tennyson are reduced to failed signposts in this "exchange," bypassed in a rush of self-absorbed observation, incomplete
thoughts and sentences, and postadolescent academic posture.

The text's critique, however, consists in no simple antagonism
toward the canonical men of literature, art, and philosophy. Rather, it
traces, with varying degrees of playful humor and sardonic sharpness, the academically superficial and egoistic gestures of reference
and invocation that in themselves establish the legitimacy of those

who quote (and misquote) the proper names, as the only proper intellectual heirs to those names.

This is but one aspect of the falsifying violence carried out in the logic of knowing. In this novel it is a violence that invariably ejects female subjectivity and art from the entire field of cultural production, while providing still more monuments to male scholarship and accomplishment, no matter how shallow or inconsistent with its own standards of rectitude. Jacob's near-complete ignorance of Greek and ancient history is no obstacle to his acting out his identification with the imagined spirit and grandeur of Greek antiquity:

> "Now let us talk," said Jacob, as he walked down Haverstock Hill between four and five o'clock in the morning of November the sixth arm-in-arm with Timmy Durrant, "about something sensible."
>
> The Greeks—yes, that was what they talked about—how when all's said and done, when one's rinsed one's mouth with every literature in the world, including Chinese and Russian (but these Slavs aren't civilized), it's the flavour of Greek that remains. Durrant quoted Aeschylus—Jacob Sophocles. It is true that no Greek could have understood or professor refrained from pointing out—Never mind; what is Greek for if not to be shouted on Haverstock Hill in the dawn? Moreover, Durrant never listened to Sophocles, nor Jacob to Aeschylus. They were boastful, triumphant; it seemed to both that they had read every book in the world; known every sin, passion, and joy . . .
>
> "Probably," said Jacob, "we are the only people in the world who know what the Greeks meant." (76)

Indeed, the narrator seems to forgive this habit in Jacob as somewhat charming, even as she continually points it out with a hardness more directed at Jacob's privileged social typology than at Jacob himself. This kind of ambiguity, in keeping with Woolf's radical leap of aesthetics from positionality, category, and criterion into contradiction, incoherence, and self-effacement, enacts the move into the negative sublime of modernism. The apparent jaggedness of the narrative oscillations between Jacob's actual speech to Bonamy and the protagonist's interior asides resolves itself within the internal logic of the novel. This pattern of oscillation is preoccupied with the contradictory presence of difference in the self-constitution of thought and position, as well as with the necessary exclusion from this process of the other's participation, rendered here by the silencing of Richard Bonamy. The narrator reorders the conceptual structure of conversation, enacting it not as a content-oriented mode of pure exchange, but instead as a profoundly solipsistic arena in which the presence of the other is necessary for the realization of different aspects of the self.

Jacob's playful nonsense stands at odds with the imago of the pompous knowing subject that others, like Julia Hedge, see buried in volumes of Marlowe in the British Museum. In Jacob's unwitting deconstruction of himself as a false guardian of Western canonicity, Woolf again floats to the surface of the narrative the disruptive play of incongruity. She distances Jacob, however slightly, further from proximity with his public image by granting him a spoken agency that removes the ground from beneath itself and becomes silly. At no point does she subsume the infinite play of difference and signification to a prescribed ideological dogma that is itself only a repetition in reverse of the dominant, specular logic of essentializing.

If positionality is thematized in the novel as necessarily always self-distant and unstable, then the opening scene, in which several simultaneous attempts at *com*position are disrupted or marred, is consistent with Woolf's narrative program of communicative and hermeneutic failure. Teardrops stain the page on which the widow Betty Flanders composes a long letter to her companion Captain Barfoot, as she sits quietly on the beach at Cornwall, and the welling in her eyes washes away her necessary sense of continuity, blurring and distorting her immediate view. Indeed, her very punctuation in the letter is "dissolved," as her intended "full stop" spreads into an indeterminate blot that throws into question the notion of "proper" beginnings and endings, and disrupts the communicative, suturing function of writing itself.

She is jarred further by the unanswered calls of her son Archer, who tries in vain to summon Jacob, his older brother. The nothingness evoked by Archer's echoing cries establishes itself as the organizing motif of the entire narrative, figuring itself not only in the concluded, but somehow unfinished letter of Betty Flanders, but also in her own disruption of another composition, of which she is the principal, though unwitting object. For as she rises from the beach and gathers her materials, concerned about the whereabouts of the still silent Jacob, she ruins the painterly field of Charles Steele, an artist working on the beach who has made the writing widow the center of his present work in progress:

> "Scarborough," Mrs. Flanders wrote on the envelope, and dashed a bold line beneath. It was her native town; the hub of the universe. But a stamp? She ferreted in her bag; then held it up mouth downwards; then fumbled in her lap, all so vigorously that Charles Steele in the Panama hat suspended his paint brush.
>
> Like the antennae of some irritable insect it positively trembled. Here was that woman moving—actually going to get up—confound her! He struck the canvas a hasty violet-black dab. For the landscape needed it. It was too pale—greys flowing into lavenders, and one star or a white gull suspended just so— too pale as usual. The critics would say it was too pale, for he was an unknown man exhibiting obscurely, a favourite with his landladies' children, wearing a cross on his watch chain, and much gratified if his landladies liked his pictures—which they often did.
>
> "Ja-cob! Ja-cob," Archer shouted. (8)

In her freedom to decide when to write and when to abandon writing, Betty shatters another autonomous project in which she enjoys no freedom whatsoever, a work of which she happens to be the central element. The singularity disrupts the whole, the totality of Steele's artwork now proven dependent on Betty's total complicity with her own negation, her own desubjectification as a silent sitter.[21] It should be observed at the same time however, that Betty's seemingly sudden and aimless movement away from her own letter to Barfoot is a movement of freedom only in the sense that she is not restricted by any external boundary. Her apparently precipitate abandonment of the letter is instead an outcome of an unsatisfactory process of labor that shuts down her progress and, in this sense, leads her away from it, making her abandonment of the letter as voluntary or autonomous an act as her uncontrolled tears moments before. While the letter appears concluded, the banality of its content ("everything seems satisfactorily arranged, packed though we are like herrings in a barrel and forced to stand the perambulator which the landlady quite naturally won't allow . . .") seems violently incongruous with Betty's tearful emotions. The divergence between her tearful affect and the content of her communication presents a chaotically unifying frame for the scene, as this split is analogous to the tortured disunity between the stable reality of her surroundings and the blurred, distorted vision that actually momentarily paralyzes her:

> Slowly welling from the point of her gold nib, pale blue ink dissolved the full stop; for there her pen stuck; her eyes fixed, and tears slowly filled them. The entire bay quivered; the lighthouse wobbled; and she had the illusion that the mast of Mr. Connor's little yacht was bending like a wax candle in the sun. She winked quickly. Accidents were awful things. She winked again. The mast was straight; the waves were regular; the lighthouse was upright; but the blot had spread. (7)

This detachment between realities resonates obviously in the distance between the two Bettys—the frustrated, representing writer/subject on the beach and the innocuous, sunbathing object of representation on Steele's canvas. Betty's movement and departure breaks the semblance of harmony within Steele's landscape and returns it to the private disunity that preceded it, destroying the coherent fiction of an undisturbed writer on the beach that would negate the truer representation of its troubled genesis. But this antagonistic rupture, by itself, does not destroy the semblance of aesthetic unity internal to Steele's work; rather, the rupture of the accidental returns the artwork to the space of uncertainty within which it inaugurates itself, and in this sense restores to it *its own language*. When Steele, in irritation, strikes onto the canvas the "hasty violet-black dab," that seems more a reflex physical action than a decisive act, the movement is true in the same way that the seeming abruptness of Betty's departure is true. It is a paradoxically random movement of freedom that is yet somehow forced, somehow coerced or reluctant, and in this way, a movement that ultimately imposes an even more nuanced and defined shape on the final result. Steele recognizes this more sublime unity within difference almost immediately:

> Steele frowned; but was pleased by the effect of the black—it was just *that* note which brought the rest together. "Ah, one may learn to paint at fifty! There's Titian . . ." and so, having found the right tint, up he looked and saw to his horror a cloud over the bay. (9)

Woolf's outrageously reflexive humor denies the artist of vision even a moment to admire his own work, as he is immediately forced to risk himself again in the face of a fresh element of difference and antagonism. Steele's deft placement of the black intrusion breaks the happily false positivity of the beach landscape, introducing an unforeseen element that does not exist on the beach, but that symbolizes dramatically the contingency that continually resurfaces on the material landscape in the form of either the shouting Archer, the disappeared Jacob, or, of course, Betty Flanders's abrupt rise and departure. It is this contingency that provides his work the semblance of its true unity, because in its very intrusiveness, it guarantees the work's necessary distance from itself. It is a potentially fatal riskiness that, as Woolf adumbrates by means of the emergent threatening cloud, must continually appear and reappear to keep the work from complacently settling for itself contentedly, and not pushing itself out any further into the violence of self-discovery.

This principle of heterogeneity and unity through dissociation not only governs at the level of her thematic content but also constitutes Woolf's narrative fabric. For at the beginning of the first cited passage, Betty Flanders enjoys an interiority that is dissipated within two sentences, her own fragmentary discourse pushed to the margins by the arrival of Steele's. But his narrative proves no more cohesive than Betty's, since his anger at her movement reverts, with only the abrupt dab of black providing a formal vehicle of transition, to his prior, single-minded preoccupation with his art. But even this concentration dissolves quickly from the immediate into the abstract, as his concerns with the specific elements of color and space before him transform imperceptibly, as do his grays into lavenders, into broader worries about the critical response to his work, his commercial status, and his local reputation.

Isolated elements of thought and material disjoin all continuity in the narrative to the degree that disjunction gradually reveals itself as the organizing principle thereof. The violence of the violet-black blot's insertion into the "too pale" landscape not only provides the thematic key toward reading Woolf's aesthetic theory of heterogeneity and dissonance; it also doubles as the technical hinge on which she is able to *enact* it, as the inclusion of the dab propels Steele from the stasis of petulant anger into the motion of interpretation. It sends the character and the narrative forward temporally, while sustaining the illusion of frozen or static time through attentiveness to the multidirectional paths (meaning path*less*ness) of his personal ruminations on his public status as an artist. Within this seemingly self-contradictory space of radical exclusion, made all the more incongruous by its very spontaneity, Steele's thoughts and associations demonstrate themselves to be oriented intensely on issues of personal anxiety revolving around self-worth. These subvert any readings of the passage arguing a dissociative, aimless "stream" of aestheticized inconsequentialities.

What is to be made of the strong motif in *Jacob's Room* of the profoundly nondialectical unanswered call, the endless call that continually tries and fails to summon Jacob from nothingness? This is the absence of the text that *is* permitted to remain an absence, the dialogue with a void that never becomes anything more. It is filled not by the actual Jacob, but rather by his potent suggestion, a suggestion that always bears the inscriptive weight of its speaker. His existence as a character is purely asymptotic, and yet in its absence and its catastrophic effect on those who are left without him, also anything but imaginary, as evinced by the urgency of their repeated, unanswered calls to him. The negative underside or remainder of the real that continually reveals itself in these numerous narratives of Jacob is each speaker's anxious imagining of Jacob's gaze itself, of each speaker's image of self as seen by Jacob. Part of the novel's pathos lies in that this image is usually marginal in itself; few seem to have made substantial impressions on the absent character whose absence now underscores the sense of liminality that already saturates the narratives of his survivors.

This sense of self-marginality takes on greater resonance with the recurring silence that answers Archer's plaintive cries of "Ja-cob! Ja-cob!" as the novel opens. These cries into the void are a device by which Woolf marks Jacob with death; from that moment on within the text, most particularly within its fragmentary glimpses of his living, his name reverberates within that primary silence. Receiving nothing in return, the call is forced to answer itself; it produces accounts of Jacob where Jacob himself fails to materialize. The silence evokes the power of language to create presence, of the discursive to figure phenomenality.

That this figural creation is a presence-ing of negativity, a purely verbal testimony to the absence for which it can never substitute, and yet *must* in every utterance, demonstrates the most shattering evidence of the text's principle of nonidentity. The call is always issued from a single narrative voice, representing to itself constructions of Jacob that are determinate and finite, and yet, as purely linguistic renderings, are utterly powerless to conjure him other than relationally. This distance itself communicates an undermining sense of untruth or failure structuring the novel, since these representations are determined and arranged not by Jacob, of course, but by his external informants who are themselves at once marginal and central to the narration, present only to their render their own "sightings" of Jacob and whose voices dissolve in the course of that rendering. They are also oblivious to what they necessarily disclose of themselves by speaking. But the narrator does not neglect to stage the anxiety and egoism that impels their speech and animates their voices.

> Nobody sees any one as he is, let alone an elderly lady sitting opposite a strange young man in a railway carriage. They see a whole—they see all sorts of things—they see themselves.

Or,

> One must do the best one can with her report. Anyhow, this was Jacob Flanders, aged nineteen. It is no use trying to sum people

up. One must follow hints, not exactly what is said, nor yet entirely what is done—(31)

For this novel, the plastic and contingent nature of discursive meaning, identity and referentiality is what constitutes and organizes our representations of all subjective and social experience, hence the text's foregrounding of the plasticity and contingency of symbolic speech and language. This practice enacts an implicit critique of naturalized conceptual and political "givens" that ignore, conceal, or otherwise remain silent upon the necessity and the reality of their own *self-giving*.

Part II

Narcissism and Nothingness

3

Maladjusted Phantasms: The Ontological Question of Blackness in Light in August

The Negro, by his presence, being on the bottom, affords society almost the only coherence that it has. . . . That means if I'm on the bottom and you can see me there, then you are not.
—James Baldwin, interviewed on the BBC program
Encounters, July 1965

The man who has not experienced the fear of death does not know that the given, natural world is hostile to him, that it tends to kill him, to destroy him, and that it is essentially unsuited to satisfy him really. This man, therefore, remains fundamentally bound to the given World.
—Alexandre Kojève, *Introduction to the Reading of Hegel: Lectures on the Phenomenology of Spirit*

The private consequences of the public mandate of cultural role-play, scrutinized with such unrelenting irony by Conrad and then by Woolf, are disclosed perhaps most graphically in the American con-texts of literary modernism. With William Faulkner's *Light in August*

(1932), we observe that the failure to "identify properly" not only unhinges every schema of social ordering but also sets into motion the
mechanisms by which such projects of power will defend and perpetuate themselves by force. In other words, the novel is largely about
how the failure to identify adequately can get one killed.

As Edouard Glissant writes in his critical reflection, *Faulkner, Mississippi,* Faulkner's work:

> is revealed as infinite, not locked in by any "answer" or solution.
> The characters in the work are not "types," determined in ad-
> vance by possible answers as conceived by the author; they are
> people prey to this gaping wound, to a suspension of being, a
> stasis, an unhappy deferral acted out through wild exuberance
> or repressed within. Whether savagely racist, pathologically an-
> tiracist, or morbidly indifferent, these people are not compelled
> by such questions, but they inhabit the vertigo.[1]

In the fugitive body of the enigmatic drifter Joe Christmas—a body
in flight from various arms of law and determinacy, including that of
racial identification since its very pigmentation cannot be cleanly ar-
rogated or disposed of in racial terms—*Light in August* localizes such
a citizen of vertigo, presenting in this character at once repetitions of
stereotypes of "blackness" and deconstructive ridicule of the anterior
demand for racialization. This is not to mention, in this same character, an opaque imagining of sexual life that makes porous whatever
boundaries are presumed to delimit the notion of "gender." The originary wound of which Glissant speaks, the primary void from which
all designations follow, is one that Joe never makes any overt attempt
to close. His own inability to account for who he is exactly, his own
anxiety of origins and belongings, never compels him to falsify himself by laying claim to any specific cultural place of home. His truth is
made evident only in his bearing, as his countenance and his rhythms
of speech and movement alone announce the depth of a personal
sovereignty secure enough in its own needs and its own deeds never
to have to publicly claim itself as such. His every utterance and every
step communicates his absolute social nonbelonging, making plain
the totality of his distance from every familiar or conventional way of

being in the Mississippi village he has wandered into. His castration at the town's hands must be read as a vengeful return of the wound that his very presence is felt to inflict on its inhabitants, for his every self-contained, indifferent gesture is, for them, a complete severing of every expectation of sociality or kinship.

Joe's customary silence and general inscrutability keep him "behind the veil" of his "negro's job" at the Jefferson, Mississippi, planing mill. But what Faulkner circulates here is doubt as to what constitutes the exact fabric of this "veil": doubt whether a "negro's job" is designated as such simply by social habituation repeated so often and so uncritically as to have by now become unwritten law, or whether its distinction somehow proceeds by some mystically and uniquely "negro" characteristic of the body performing it. The very *form* of Joe's intrusion as a figure of otherness into a social texture of white, masculine homogeneity antagonizes his new judges, presenting them not only with an unapologetic object of incomprehensibility, *but also with a specific stylization of aporia* that is mocking as well as menacing. His idiom of communication is not shared with the townsfolk; it is outside the boundaries of common exchange, opening a fissure with the very logic of communication itself. The inscrutable cut of his carriage unhinges the promise of immediate clarity that inheres in the common speech that organizes Jefferson life, moving instead into the opening of profound absence that such language works so assiduously to close.

Where James Wait's appearance on the deck of the *"Narcissus"* scandalizes its crew because of their inability to properly assimilate his indifference to the very idea of assimilating, Christmas's arrival in this small Mississippi village seems to transmit a silent danger, a palpable if unspoken threat to the status quo:

And the group of men at work in the planer shed looked up, and saw the stranger standing there, watching them. They did not know how long he had been there. He looked like a tramp, yet not like a tramp either. His shoes were dusty and his trousers were soiled too. But they were of decent serge, sharply creased, and his shirt was soiled but it was a white shirt, and he wore a tie and a stiff-brim straw hat that was quite new, cocked at an angle

arrogant and baleful above his still face. He did not look like a
professional hobo in his professional rags, but there was something definitely rootless about him, as though no town nor city
was his, no street, no walls, no square of earth his home. And
that he carried this knowledge with him always as though it were
a banner, with a quality ruthless, lonely and almost proud. (32)

Joe's contradictory presentation of a man who looks "like a tramp, yet
not like a tramp," whose trousers are soiled, yet expensive and sharply
creased, whose shirt is soiled, and is yet still a dress white shirt, bespeaks a fragmentation that refuses to account for its sundered condition, as if this is a condition of deficit. It refuses to disintegrate into
pure abjection, maintaining a sense of self-unity by expressly *not*
masking over any single one of the incongruous elements of appearance that simultaneously announce and splinter him. He instead allows his soiling to speak itself as a singularity reflective of his lived
reality, itself absolutely equal to some distant moment of affluence to
which the serge trousers, stiff hat, and white shirt testify from behind
the present embodiment of destitution they now project.

Christmas's poverty occludes any material ascesis that would literally whitewash him, remove his dirt, and, in so doing, strip away a
central layering of his own historical and living matter—matter that
makes visible the tangible discontinuum of any actual history. Within
the expensive fabric of the clothes, the soil literalizes the transient
sedimentation that his character enacts, a visible residue of differentiality that negates any broader concept of coherence by which he
would be explained. In the body of Christmas, the sedimentation of
temporal experience collapses on itself as a mass of visible contradictions that discloses its disunity as its signature, and is, in this sense, to
be seen as an irreducible unit of chaos. This self-expressivity of self-
absence is the molecular "banner" of nonidentity that is "carried with
him always" and which "ruthless(ly)" communicates itself to those
who try to dictate its unification.

As the text demonstrates its own groundlessness in its disinclina-
tion to classify Christmas, it performs the noncomprehension that
surfaces within the mill workers themselves during their initial encounter with him. The impoverished stranger is measured under
their gaze, the totality of his material lack evident from the filthy con-

dition of his clothes. Yet it is this very sense of complete defeat that enables the intensity of the gaze by which he equalizes himself, fixing the men in his silent stare, despite his seemingly not being "positioned" or "entitled" to do so. The silence that accompanies this unwavering gaze is at once the *promise* and the *execution* of the danger he represents; it is the sound of a failed identification, a refuted interpellation, and is therefore the sound of a thwarted and dispossessed politics of domination—the sound of what is not already given. Its mute refusal to account for itself is an insolence before the "law" of proper identification—mandated and articulated by the workers' dumb gaze alone.

For the immediate question that leads them into "baffled outrage" at his image is of how a being so beaten can derive the "agency" necessary to gaze on another without fear, as if he is its master, and not its slave. By all external indication, save his "baleful" look, Christmas is vanquished. But the terms of his experiential vanquishing are the same by which he is able to attribute a sense, however fleeting and insubstantial, of irreducible value to himself. This is evinced by the phenomenality of his very survival, even conquering of personal destitution; his filth and dress function as coequal signatories to his unique emergence as an evanescent, defiantly self-refusing presence. The apparent oxymoron of his presence is deconstructed by its formal terms, which liquidate the assignations by which Christmas would be symbolically disposed, subsumed under one cultural identification or another. Constituted as he is by visible oppositions and absences, sartorially as well as epidermally, such overdetermination cannot bear its own weight, and in his movement beyond such categories, his radical difference as a thinking force materializes.

Barbara Ladd glosses Glissant's useful notion of Creolization in her discussion of other marginalized Faulkner protagonists, finding the pivot into their ontological break from domination less in their tonality of skin than in the totality of a historico/intellectual engagement with life events that give shapes and make impressions that cannot be explained or classified by such schemes as "race":

> Glissant is himself an "Other American" writer of French and African descent, a creole. When Glissant speaks of the creole and of creolization, however, he speaks more broadly and more

figuratively, not only to suggest "metissage," a mixing of races, but also the "long-unnoticed process of integration and regeneration" to which it gave birth; "creolization," Glissant writes, "adds something new to the components that participate in it." For Glissant, William Faulkner is creole, despite his U.S. citizenship and predominantly British ancestry, by virtue of his identification with the Other America of the U.S. South and his immersion in its own process of cultural and racial regeneration. . . . When seen as a representative of Euro American rather than Other American literary traditions, Faulkner has been read as a writer embedded in the universalizing Western Historical vision. In other words, he has been interpreted in terms of a specifically Western concept, associated with Hegel, which maintains that human and cultural events are part of and the product of a transcendent and rational force that encompasses and gives direction to those events. . . . But for Faulkner, as for many other writers of the "Other America," there is, for good reason having to do with the experience of slavery and colonization, little sense of an actual investment in this History. . . . As Glissant himself has demonstrated, in speaking *as* a Creole, one speaks from the intersection where History confronts and is confronted by the histories of the colonized, the dispossessed, the exiled. . . . For Glissant, the voice of William Faulkner speaks from this intersection against History—surrounded by and marshalling the voices of the Other America.[2]

As the object of the workers' wonder, Christmas's consolidation of contradictory impressions transfixes them in the attempt to understand and to master an indecipherably "Other" presence beyond immediate assimilation. In the Lacanian distinction between the eye of the subject and its gaze onto an external object, the subject unwittingly sacrifices itself to its will to subordinate the object of its gaze, as such subordination helps constitute the realization of the subject's self-certainty.[3] However, that subject cannot grasp the already accompanying truth, that in remaining outside the field of what its eye perceives, it is invisible to itself in the act of looking. It presumes instead the clear solidity of its own position, the supreme vantage point at which its being is unquestioned and at which the absolute, pure objecthood of all within the visible is "given." The look returned from the object in this instance, however (Christmas), is a violent intersubjective and aesthetic cut that reduces that of his judges (the workers), and also of the novel's reader, to a mere, rank object itself, one that cannot hope to determine the singular place of otherness within Christmas from which their looking is so effortlessly refigured and reprojected as an object. The workers' anxiety of mastering the aporetic presence of Christmas is arrested by the returned gaze in this dialectic and the men are left in a black hole of wonder *and* hatred. Their wonder orients around the new inexplicability, while their visceral hatred is a response to the formal structure of its intrusion. It is hostility at the specularization of this "foreign" other's indifferent self-presentation, at the smoothness of its calm, seemingly impossible self-possession—which in itself fractures and distorts the world of solidity and coherence they have so completely fashioned for themselves.

Again undermining its own authority, the narrative suggests a specific position for the racialized, this being the "negro's job," only to fill it with a character who appears impossible to racialize. As the nature of this particular job shoveling sawdust is evidently so menial that only a "negro" would accept it, and its very baseness reinscribes tautologically the function of the constructed division of "negro" from "white," it would seem that a suitable "negro" would have been found beforehand to perform it. For any "white" man to perform the job would suggest a certain "negro-ness" on his part—not a desirable projection in Jefferson, Mississippi. But the job is not occupied by any actual "negro" when Christmas arrives, and his insertion into the position, despite his not being thought to be "negro," supports not only the question of whether anyone taking the job would be figured socially as somehow analogous to such an abject "negro" but also how and why the position came to be so designated originally. Christmas's name and his "parchment-colored" skin generate abundant speculation as to how to frame him socially:

"His name is what?" one said.
     "Christmas."

"Is he a foreigner?"

"Did you ever hear of a white man named Christmas?" the foreman said.

"I never heard of nobody a-tall named it," the other said.

And that was the first time Byron remembered that he had ever thought how a man's name, which is supposed to be just the sound for who he is, can be somehow an augur of what he will do, if other men can only read the meaning in time. (33)

The very name "Christmas" deflects safe conceptualization, under- mining again the Hegelian logic by which the linguistic abstraction of naming would vaporize the named thing itself. The strangeness of Christmas's name enables him a literal escape from the totalizing power of social abstraction, as he can be figured only as something "foreign," a marginally recuperative gesture in which the indetermi- nacy of his name echoes in sound the "inconclusiveness" of his skin color, which itself eludes any "proper" racialization.[4] "Christmas" as a surname fails to register meaningfully within a system of representa- tion in which "a man's name is . . . just the sound for who he is," in which the sovereignty of aurality would give itself over to the cultural imperative of social exchangeability and make itself absolutely iden- tical with the object it would slavishly denote. No one appears able to explain why Christmas's name, or rather its sound, is not congruous with his "insufferable, baleful" appearance, and the imaginary dis- tance between the signifier and the evident "signified" disrupts the local hermeneutic system, forbidding the workers' identification of him with any image of familiarity or even comprehension.

While his very introduction subverts the identifying, explanatory function of the name, Christmas's embodiment of his "banner" of nonidentity is unfurled visibly in the flat, (anti)expressivity of his face, a silent participation within the matrix of symbolic exchange that his presence transfigures so traumatically elsewhere. The "still," "inscrutable" expression is interpreted by the men as "darkly con- temptuous" and "insufferable," while even his inanimate hat takes on a "baleful" character. His very quietude and blank inscrutability an- tagonize the regulatory character of what Butler terms the "discipli- nary production of the subject,"[5] meaning only that his silence registers as such a hostile threat because it directly repudiates an authority of designation always assumed by those gazing on him. This authority would presume the power to name or interpellate him as an object of safe representation and thereby win his allegiance for having recognized and approved him. Their fear and hatred reflect not only their bewilderment before the aporia he represents, but also an intolerance for that aporia's apparent lack of innocence, its utter lack of fear or humility before *them,* its absolute absence of any need for them. Their hostility is the function or the outcome of a narcissistic desire to see in Christmas's expression a clear acknowledgment of their power, a desire thwarted by the ever-present signature of death that is his still, dark expression:

> They did not know who he was. None of them had ever seen him before. "Except that's a pretty risky look for a man to wear on his face in public," one said. "He might forget and use it somewhere where somebody won't like it." (32)

As the narration abandons itself suddenly, failing to maintain itself before this rejection of self-posited authority, and giving way to the hateful interruption of one of the nameless workers, so too does that worker forget the specificity of his own hostility; in so doing, he bespeaks his own terror of Christmas. His speech originates from a bruised narcissism that sarcastically masquerades itself as a warning advisement, as if Christmas's "look" is approved locally but might subject itself to dangerous misinterpretation elsewhere. The worker projects the actual labor of his violent wish for Christmas onto a contingent, fictitious "somebody," conveniently unavailable to physically remove the "look" that, in immediate reality, is not a "risky" one at all for Christmas, given the town's anxiety about his presence. For the "formal" texture of his countenance and appearance is an intrusion of aesthetic otherness that in itself establishes concrete proof of an experiential and political difference separating him hopelessly from this culture.

The substance of this presumably formal gulf of difference between the now openly contentious subjects inheres in the material cost of the "other's" persistence within a zone that finds itself unable to refigure him into any mode of comfortable assimilation and at the same time cannot permit his difference to remain difference. But Joe's' undigestability is only the outcome of that culture's prior insistence on constructed, doctrinal difference as a way to wield power; his withdrawal and elusiveness is the strange and bitter fruit of that egoistic insistence. In other words, the very "race" discourse that has historically excluded and "niggered" him personally into a threatening repository of undefinable excess and nothingness at once is now collecting painfully on its self-investment.

By the time he arrives in Jefferson, Christmas has already survived his own obliteration many times, beginning with the death of his mother as he is born, her murderous punishment from her father for giving birth to a supposedly "black" child. The forfeiture of his original name contributes to his social alienation in the orphanage in which he lives until he is five, and where he is introduced to the concept of being a "nigger," the primary name by which the other children refer to him. The repressive family regime of his adoptive father McEachern reinstitutionalizes the renunciation of his own particularity for the next thirteen years, as the father demands unquestioning conformity to his rules. The blur of the following fifteen years, after his departure from that house, is described as a long interminable avenue along which he ran in wishful escape from his own negation:

> From that night the thousand streets ran as one street, with imperceptible corners and changes of scene, broken by intervals of begged and stolen rides, on trains and trucks, and on country wagons with he at twenty and twenty-five and thirty sitting on the seat with his still, hard face and the clothes (even when soiled and worn) of a city man, and the driver of the wagon not knowing who or what the passenger was and not daring to ask. The street ran into Oklahoma and Missouri and as far south as Mexico, and then back north to Chicago and Detroit and then back south again and at last to Mississippi. It was fifteen years long . . . (223–24)

Moving seemingly without end or even evident direction are these sentences themselves, installing the readerly experience of a life anchored by nothing, promising nothing and aimed toward nothing. Able to live anywhere, Christmas is also able to leave anywhere, attached to no home and no particular other. Even as he finds himself tramping across the country in a life of perpetual dislocation, his indeterminate self-presentation refuses any egoistic specularization from the outside, does not permit the other to see itself reflected in his countenance, and turns the quizzical, helpless gaze of that other on itself. Unable at any point to assert the agency by which he would determine his own broken path or even the mode of his transport, dependent utterly on the material health of another from whom he can beg or steal, he appears always already conditioned to the social status of nonbeing. The only guarantor of his singularity is the veritable inscription of rejection and lack in his stony, facial blankness. His overdetermined presence, underscored as always by his silent refusal of self-accountability, transmits not only the silent threat that so unnerves Jefferson but also a greater mystery surrounding the history of his own suffering—a suffering whose detail he does not disclose and whose enigma averts all explanation. As Joe's image is so overloaded with visibly discrete narratives as to defy any one imposition of unitary meaning, it blocks interpellation at the same moment that it demands it.

What is required on the part of the townspeople of Jefferson is the abyssal nonvocabulary of self-risk and self-negation; it is Joe Christmas's language, one to which they can have no access whatsoever, grounded as it is in the experience of death. Remembering Blanchot's axiom, later refigured by Bataille and again by Agamben, that imaginings of death within the social can be asserted only representationally, that the concept of death can take shape only through the necessary, but falsifying, distance of identification with the dead, the chasm separating Christmas from culture becomes perceptible. For Christmas has, in Kojevian fashion, experienced the risk of his life and its loss within the symbolic matrix of culture. He has come to embrace, indeed to live, a nothingness and continual self-annulment that others cannot yet imagine:

"Ain't you going to knock off," Byron said.
    The other expelled smoke. Then he looked at Byron. His face was gaunt, the flesh a level dead parchment color. Not the skin:

the flesh itself, as though the skull had been molded in a still and deadly regularity and then baked in a fierce oven. "How much do they pay for overtime?" he said. And then Byron knew. He knew then why the other worked in the Sunday clothes, and why he had had no lunch with him either yesterday or today, and why he had not quit with the others at noon. He knew as well as if the man had told him that he did not have a nickel in his pockets and that in all likelihood he had lived on cigarettes for two or three days now. Almost with the thought Byron was offering his own pail, the action as reflex as the thought. Because before the act was completed the man, without changing his indolent and contemptuous attitude, turned his face and looked once at the proffered pail through the drooping smoke of the cigarette. "I ain't hungry. Keep your muck." (35)

What Byron fails to grasp is that for Christmas, the giving of the gift, of help or charity, amounts only to an imposition, to the establishment of a dialectical social relation and therefore to the responsibility of a response. Acceptance of Byron's offering would efface the experience of his starvation and lack, the only kind of experience that registers within Christmas as singularly his own. His nothingness functions as the deepest evidence of his free subjectivity and his narcissism. To displace it with Byron's lunch would open a space of shared recognition between the two, a symbolically self-negating relation in which a "virginal" outsider, with no conception of how Joe has labored to forge his difference, could remove that difference by abstracting Joe into the grateful recipient of a good deed, an unlucky comrade in need. Byron cannot conceive of nothingness as a livable condition, while for Joe the inability to integrate material lack and degradation into the very center of one's experience means excluding an entire sphere of reality from consciousness. It is consistent with his violent rejections of his foster mother's acts of kindness during his childhood in the McEachern home. He cannot allow himself cultural subjectification by these conventional terms of ideological trade, cannot step into the prefabricated role or position of beneficiary, while knowing that to accept the occasional charity conferred in the social is also to legitimate his exclusion therefrom, and to validate its systematic practices of the refusal of difference. His adaptation to the position of beneficiary can only reinforce the cultural logic that has worked to marginalize him in the first place. Acceptance of the food would amount to a desubjectification for Christmas, having not to do with any humanistic notion of "losing face" or pride, but instead with the loss of the experiential value of surviving void, of becoming through the lived history of material abandonment and helplessness.

Rather than a momentary condition of illness discoloring his face, the pallor of death he wears is a permanent and constitutive feature, structured into "the flesh itself" and as timeless as the parchment to which it is likened, as Faulkner puns the body into a final, non-palimpsestic bearer of text—a bearer of the specific, historical experience of abandonment and death. Finitude is naturalized in the body of Joe Christmas, not only in his visage but also in the pendulous, absolute rhythms of his work, his step, and his speech, utterly dependable in its inescapable "deadly regularity" and accentuated by the absence of any self-explanation.

> He did not talk to any of them at all. And none of them tried to talk to him. But they were all conscious of him, of the steady back (he worked well enough, with a kind of baleful and restrained steadiness) and arms. (34)

When he is assigned a partner, the buffoonish Brown, the deathliness of his rhythmic silence becomes even more pronounced as a function of contrast:

> They both turned and looked down at the sawdust pile, where Brown and Christmas labored, the one with that brooding and savage steadiness, the other with a high-armed and erratic motion which could not have been fooling even itself.
>
> They had been watching the two of them down there since the day when Brown went to work: Christmas jabbing his shovel into the sawdust slowly and steadily and hard, as though he were chopping up a buried snake ("or a man," Mooney said) and Brown leaning on his shovel while he apparently told Christmas a story, an anecdote. Because presently he would

laugh, shout with laughter, his head backflung, while beside him the other man worked with silent and unflagging savageness. . . . Then he would lean upon it again and apparently finish whatever it was that he was telling Christmas, telling to the man who did not even seem to hear his voice. As if the other were a mile away, or spoke a different language from the one he knew, Byron thought. (39–40)

Through the foregrounding of his "savage" physicality, the relentless stroke with which he labors in null disregard of all humanity, indeed, seeming to want to "chop it up," Christmas is distanced from the field of common communication in general. The assumption of his complicity in an ideological arrangement predicated on the annihilating transfiguration of the unknown is quietly but savagely refused in favor of his textual function as an agent of death, signified by his nullifying silence and equally absolute steadiness in service to nothing visible. Joe's disruption of his own ideological subjection, his inability to be properly assimilated into the social is bound organically to his originary loss, the denial of maternal recognition that works to destructure his narcissistic need for recognition from without. His characteristic social evanescence, metaphorically represented by the recurrent motif of the silently vanishing flame of the match with which he lights a cigarette, is itself a figure of pronounced repetition by which the text's central character is discovered only as he disappears, not so much in retreat from, as in refutation of recognition. His own sense of self-discovery or self-invention lies in his interpretation of this freedom from sociality as something earned existentially through a pained, intensive labor that he alone can comprehend.

Joe's expressionless, silent refusal to cry as a five-year-old, during a prolonged beating from the austere McEachern for failing to memorize assigned passages from the father's Presbyterian catechism, portends the committed, savage (and futile) labor of disengagement from the ideological that will mark him so distinctly later. Endurance of the external savagery visited on him is itself an equally structured personal savagery that enables him to "work through" his fear of material punishment and in a real sense to help determine his own terms of subjectification through indifferent subversion of cultural demands of placement and category. Having absorbed a lifetime of rejections, he has not formed conventional aspirations of recognition or material health but has instead attached himself to the negative underside of these, seemingly relishing in the possibility of his nonbeing, constructing for himself the paradoxical nonidentity of a brilliantly lit match.[6]

His commitment to his own formal terms of existence expresses itself in self-contradictory modes, even in its most violent moments, as Byron relates to Reverend Hightower an episode involving Christmas and a drunken Brown. The two have been operating an illegal whiskey enterprise that Brown's loose-lipped braggadocio is about to compromise on a Saturday night in the barbershop:

> And Christmas saying in that quiet voice of his that ain't pleasant and ain't mad either "You ought to be careful about drinking so much of this Jefferson hair tonic. It's gone to your head. First thing you know, you'll have a harelip." Holding Brown up he was with one hand and slapping his face with the other. They didn't look like hard licks. But the folks could see the red even through Brown's whiskers when Christmas' hand would come away between licks. "You come out and get some fresh air," Christmas says. "You're keeping these folks from working." (80)

With brutality sedimented alongside an equally passionate restraint in the single body, Christmas denies his audience whatever preestablished humanistic harmony is expected even in the figuration of absolute or radical otherness. His atavism is disturbingly offset by his "quiet" property of gentility, an assassin's ironic charm by which enormous capacities for violence and bloodletting are at once foregrounded and softened. The quiet voice that "ain't pleasant and ain't mad either" is the utterance that bespeaks the life of a machine, the neutral drone of finitude's voice, the deadly enunciation of the "underside" of life to which his "human" antagonists have no access. The passionless sound of his voice and the deathly content of his speech itself are issued from an already negated subjectivity that animates itself in its violence on another (Brown), whose loudly theatrical gestures would themselves positivize Christmas, identifying him distinctly in figure and deed before the regulatory machine of cultural positionality—and also, of course, before the codified laws forbidding private whiskey enterprise that he transgresses.

Even the actual violence itself is delivered in terms of self-restraint, the "short, hard, vicious blows" that he slowly "measures out," transmitting not only physical pain and damage, but also communicating the silent promise or potential of an even greater violence that is for the moment harnessed, mediated, and controlled. Christmas's labor of serious violence is a repressed desire, an arrested means of self-establishment that at the same time keeps him hidden, concealing the vastly greater violence of which he is capable and that discloses itself later in his murder of Joanna Burden. Christmas refuses to positivize himself as the brute Other he is feared to be, precisely because doing so would immediately consume and terminate the public fear that enables him distance and nonidentity. It would extinguish the fear of the unknown that he has cultivated as an object of negative recognition and make known the limits of a violence more pervasively frightening and paralyzing in the imaginary than it is in reality.

Denying himself the pleasure of this immediate consumption, forbidding himself indulgence of the brutality that would demystify him and reduce him to an object of social certainty, Christmas sustains a profound narcissism that in its impenetrability, its refusal of external identifications, prohibits any objective truth value that would define him. What his solipsism augments for him cannot be called pleasure of any kind but only a deepening of his experience of exclusion, of an asociality at once libidinal and involuntary that marks him as an agent of death. He resents the authority by which others assume positions of superiority from which to offer help and gifts, detesting the determinism and arrogance that he believes to organize such gestures. Just as in one childhood scene he dumps the tray of food his adoptive mother prepares for him, effacing the labor by which she tries to demonstrate her pitying love for him, so does he decide to kill Joanna Burden, telling himself repeatedly, "She ought not to have started praying over me." His sense of envelopment by a social sphere that would preserve itself by appeasing him works constantly toward his extrication therefrom, reluctant though it may be. In one scene, he wanders aimlessly through town and, before realizing it, finds himself in the "negro" section, where a strange sense of communion emerges within him, one that must quickly be foreclosed:

Then he found himself. Without his being aware the street had begun to slope and before he knew it he was in Freedman Town, surrounded by the summer smell and the summer voices of invisible negroes. They seemed to enclose him like bodiless voices murmuring talking laughing in a language not his. As from the bottom of thick black pit he saw himself enclosed by cabinshapes, vague, kerosenelit, so that the street lamps themselves seemed to be further spaced, as if the black life, the black breathing had compounded the substance of breath so that not only voices but moving bodies and light itself must become fluid and accrete slowly from particle to particle, of and with the now ponderable night inseparable and one.

He was standing still now, breathing quite hard, glaring this way and that. About him the cabins were shaped blackly out of blackness by the faint, sultry glow of kerosene lamps. On all sides, even within him, the bodiless fecundmellow voices of negro women murmured. It was as though he and all other manshaped life about him had been returned to the lightless hot wet primogenitive Female. He began to run, glaring, his teeth glaring, his inbreath cold on his dry teeth and lips, toward the next street lamp. . . .

Then he became cool. The negro smell, the negro voices, were behind and below him now. . . . He went on, slowly again, his back toward the square, passing again between the houses of white people. There were people on these porches too, and in chairs upon the lawns; but he could walk quiet here. Now and then he could see them: heads in silhouette, a white blurred garmented shape; on a lighted veranda four people sat about a card table, the white faces intent and sharp in the low light, the bare arms of the women glaring smooth and white above the trivial cards. "That's all I wanted," he thought. "That don't seem like a whole lot to ask." (114–15)

His absent stroll into Freedman Town awakens an anxiety of a "return" to the "lightless, hot, wet primogenitive" womb, the locus of his simultaneous introduction to life and to death. Though his biological mother is "white," she is banished into the a-subjective realm of the "nigger" after being impregnated by a man of indeterminate ethnicity.

This "niggering" costs her her life when her father refuses to take her to a hospital to give birth, and she dies as Joe enters life. His panic during his inadvertent traipse through Freedman Town stems not only from a renewed sense of the peculiar racial abjection that he has largely escaped during his life, but also from the sudden, even violent, sense of noumenal familiarity and warmth that mists over him now, an involuntary sense of belonging that he has always lived without.

As the surrounding sounds and smells of "blackness" impress themselves on him, he is lifted out of the sheer discursivity that institutes such notions as "race" or "whiteness," and is thrust into a primal totality of the sensory. He ingests the "breath" of abyssal night that so "fluid(ly)" moves "from particle to particle," until it is one with him, an energy fusing him with the molecularity of a nondefined "black life," of opaque voices and movements. This "blackness," felt as it is within the nocturnal "black pit" of faceless, "bodiless" people who at the same time change the very air itself, transforming the atmosphere with intensities indifferent to prelegislated valuation is nothing at all "racial," but is instead a processuality of a profound, insistent *nonexclusivity* of color, sound, light, and *thinking*. Joe is "returned," via this textual de-essentialization of the lived "blackness," of night to a primary sociality that he has never properly known—and it is more than he can bear. He flees immediately to the familiar, "cold, hard air of white people" on the other side of town. His oneness with Faulkner's seemingly essentialist notion of "black life" would liquidate the spectral liminality that he enjoys in the "whiteness" of dominant American culture; it would melt his overdetermined particularity into the "fluid," "bodiless," "inseparable" totality of abyssal "blackness" against which his body has always stood in visible contrast.

Tearing himself out of this enveloping blackness, Christmas repeats the gesture of elusiveness and escape that so characterizes him, refusing enclosure within the threatening terms of symbolic abstraction. This marks a turn away from the brutality and savagery with which, as an adolescent, he makes himself complicit with the power of whiteness during his attack on an anonymous black woman with whom he and five friends have just "taken turns" sexually. "[S]melling the woman, smelling the negro all at once," sensing "something, prone, abject," Joe's reaction, as Richard Moreland puts it sharply, "recalls and focuses the larger social dynamic." In the text, we learn that "He kicked her hard, kicking into and through a choked wail of surprise and fear" (156–57). In Moreland's well-tuned assessment, "Joe's and the other boys' attempt to overcome their own confusion and fear have violently assigned that confusion and fear to her, to be overcome by dominating her. Their white manhood depends upon that domination."[7] While his techniques of extrication from blackness appear to have transformed by adulthood, what remains is the affective horror and enrapture of entropic "black" smells and sounds that would imbricate him within a situatedness of belonging.

This escape from sociality, no matter how loving or altruistic, is literalized earlier in the text as he again wanders through the darkness, meditating on the obliterative kindness represented by Joanna Burden. His spinsterish lover is obsessed with "bettering" him by institutionalizing his intellect and sending him to law school—a "nigger" law school at that. To make matters worse, she makes a show of praying for him. Christmas is outraged to realize that he is an object of pity under her gaze of condescension, and is again resistant to any form of external confinement, whether discursive or material:

> "But she ought to have had better sense than to pray over me."
> He began to curse her. He stood beneath the dark window, cursing her with slow and calculated obscenity. He was not looking at the window. In the less than halflight he appeared to be watching his body, seeming to watch it turning slow and lascivious in a whispering of gutter filth, like a drowned corpse in a thick still black pool of more than water. He touched himself with his flat hands, hard, drawing his hands hard up his abdomen and chest inside his undergarment, It was held together by a single button at the top. Once he had owned garments with intact buttons. A woman had sewed them on. That was for a time, during a time. Then the time passed. After that he would purloin his own garments from the family wash before she could get to them and replace the missing buttons. When she foiled him he set himself deliberately to learn and remember which buttons were missing and had been restored. With his pocket knife and with the cold and bloodless deliberation of a

surgeon he would cut off the buttons which she had just replaced. (107)

This exemplifies the acutely egoistic labor of self-liberation from the
other's grasp, the shattering of the social bond implied by the admin-
istering of "gifts" that silently institutionalize the dialectic of recipro-
cation, gifts that in themselves mandate their return and confer the
obligation/interpellation of the recipient. Christmas realizes himself
in the surface signature of his independent nothingness, the sundered, ruined undergarment that testifies at once to his abandonment of identity and to his profound narcissism. Functioning as a
direct foreshadowing of the violence to come when Christmas slashes
Joanna's throat, this eroticized scene in which the buttons are cut
away replaces the touch on his bare skin of the nameless, all but ef-
faced "woman" of a long-distant "time" with his *own* lingering touch,
a caress by which he actualizes himself without the validating social
gaze or sexual response of another. His apparent onanism is not simply a withdrawal from the power dynamics structuring the fight between self and other over the determination of one's own self-agency;
it is a product of an earlier degradation, a prior subservience to the
concept of sociality itself. His absence emerges only after periods of
social alienation in the orphanage and under McEachern's roof, during which he learns that he is desired only as a mirror of the other and
not for the diversity of impression that he singularly enacts. His refusal to acknowledge "the woman's" gift of the sewn buttons is his
recognition of the terror of the other that, to this point, he has managed to overcome, the destroyed garment the evidence of his "survival" of a former servitude to ideology.

His emergence as an anthropomorphic incongruity is concretized
in the next paragraph as his very body contests the imperative of
assimilation:

He passed through the broken gate and stopped beside the road.
The August weeds were thightall. . . . After a time a light began
to grow beyond the hill, defining it. Then he could hear the car.
He did not move. He stood with his hands on his hips, naked,
thighdeep in the dusty weeds, while the car came over the hill

and approached the lights full upon him. He watched his body grow white out of the darkness like a kodak print emerging from the liquid. He looked straight into the headlights as it shot past. From it a woman's shrill voice flew back, shrieking. "White bastards!" He shouted. "That's not the first of your bitches that ever saw . . ." But the car was gone. There was no one to listen (107–108).

While Christmas admits elsewhere in the text to not "really" being certain of any "black" ancestry, his antagonistic cry of "white bastards" seems to imply his belief that he is something other than "white." The irony undercutting any solid inference of his "blackness" from the statement inheres in the vulgar truth value of the second term of the epithet: "bastards." Jutting out of the inky, "liquid" black woods, his pallid whiteness takes on a stark definition that animates into the illusion of intense color its customarily "dead," "parchment-like" look. Against the wild blackness, the contrast of his naked skin scandalizes the passing "white" woman whose "shrieking" is an aural cut on a specular history of racialization, resounding for Christmas the eternal cultural hypocrisy that has circumscribed his entire life, reopening the originary wound of his nigger-ing. The piercing shriek is only a haunting echo of Joe's expulsion from the sphere of "white" legitimacy that he imagines as his lost birthright.

He remembers that in his teens he would often racialize himself as a technique of sexual seduction on "white" women, telling them that he was actually a "negro," thus tingeing his sexual encounters with the illicit excitement of penetrating (and perpetuating) racialist social boundaries, heightening his inner sexual confidence by way of a "blackness" that is, for him, a complete externality. This continues until one of his sex partners informs him that she has actually slept with black men before, thereby deflating his auratic sense of unique exotica and also removing from his consciousness the false notion of white, female sexual purity. For Joe, the passing shriek is testament to a false innocence, as he projects onto the woman in the car his generalized view of (white) female hypocrisy, suggesting that she has seen naked "negro" men before. However, he too must necessarily escape his own gaze and thereby miss the fact that as she passes him in the car, she can't know that it is probably a naked "negro" she sees emerging from the dark wood. The fact of her own rank objectification nearly escapes scrutiny altogether, her status as merely one of "your bitches" effacing her entirely from his response; he is speaking not to her, of course, but to the white men with whom he is violently engaged, as Fanon reminds us, in struggle for her paradoxically abjected and exalted possession. His is a response to a shriek that sounds—and repeats—the history of another abjection; a sound defining an ethos of dehumanization, enslavement, and murder.

As Joe's whiteness materializes plainly against its contrasting frame, only to sense within itself the trace of the otherness it has just shed, so too does it urgently attempt to organize itself into a rejoinder to that same anxiety when he walks out of Freedom Town. The uneasy oneness that binds him at the level of sensation as he enters all but disappears as he exits, his long, anxious walk through the community another example of his "working through" or overcoming his terrors instead of turning around and avoiding them. What lingers, however, is the unshakable sense that he has just left the scene of his beginning:

> But he did not look back until he reached the crest of the hill. Then he could see the town, the glare, the individual lights where streets radiated from the square. He could see the street down which he had come, and the other street, the one which had almost betrayed him; and further away and at right angles, the far bright rampart of the town itself, and in the angle between the black pit from which he had fled with drumming heart and glaring lips. No light came from it, from here no breath, no odor. It just lay there, black, impenetrable, in its garland of Augusttremulous lights. It might have been the original quarry, abyss itself. (116)

Faulkner's naturalization of the "black pit" as an organic space of death and negativity must be read at the same time as a description of an "in between," a blackly interstitial space within an angle separating and connecting the bright ramparts of town with Freedman Town, an affectless, null membrane of another pure blackness, as filled with possibility of origins as it appears barren of all life. In its inky impenetrability, in its mute indifference to all attempts at decipherment, it not only provides a certain spatial analogue to Christmas's own "inscrutability," but also sounds a return to that originary zone of potentiality theorized by writers throughout this book.

This zone's difference from those of the distinctly "Negro" smells, sounds, energies and movements so frequently described by Faulkner's narrator is striking in its ambiguity. For while there are numerous references to an experientially palpable, if never actually concretized "blackness"—such as when Joe, in bed with a black woman, wants to ingest "the dark and inscrutable thinking and being of negroes"—once more, as in Conrad, the absence of substantiality underscored in every such instance speaks the idea that determinate knowledge itself is what is at stake in the narrative.

The pit's absence of light and sound also demonstrates, as suggested just above, Christmas's uneasy acceptance of death as an originary precondition of his life. Its void of light corresponds to his "dead" "parchment"-like expression; the pit's impenetrability matches his own at the level of speech and countenance.

Joe makes plain that the idea of identity is real only in its movements and actions—as evinced by the extreme responses provoked by his very utterances and silences, by his effortless destabilization of every social structure that attempts to subsume his heterogeneity to one determination of "race," of "class," of "origin," or another. His very flesh is a "banner" of nonidentity, in that it exposes the possibility, even the likelihood, of his subjective untruth, of his essential core hollowness. Nonidentity is the walking signifier read in his "dead" facial expression and in the "contradictory" diversity of his physicality and dress. The reality he produces is never compromised by the modes of its expressivity, but is instead the outcome of that expressivity. Christmas's body is the very emblem of nonrecognition subverting the entire field of cultural identifications and assignations. It effectively empties such classificatory notions as "race," to which the townspeople adhere so zealously—the ones without which they descend back into the abyssal black pit from which, they fear, they originate.

4

The Business of Dreams: Retailing Presence in Miss Lonelyhearts

By emphasizing the "heart of gold," society admits the suffering it has created. . . . The pathos of composure justifies the world which makes it necessary.
—Max Horkheimer and Theodor Adorno, "The Culture Industry: Enlightenment as Mass Deception"

The wreckage of all beliefs and all doctrines, the exposure of all commodities and all policies as nothing more than techniques of mass hypnosis and mass deception, forms the basis of the later work of Nathanael West. What his literature makes real is the incessant encroachment of unreality, the perpetual deferral of the spontaneous, individual experience promised by the endless projection of commercial images that bombard virtually every moment of daily life. In West's work the only survivors are those starving hordes who accept everything as it is presented, and those few who resist the banality of modernity but are functionally unable to reshape it. The protagonist of *Miss Lonelyhearts* (1933) exemplifies the second kind. Aching to revoke the disintegration and entropy that West stages as the simultaneous genesis and outcome of modernity's convergence of inherited values and hypercommodification, Lonelyhearts searches narcissistically for some self-affirming role of propriety and meaning that would remain impervious to an urbanized culture of infinite divisibility and individual ineffectuality.

West concretizes this modernist decomposition thematically by making his New York a splintered framework of physical deformation, widespread poverty, and rapidly dissolving precepts of "morality." The city is a swarming antistructure that, in the multiplicity of its facades and fronts, presents an infinite wave of terror against which Lonelyhearts's aspirations of monadic simplicity and purity take antagonistic shape. The text scatters an entire inventory of strategies that recirculate, even as they ridicule, multiple clusters of rhetorical idioms and discursive habits of domination. These are speech acts of commerce, state power, and media, all of which are aimed at exploiting modernity's crisis of dissipation—exacerbated in this context by the Great Depression.

Lonelyhearts's perception of this endless dissolution is not external to its societal object but is, rather, the conceptual determinant thereof. The culture of material fragmentation is not an independent, exterior force that simply frames its subjects, but is instead the product of an anterior subjective disposition toward stable valuation, meaning, and order. Lonelyhearts blinds himself to the paradox of identity that envelops him, failing to acknowledge that the only possible source of his would-be benediction is the same mass-mediated community that so nauseates him and that the recognition he so desires is located only within the province of the chaotically commercialized sociality he so desperately loathes. He aims to eliminate private incomprehension and self-contradiction through the linguistic appropriation of a positive ethical ethos that he urgently wants recognized publicly as such. In so doing, he confirms his need for the authorization of the same entropic culture from which he seeks extrication. In this sense, he is a continually self-suspending character, thwarted over and again not by the patent refusal of whichever ideological alternative he tries to appropriate, but by his repeated self-exposure to the empty *promise* of an authority in which, as he finds only belatedly, he cannot trust because it does not exist.

In the counterpoised characters of the advice columnist Miss Lonelyhearts and his supremely cynical editor, Shrike, the text recasts the symbolic regimes of religion, morality, and art as cultural sandcastles that petrify themselves, by way of exploitation of mass suffering, into eternal prisons of ideological law. West's short meditation on the psychic violence necessary even to eliminate these forms of violence compels Harold Bloom's observation of "Miss Lonelyhearts . . . as the perfected instance of a negative vision in modern American fiction," surpassed only by the very "greatest" works of Faulkner himself.[1]

Faulkner's Joe Christmas invests in his own symbolic deferment of self within sociality, recognizing his own living "death" as the paradoxical cornerstone supporting his terrifying power as a nonassimilable figure. His insistent nonidentity within a regulatory sphere is read here as a necessary precondition of individual self-becoming. But Miss Lonelyhearts assiduously resists the personal risks of nonidentity, staking himself instead on the possibility that some exterior truth or meaning to which he might seamlessly attach himself will soon be revealed to him—either through Christ, art, nature, or through various, even contrasting principles of morality. These avenues of borrowed self-actualization are effortlessly exposed as such by Shrike.[2] But Lonelyhearts holds fast to his abstract idealism with a tenacity that discloses his passion not only for continuity, but also for self-abrogation, as he continually tries to discover himself in whatever external discourses of ultimate truth make themselves available. In this way, he is hardly different from the millions he simultaneously pities and fears: his readers, who naively seek to find life answers in the commodities and "opportunities" promised by everything from advertisements lining the walls of subway stations to the trite imbecilities that appear in Lonelyhearts's advice column. These practices of cultural persuasion sustain the promise of their mythological functions of solution, while never revealing any evidence of same. The fictiveness of this promised unity is concealed by the very anteriority of transcendent unity's status as an "oceanic" object of desire within Lonelyhearts. In other words, he constantly renews identifications with external representations that on the sole basis of their cultural projectedness, are presumed greater and more certain than the self.[3]

In the novel, the falsity of this consonance emerges in an early passage, as the mutilated Christ statuette in Lonelyhearts's Spartan room appears to mock its very disfiguration at his hands, seeming to demonstrate its transcendent strength and internal perseverance, despite its physical ruin. It also gives monument to the rarely seen, resistant impulse within Lonelyhearts that would refuse easy complicity with social convention and cliché:

> Miss Lonelyhearts went home in a taxi. He lived by himself in a room that was as full of shadows as an old steel engraving. It held a bed, a table and two chairs. The walls were bare except for an ivory Christ that hung opposite the foot of the bed. He had removed the figure from the cross to which it had been fastened and had nailed it to the wall with large spikes. But the desired effect had not been obtained. Instead of writhing, the Christ remained calmly decorative. (8)

Stripped as it is of its relationship to the cross, the Christ figure is momentarily "disembodied," torn from customary unity with its framing structure, the total image of which, in the commercial ubiquity of its representation, ultimately reifies the nature and specificity of Christ's execution. Lonelyhearts's critical intervention takes issue with the cultural costs of this standardized representation, as the symbolic rendering of the crucifixion is itself a specified, textual event that is also necessarily a strategy and an attitude toward an historical moment.[4] His gesture is a way to reconcile oneself toward the historical event and establish a sense of meaning therein, or to inscribe oneself hermeneutically in history. In the image of the writhing Christ, Lonelyhearts wants to see some mirroring validation of *himself*, a representational effect that would justify his own intensely personal sense of agony and fracture in a culture whose suffering is the dominant source of his own private suffering.

That the newly disfigured statuette remains "calmly decorative" confirms instead, however, the smug implacability of commercialized conviction that secretly lies at the foundation of organized religion, buoyed by the pervasive need for such representations of eternal truth and strength. This need is cynically satisfied by the artificial "calm" that is only a wishful reprojection of synthetic lifelessness in a hypercommodified social sphere. Lonelyhearts's revision is aimed at removing the death of Christ from its own reassuring institutionalization and simplistic readability as a text of suffering and sacrifice, as he seeks to disrupt the process by which the text of the passion is reduced to religious cliché. His graphic displacement of the text of crucifixion in statuette is antagonistic to the easy systematization of a historical event whose individual meaning is crucial in his own formation as a subject. Lonelyhearts wants to see in the Christ figure some specific registration of the fresh pain inflicted by the new spikes—but to his disappointment, the expression of the inanimate thing does not change. For the believer, the figure's placid indifference to the scandal of defacement and the pain of fresh mutilation is testimony to the eternal strength and transcendence ascribed to Christ and Christianity. Its force endures even in the face of incessantly renewed cultural fragmentation and absence of meaning, represented by the room that somehow remains "full of shadows," despite its relative emptiness and solitary occupancy.

As Lonelyhearts's sense of selfhood is conferred through his willing subjection to an ideological matrix of objectifying interpellation designed within culture for the very purpose of its own self-realization, he comes to "hail" and to recognize himself on the terms of the money culture he simultaneously loathes and supports:

> He got undressed immediately and took a cigarette and a copy of *The Brothers Karamazov* to bed. The marker was in a chapter devoted to Father Zossima.
>
> "Love a man even in his sin, for that is the semblance of Divine Love and is the highest love on earth. Love all God's creation, the whole and every grain of sand in it. Love the animals, love the plants, love everything. If you love everything, you will perceive the divine mystery in things. Once you perceive it, you will begin to comprehend it better every day. And you will come at last to love the whole world with an all-embracing love."
>
> It was excellent advice. If he followed it, he would be a big success. His column would be syndicated and the whole world would learn to love. The Kingdom of Heaven would arrive. He would sit on the right hand of the Lamb. (8)

Miss Lonelyhearts conflates the unconditional love prescribed in Dostoevsky's passage with one that is at the same time uncritically imagined, an oxymoronic interpretation that nullifies *the very fact of unconditional love's own self-decisiveness*. As a newspaper advice columnist he would transform this love from a dialogical instrument of wonder, aimed at beholding divine mystery, into a crass strategy for commercial success that would conveniently coincide with its function as a tool of individual comprehension or mastery, culminating in social uniformity. The beatific ideal of universal love is crucially premised, for Miss Lonelyhearts, on an eradication or suppression of individual distinction that would ironically happen to guarantee his own, since his quite public advocacy of universal love would elevate him prominently, indeed, to the "right hand of the Lamb." To love man altruistically, "even in his sin," however, would presumably mean first recognizing the sedimentation of sin within man, and then deciding to embrace it on its own terms—a truly unconditional love, premised on embrace of the incommensurability and radical singularity of the other. Miss Lonelyhearts, however, is narcissistically concerned with bearing an undifferentiated, unreflected love to the mass population, as a purely imitative and instrumentalist strategy of godliness. The value of universal love, for Miss Lonelyhearts, lies not so much in its own concept and forms, but in its character as a "*semblance* of Divine Love," in the fact of its mimetic relation to the ideal of God's own practice of love (my emphasis).

The Dostoevsky passage functions as an access code to Lonelyhearts's own desire, a code by which he is enabled to materialize his own long-standing, egoistic identification with Christ. This mimetic identification subordinates the altruistic ideal of universal love to a narcissistic self-idealization that ironically abolishes the desiring self even as it brings that self into being. This is to say that Miss Lonelyhearts preserves a sense of ideal selfhood only by abandoning, as a condition of his identification with Christ, the notion of self.[5] His wishful self-revision as an altruistic Christlike figure is compromised hopelessly by the same egoistic desire structuring this overidentification—the hunger for public recognition as such a figure. At the same time, his idealization of Dostoevsky's universal love removes the specters of difference and sin in the other (the very otherness of that other) that a true, altruistic love would embrace. His true desire, as such thinkers as Kojève and Borch-Jacobsen elaborate independently, reveals his core "nothingness," his constitutive anxiety:

His vocation was of a different sort. As a boy in his father's church, he had discovered that something stirred in him when

he shouted the name of Christ, something secret and enor-
mously powerful. He had played with this thing, but had never
allowed it to come alive.

He knew now what this thing was—hysteria, a snake whose
scales are tiny mirrors in which the dead world takes on a semblance of life. And how dead the world is . . . a world of door-
knobs. He wondered if hysteria were really too steep a price to
pay for bringing it to life. (9)

West's Freudian homage aestheticizes the primary character of hysteria, articulated by Christopher Bollas as a mode of sustaining and
"mirroring" one's own history, "of recalling the people and events of
the past," by performing it oneself in the present, demonstrating
"histrionics a skillful means of portrayal."[6] In other words, West narrates the central void at the core of both mass culture and individual
subjectivity. It is only a network of egoistic anxieties within the child
that is first "stirred" by the "name" of Christ, a crucial, yet nameless
"something" within, only reachable by means of another name or
image, an anonymous "something" that covets its own conversion
into some powerfully solidified presence. The future Lonelyhearts is
captivated by a signifier without any concrete referent, and the totality of his identification with what is suggested by the name helps him
to institute himself as a complete subject in the *image* of Christ. He is
given himself by the name of Christ, without which he remains a
being in negative suspension.

This primary identification grounds a pattern of attempts at self-
realization for Lonelyhearts. Investigating a range of cultural arche-
types that extends from the "romance" of sexual and alcoholic
dissolution to a near-fundamentalist religious asceticism, he seeks
himself within paradigmatic orders of truth that, in their very representations as ideals, actually foreclose any possibility of private,
noumenal difference they might otherwise provide him. By this I
mean that Miss Lonelyhearts's embraces of Christianity—and later of
sex, suffering, and art—presume an absolute sanctity in the conception of each that refuses the sedimentation of actual, social experience within any. He thereby fetishistically converts spirituality,
decadence, and art into nondialectical zones of pure otherness *by*

which to abjure the painfully disjunctive material conditions of modernity that confront him in his daily work.

In attempting to exchange social realities of anthropomorphic disfiguration, fragmentation, and impoverishment (literalized by West's notorious "grotesques") for idealized conceptions of individual absolution and redemption, Miss Lonelyhearts oversteps the anterior abyss from which strategies of religion, morality, and art necessarily emerge as discursive means of closure. The increasingly pained sincerity with which Miss Lonelyhearts attempts to meet his responsibilities as advice columnist at the New York *Post-Dispatch* is nothing less than his effort to assume, nonparodically, the psychoanalyst's illusory position of absolute knowledge of self and other. Unlike the analyst, Lonelyhearts engages seriously the notion of his certitude and is therefore tortured by a paralyzing sense of ethical responsibility to a public addicted to its own material exploitation by a cynical, commercial complex of cheap, sensational journalism and rampant advertising, as exemplified in this passage:

> What had happened to his great understanding heart? Guitars, bright shawls, exotic foods, outlandish costumes—all these things were part of the business of dreams. He had learned not to laugh at the advertisements offering to teach writing, cartooning, engineering, to add inches to the biceps and to develop the bust. He should therefore realize that the people who came to El Gaucho were the same as those who wanted to write and live the life of an artist, wanted to be an engineer and wear leather puttees, wanted to develop a grip that would impress the boss, wanted to cushion Raoul's head on their swollen breasts. They were the same people as those who wrote to Miss Lonelyhearts for help. (22)

Powerless to critique what even he sees as the manufacture and merchandising of desire, indeed, the production, and retailing of dreams themselves, Lonelyhearts's counsel is customarily abstract in its avoidance of detailed practical immediacies.[7] He instead attempts to recover "the soul" of an audience more preoccupied with eliminating tangible sources of material pain than with a sublimation that refutes or ignores the specificity of its suffering—a sublimation that therefore undercuts its own accomplishment. He continues to take a binary view of the relation between subject and capital in which the latter exploits the weakness of the former, failing to see that the "dream industry" is *not* a purely external agent in the life of the individual modern subject, but is rather a cynically reifying strategy of lending meaning and concretization to an *anterior* craving for a potency and distinction of self from other.

West's figuration of this desire of self is routed ironically through externalities, as the advertisements offer nothing other than the possibility of a "new" existence through identification with a projected image operating at pleasurable distance *from oneself*. In promising, through the otherness of the transformed body, or the new gift for writing, a more desirable self, this retailing of identity conceals the necessary murder of the present self—a strategy repeated clearly by Lonelyhearts in his own relation to Christianity and every other sphere in which he invests. The advice column reflexively plays on the desperation for identity and resolution in a society hopelessly dispersed by the seductive network of capitalism, one that profitably orients the egoistic desire of newspaper readers toward marketing and consuming their own material suffering on the advice page. The anonymous signatures and shattered syntax of Lonelyhearts's readers are instead the true signatures of a culture industry that realizes its greatest power at the moment when the individual subject is in complete agreement with its use against the singularity of its own experience. Lonelyhearts is aware that this cynical matrix achieves supremacy when the private, libidinal interest of the individual subject coincides with its market function as a product; yet he is powerless to mount an actual critique of this state, dependent as he is on its satellite, Christianity, for any sense of his own difference. Reduced to an object of its own enjoyment, the suffering of West's modern subject diverts that being's attention from the real sources of its abjection. This relation is concealed from the consuming subject by its own desire, as it reads its own substantiality in the degradation of the letters of others; while finding solace in Miss Lonelyhearts's responses to its own.

This relation is also hidden from Miss Lonelyhearts by the messianic conviction of his own centrality to the lives of his "public."

Compromising this conviction is his own anonymity before an audience that knows nothing about him beyond his professional function. The false name that inscribes its own functionalist reality is also a metaphorical rendering of Lonelyhearts's inability to assert an identity or a practice that is not already scripted elsewhere within culture. His undisclosed actual name is liquidated by the pseudonym "Miss Lonelyhearts," as he submits to the commercial pressure of preserving a professional identity that alienates him further from a sense of self—an identity that at the same time institutionalizes him as a public figure of distinct, if masked operation.[8] His forced regurgitation of trite cliché in response to his readership operates not only as the public guarantor of his commercial popularity but also as the private concealment of his own profound self-anxiety, a private void simply cemented over by the pseudonym. The distant amusement he originally finds in his public's letters, and the hackneyed cynicism with which he answers them, quickly gives way to a dogmatic insistence on authenticity and purity that necessarily presumes its own viability, as well as the stability of the secret subjective ground from which it issues. Blocking any hope of "cure" for his readers is Miss Lonelyhearts's blindness to his own insufficiency in this respect. His adherence to an abstract ethical program denies the specificity of the immediate plea of his individual "analysand," the anonymous solicitor of corporate "advice" who also abolishes his or her own singularity in the very gesture of such solicitation:

> Although the deadline was less than a quarter of an hour away, he was still working on his leader. He had gone as far as "Life *is* worth while, for it is full of dreams and peace, gentleness and ecstasy, and faith that burns like a clear white flame on a grim dark altar." But he found it impossible to continue. The letters were no longer funny. He could not go on finding the same joke funny thirty times a day for months on end. And on most days he received more than thirty letters, all of them alike, stamped from the dough of suffering with a heart-shaped cookie-knife. On his desk were piled those he had received this morning. He started through them again, searching for some clue to a sincere answer. (1)

Cut as they are from the universal and undifferentiated "dough of suffering," the plaintive queries of Miss Lonelyhearts's readers reveal—in their very disclosure to a faceless commercial institution as notoriously bereft of individualized empathy as a big-city daily newspaper—their absolute complicity with a capitalism that depends for its own survival on the pervasiveness of the individual need for resolution and understanding, no matter how prefabricated and homogenized. Paradoxically, what makes these letters perfectly "alike" on one level is the unrelieved specificity of their purely individual horror and pain. The singular experiences of poverty, disease, and abuse endured by each writer of each letter constitute for Miss Lonelyhearts a materially uniform terror, an accumulation of narratives that has been multiplied so many times in epistolary form as to lose *all* specificity and to blur into an amorphous mass of undifferentiated abjection.

Isolated moments of experiential poignancy and suffering congeal for their reader into a distant aggregate of collective banality and degradation. They sacrifice their own unique content, merging themselves with one another by submitting themselves to the "heart-shaped cookie knife" of their self-plasticizing "signatures." These signatures transform the particularity of each writer's torments into assimilable, everyday cultural realities that indeed gain commercial value in terms of their public readership. By means of such falsifying signatures as "Desperate," "Disillusioned" and "Sick-of-it-all," the writers of these letters convert the difference of their agony into universal familiarity. Such signatures introduce the unique sufferings to which they attest, into a vocabulary of social sameness and therefore into a certain social acceptability, enabling the normalization of cultural atrocity within the pages of daily "journalism." This amounts to a commodification of abjection. Realities of child molestation and deforming malnutrition become standardized amusement when made attributable to an informant whose signature translates his or her pain into a false idiom of commonality.

A signature like "Sick-of-it-all" reduces unsharable, distinct experience to a vehicle for popular identification at the level of common mood or disposition. Miss Lonelyhearts refuses the self-negating dialecticism of his public's letters to him, keeping himself blind to the impossible relation between their unique contents and their stock signatures. For within this gap lies the individual truth of each letter: the irreducible desire for the public recognition of the letter-writer's personal struggle. The horror of this desire is its self-sabotaging, since each letter is addressed to the equally anonymous Miss Lonelyhearts, thereby rendering unattainable any hope of fully realized recognition by another, of the writer's own particular suffering. This embodies what Alistair Wisker characterizes as the novel's principle of making "absurdity of norms," and of "Miss Lonelyhearts' attempts to normalize the pain."[9] Again, Shrike is on hand to spell out the structure of this cycle.

> This one is a jim-dandy. A young boy wants a violin. It looks simple; all you have to do is get the kid one. But then you discover that he dictated the letter to his little sister. He is paralyzed and can't even feed himself. He has a toy violin and hugs it to his chest, imitating the sound of playing with his mouth. How pathetic. However, one can learn much from this parable. Label the boy Labor, the violin Capital and so on. (53)

Lonelyhearts is disgusted by his public's willing debasement of itself, its effacement of its own singularity in its dependency on equally anonymous, corporatized prescriptions of health, contentment, and imagination, ruminating that "Although dreams were once powerful, they have been made puerile by the movies, radio and newspapers. Among many betrayals, this one is the worst" (39). His conjuring of an organically pure past, now supplanted by a faceless culture industry that dictates the terms of individuality to the mass in the function of the cookie-knife, is echoed by Shrike's invocations of Shakespeare and Beethoven, antiquity and the Renaissance. The works of these artists and epochs constitute for him mere vessels of transport from the immediate wasteland of culture. At the same time, Lonelyhearts's construct of prior glory is undone by commerce's cynical appropriation of that seemingly purer past. The facelessness of the newspaper is not faceless at all, but is constituted by willful singularities who adapt themselves to the conditions of conformity under a cultural cookie-knife, thereby revealing themselves also as its products:

Miss Lonelyhearts stopped listening. His friends would go on telling these stories until they were too drunk to talk. They were aware of their childishness, but did not know how else to revenge themselves. At college and perhaps for a year afterwards, they had believed in literature, had believed in Beauty and in personal expression as an absolute end. When they lost this belief, they lost everything. . . . Like Shrike, the man they imitated, they were machines for making jokes. A button machine makes buttons, no matter what the power used, foot, steam, or electricity. They, no matter what the motivating force, death, love or God, made jokes. (15)

These newspapermen are, of course, no more faceless than the despairing New Yorkers who read them. They are individuals who comply with their own reification into bloodless agents of sameness and profit. They realize, like Shrike, that art is only more material for the cookie-knife, to be cut and used journalistically in forms of aphorism and platitude. They convert themselves into nonthinking robots of automatic production and response in much the same way that their readers seek to convert themselves into uncomplicated, easygoing, cultural automatons by actively soliciting and incorporating the pablum advice of an anonymous newspaper column whose only interest is in sustaining and capitalizing on the public despair it is presumed to help alleviate.

Miss Lonelyhearts's immediate inclination is to paper over the vast divide between his solicitors' self-flattering representation and their palpable desire to eliminate their collective impotence with the equalizing solution of religion—"Christ was the answer" (2). The solemnity of this formula, the very utterance of which imposes a final, transcendental "solution" on problems that lack even the means to articulate themselves as such, strikes the precise note of authority, is itself the verbal mechanism necessary to communicate the sense of knowing and power that will seduce this public endlessly into investing its belief, thereby perpetuating the force of this cycle. Such abstraction, operating as an actual, viable corrective, denies the pathos of the distance between the graphic specificity of the *writing* of the writer's agony and the anonymous signature's whiting out of that experience as something uniquely the writer's own:

Dear Miss Lonelyhearts—

I am in such pain I don't know what to do sometimes I think I will kill myself my kidneys hurt so much. My husband thinks no woman can be a good catholic and not have children irregardless of the pain. I was married honorable from our church but I never knew what married life meant as I was never told about man and wife. My grandmother never told me and she was the only mother I had but made big mistake by not telling me as it don't pay to be inocent and is only a big disappointment. I have 7 children in 12 years and ever since the last 2 I have been so sick. I was operatored on twice and my husband promised no more children on the doctors advice as he said I might die but when I got back from the hospital he broke his promise and now I am going to have a baby and I don't think I can stand it my kidneys hurts so much. I am so sick and scared because I can't have an abortion on account of being a catholic and my husband so religious. I cry all the time it hurts so much and I don't know what to do.

Yours respectfully
Sick-of-it-all (2)

Anchoring this seemingly schizophrenic communication, girding its unpunctuated assemblage of discontinuous thoughts into a steady stream of directed discontent, is the localized site of literal, bodily agony, the letter's point of departure and return. The woman's body is the initial object of, and ultimate sacrifice to, the terms of religious and political ideology that finally compel her tortured plea—a plea whose own figuration provides some explanatory narrative by which to simultaneously account for and offset the tortured body's helplessness. The writer's broken language speaks the unique experience of pain that contradicts her mere object-status as a birth-machine in service to a Catholicism that denies its female constituency any recognition of its thinking. The pain that results from the overuse of this machine paradoxically forces the body into accounting for its own sick condition, into enunciating its self-sacrifice to an ideological principle that conveniently oversteps the individuality on which it actually depends. Now living the negated, unspoken experience of what she "never was told" of marriage, she testifies to the anxiety that compelled her subjection thereto and, in so doing, unwittingly admits her choice of this life. She regrets her ignorance of the larger implications of Catholic marriage, or her "innocence" (a claim of violated purity), but she remains silent about her prior acquiescence to such conventional imperatives once they began to manifest themselves in her marriage. She conceals her knowing complicity with her own interpellation into the object position. Her adoption of her own subjection, her prized emergence within the symbolic as "wife," "mother," and "good Catholic" comes at the price of an imposed physical suffering—at the price of the literal reappropriation of her material body.

This demonstrates that the threat of symbolic depropriation of subjective experience is absolutely supported by the promised material consequence of a profoundly asymbolic, nondialectical pain within the body, whose specific sufferings are, like death, absolutely unique, untranslatable, and not communicable. What emerges in this tortured, all but indecipherable writing and in its silences, is the experience of what Lyotard calls "the inarticulate," a scene that extends the problematic of his juridical differend into a circulatory communicational zone in which a somehow proper articulation of the intensity of this suffering would actually reopen the wound itself—would, in other words, effectively mutilate further the experience of the abjection, rendering utterly banal an experience whose texture defies assimilation into everyday speech.[10]

Dashed into a convenient desk drawer, no sooner does "Sick-of-it-all's" letter disappear from view than it is replaced with another narrative of suffering, this one penned by sixteen-year-old "Desperate" who, having been born "without a nose," now watches in loneliness as her friends go dancing on Saturday nights with dates. She is denied even the satisfaction of a visible tormentor, as her organic disfiguration presents a ready-made logic for the constant of her social rejection and isolation:

I have a big hole in the middle of my face that scares people even myself so I can't blame the boys for not wanting to take me out. My mother loves me but she crys terrible when she looks at me. (2)

To recognize the hole in her face as lack, "Desperate" must already have emerged from a social structure in which absence is assigned abjected value, in which ideals and meanings are attached to notions of beauty and ugliness, presence and absence, symmetry and disjunction. These broader notions are insufficient to address the specificity of her suffering, and are yet, as ideals beyond her reach, responsible to some degree for that suffering, for her inability to claim any identification with the "whole" that grounds itself as cultural normativity. This is the aspiration of each singular visage or appearance, much as Adorno says that the individual artwork reaches in its particularity for the greater Platonic idea of Beauty. The reality of "Desperate's" identification with the norm of facial symmetry does nothing to modify the impossibility of its access. "Desperate's" acceptance of the truth premises of these discursive oppositions validates to her the logic of her own exclusion from sociality, even while the very abyss of her face undermines any truth value in the notions of balance and agreement she so idealizes.

The perfectly symmetrical face functions in reality as an attitude before a social situation; it is aimed at concealing a subjective uncertainty within the social, and therefore it operates in the exact manner of a mask. The otherness of her appearance, shocking even to her, is itself the greatest confirmation of the ideological domain of sameness and normativity from which she is expelled. Her facial vacuum constitutes a difference that legislates its own banishment from a consensus of norms predicated on the reliability of notions of presence and symmetry that, in their status as ideals, simultaneously disclose and conceal their own distance from reality. This consensus is violated by the intrusion of a foreignness within which the ideal can see no admiring reflection of its own coherent agency; within which it can see only a distortion or deformation of itself. While "Desperate's" fragmentary visage is for West the truest mirror of the gaping abyss at the foundation of cultural dogmas of beauty, morality, and so on, that this truism should escape the grasp of cultural norm is consistent with its self-perpetuating logic. As the noseless girl is ignored because her differentiating presence disrupts a culture with no vocabulary to address its own rejection by the appearance of an internal "deformation," an aporetic otherness whose agency counters its own, so must that culture elide the negativity of self-critique and seal over its inconsistencies.

For Lonelyhearts, religion would provide the perfect vehicle for such elision, if not for a strange paralysis; "Christ was the answer, but if he did not want to get sick, he had to stay away from the Christ business" (3). Ironically, the material remainder of bodily illness that exceeds the noumenal jurisdiction of Lonelyhearts's typically abstract "law" of Christ, returns to him in much the same way it visits "Sick-of-it-all"—as the paradoxical symptom of its own need. She ruins her body as a condition of winning the recognition of being a good Catholic, and Lonelyhearts will become literally sick if he suggests that she resubmit herself to Christianity's terms. This abstract law, like any ideological positing, exteriorizes a private anxiety of identity into a public order of propriety that happens significantly to depend upon its ethical arrest of others. It is Lonelyhearts's wish here to offer Christ to his suffering readers as an anchor of stability and meaning. His discourse cannot address hope to speak to the local idiom of bodily pain, and confines itself instead to metaphysical abstraction and the legislation of unseen values. He divides the idea of subjectivity from the body, forgoing self-phenomenality in pursuit of an idealism that asserts the form of an imperative, with regulatory power over the corporeal. This hierarchy of values in which the invisible marginalizes or excludes the tangible actually registers in Lonelyhearts's own appearance:

> Although his cheap clothes had too much style, he still looked like the son of a Baptist minister. A beard would become him, would accent his Old Testament look. But even without a beard no one could fail to recognize the New England puritan. His forehead was high and narrow. His nose was long and fleshless. (4)

This fleshless quality represents the completeness of his wish for sublimation, the total disappearance of the actual body, whose hindering presence makes impossible the ideal of existence in pure accord with religious or metaphysical principle. His own sartorial signing betrays the truth-value of his ideal, however, by resingularizing the body its meaning would presume to renounce. Even a nondiscursive representation of puritanism undermines the content of the puritan ideal, reliant as such communication is on a concentrated stylization devoted more to the representational figure than to God. The imperatives of "oceanic" unity that take shape in "fleshless" discourses of religion and morality tend to obscure the secret insecurities of self that originally demand them, never more so than in subjects like Miss Lonelyhearts and his readers, for whom a forgetting of the body and the entire immediate field of the corporeal is a satisfactory strategy. At one point, as he walks the streets in isolation, he realizes that "he had completely forgotten sex," his habits of solipsism by now firmly established, as West comments ironically on the conventional protocols of modernist alienation. For Lonelyhearts also remembers "that at college, all his friends had believed intercourse capable of steadying the nerves, relaxing the muscles and clearing the blood" (18). In other words, the most direct avenue toward stability and reunification of self is through the material experience of the other, the best means of establishing a "clearer," "steadier" sense of solid selfhood, through sexual dissolution within another, not through Lonelyhearts's customary performances of brooding and isolation in the pained quest for self-revelation.

That he knows "only two women who would tolerate him"—the conventional Betty and the embittered wife of his editor, Shrike—suggests the impenetrability of his self-obsessed character, his inability to share himself, to subordinate to sociality his preoccupation with his own desperation. Even in his relations with these two women, Lonelyhearts's greatest difficulty lies not in executing his platitudinously altruistic advice of "understanding" and mutual cooperation, but in extracting a solid recognition of self.[11] He seeks a mirror that will somehow not reflect his contradictions but project only his desired unity, a sounding board that will return to him a sense of consonance—which only means that each relationship is as grounded in egoistic illusion as is his own sense of agency:

> Then he remembered Betty. She had often made him feel that when she straightened his tie, she straightened much more. And he had once thought that if her world were larger, were *the* world, she might order it as finally as the objects on her dressing table. . . .
> She came to the door of her apartment in a crisp, white linen

dressing-robe that yellowed into brown at the edges. She held out both her hands to him and her arms showed round and smooth like wood that has been turned by the sea.

With the return of self-consciousness, he knew that only violence could make him supple. It was Betty, however, that he criticized. Her world was not the world and could never include the readers of his column. Her sureness was based on the power to limit experience arbitrarily. Moreover, his confusion was significant, while her order was not. (11)

In order to safely reconcile the apparent fact that she possesses effortlessly the easy sense of control and knowing he so craves, Lonelyhearts dismisses as "limited" and incomplete her smaller, "insignificant" world, indeed forbidding its qualifications as "a world" altogether. It is a narrow, insignificant space when considered alongside the magnitude of *his* world—"*the* world"—that evidently measures the enormity of its dimensions in the fact of its unmanageability, its infinite divisibility, its refusal to be ordered. He conveniently forgets that Betty "straightened much more" when straightening his tie, providing him a sense of inner stability that is absent without her guidance and, therefore, anything *but* "inner." It is this absence that therefore throws into question his ability to distinguish between the different kinds of "world" he constructs now in an effort to justify his monumentally "significant" confusion before the image of Betty's comparatively "minor" mastery. He overlooks a further irony in this narcissistic justification, for his criticism of Betty originates in what he views as the mere utilitarianism and arbitrariness of her techniques of "order," all turned in the service of fashioning some small dimension of controlled cohesion. In dismissing her practice of organization as an "arbitrary" device of smallness and limitation, he misses its necessity as a compromise strategy on a world that exceeds all grasping. At the same time, the "round and smooth" properties of her waiting arms communicate to him the seamless perfection of closure and envelopment, representing to him the instruments with which he would like to embrace and calm a fractious, radically multiple culture, applying her knowing, healing touch to an ever-fragmenting modernity. He fails to see, where Betty does not, that these instruments are only two, and that the object of their actual embrace is merely one.

At one point, Lonelyhearts ruminates on this impossible infinitude before a pawnshop window, unable to resist the impulse to impose order on materials that defy even the unity threatened by language:

> He found himself in the window of a pawnshop full of fur coats, diamond rings, watches, shotguns, fishing tackle, mandolins. All these things were the paraphernalia of suffering. (30)

But the multitude of unrelated objects and the absoluteness of their differences renders this platitude too hollow even for Lonelyhearts, as he begins to consider the peculiar anxiety that demands of every situation a certain mastery and unitary comprehension:

> He sat in the window thinking. Man has a tropism for order. Keys in one pocket, change in another. Mandolins are tuned GDAE. The physical world has a tropism for disorder, entropy. Man against Nature . . . the battle of the centuries. Keys yearn to mix with change. Mandolins strive to get out of tune. Every order has within it the germ of destruction. All order is doomed, yet the battle is worth while.
>
> A trumpet, marked to sell for $2.49, gave the call to battle and Miss Lonelyhearts plunged into the fray. First he formed a phallus of old watches and rubber boots, then a heart of umbrellas and trout flies, then a diamond of musical instruments and derby hats, after these a circle, triangle, square, swastika. But nothing proved definitive and he began to make a gigantic cross. When the cross became too large for the pawnshop, he moved it to the shore of the ocean. There every wave added to his stock faster than he could lengthen its arms. His labors were enormous. He staggered from the last wave line to his work, loaded down with marine refuse—bottles, shells, chunks of cork, fish heads, pieces of net. (31)

Everyday, practical mechanisms of fictive order, such as the separation of keys from change, are characterized by Frank Kermode as "necessary fictions," crucial to the navigation of temporal culture, to the processes of interpreting and of making oneself interpretable to others.[12] False shapes are attributed to groups of objects in the relation of a story for metaphorical effect, but this effect has value only in its ultimate self-referentiality, in its internal function as a device of figurality in the act of stylized representation. What disturbs Miss Lonelyhearts is the final incommensurability of figuration to "reality," the "phallus" of old watches and rubber boots for example, being an imaginary narrative powerless to subordinate any others or to register as the definitive representation, its final status as merely one narrative among many. Unlike the incongruous objects assembled one against the other, these individual narratives emerge as strategies of shaping and determination, becoming warlike with one another, each competing for a recognition of sovereignty from the other, each claiming in itself a private consistency that perfectly absorbs and perfectly reflects the broader ideals of order imposed from elsewhere. West's concluding imagery of the trash-filled waves on the shoreline can be read as a Paterian homage both to the incessant flow and repetition of difference that washes away any mimetic narrative of centered meaning, such as the "phallus" of watches, the "heart" of umbrellas, the "diamond" of musical instruments, or even the "cross" composed of them all—and simultaneously, as the inescapable final word of an Eliotic modernity, a picture of the phenomenal excess or waste that provides the only material substance of such allegories.[13]

Dismissing Lonelyhearts's metaphysical idealizations, Shrike ridicules the younger man's naiveté. But his own valuations of cynicism, aestheticized hedonism, and sensory dissipation aim only at counterthrust instead of actual deconstruction; Shrike would replace the metanarrative of God, salvation, and morality with another, albeit doomed, metanarrative of universal subversion that defines itself only in its negating relation to the social spheres of convention and legitimacy it would displace. Shrike's equally ideological elevation of art and hedonism above religion depends on the permeability of the aesthetic and the sexual, on an interaction between a sexuality both augmented and undermined by its aestheticized other, and an art unpretentiously inextricable from its social atmosphere. However, the very mediation of his testimony reveals the corporeal fragility of both art and sexuality, demonstrating the irreducible otherness of each experience, ungraspable by language, yet necessarily subjected to language:

> Shrike ignored the interruption. "You're morbid, my friend, morbid. Forget the crucifixion, remember the Renaissance. There were no brooders then." He raised his glass, and the whole Borgia family was in his gesture. "I give you the Renaissance. What a period! What pageantry! Drunken popes . . . Beautiful courtesans . . . Illegitimate children . . ."
>
> Although his gestures were elaborate, his face was blank. He practiced a trick used much by moving-picture comedians—the dead pan. No matter how fantastic or excited his speech, he never changed his expression. Under the shining white globe of his brow, his features huddled together in the dead, gray triangle.
>
> "To the Renaissance!" he kept shouting. "To the Renaissance! To the brown Greek manuscripts and mistresses with the great smooth marbly limbs . . . But that reminds me, I'm expecting one of my admirers—a cow-eyed girl of great intelligence." He illustrated the word *intelligence* by carving two enormous breasts in the air with his hands. "She works in a book store, but wait until you see her behind." (6)

The Dionysian character of Shrike's colorful monologue is counterpoised by his colorless deadpan, "the dead, gray triangle" of his face a dark memorial to the transient, temporal truth of sensuous art he has devoured in the same way he has consumed women sexually.[14] Both the aestheticized products of the Renaissance and the local objects of carnal consumption that sacrifice themselves to his vampiristic tastes strip each other of their particularity in the graveyard of satisfaction's dull finitude. Not only does Shrike feast on the vibrancy of art and sex, offering no contribution of his own to the "pageantry" of culture, but as a sepulchrelike receptacle of exhausted aesthetic and sexual texts, he also disappears any distinction between the two, conflating the brown Greek manuscripts with the brown limbs of the sexually objectified women who bear them.

The "intelligence" signified by the presumed bookishness of his particular woman at the moment is measured by the size, shapeliness, and availability of her breasts and buttocks to Shrike, whose deadpan expression communicates the ultimate sameness and indistinguishability of each of these favored "texts," once they have been consumed. The artwork and the woman are therefore neither new nor particular for him. The promise of happiness is deadened by the actual experience of its satisfaction. Shrike can report descriptively on the distant joys provided by each, consigning the specific properties of each to language and memory, in much the same way that he can now only speculate wearily on whatever repetitions of satisfaction they will give in the future. In his very speech, art and sex communicate themselves as absent, necessarily arrested and atrophied by a language hopelessly separate from the secret internal life of each. Like the undead vampire, he is therefore able to testify to both the uncertainty of the promise and the dead culmination of its resolution, to speak of life from a vocalizing position of death, to speculate on the future as a mere repetition, as an object of the past.[15]

His position is signified by the grayness of his countenance, a sedimentation of promise within the certainty of its annihilation in its very lived experience, a worn-out experience that establishes not only Shrike's own negative authority, but also the constitutive differentiality of each category of experience described.[16] His abstracting the specific works of Renaissance art into a broader, generalized notion of classical accomplishment and beauty opposes the animate functionality of each work. Such mimetic reportage constitutes a descriptive enterprise that obstructs the mobility of each work's private logic, the all-but-imperceptible life force or imaginative bloodstream that, as Adorno writes, is necessarily aimed at undoing the vague concept of Art by "express(ing) the whole of Beauty" in its own ineffable singularity.[17] Shrike's Greek manuscripts sacrifice their reality to a larger concept of beauty and pleasure that not only subsumes their particularity to language and category, but that also includes sexuality as an analogous source of pleasure. He conjures an orgiastic, sensory overload in which the artwork and the sexual object are decontextualized and collapsed in their functions of amusement, and finally in their exhaustion.

Ultimately for Shrike, however, art extricates itself from its bodily confusion as the artist and gentleman should only permit himself to "use the girls upstairs" (25), insignificant as they are to the eternal joy of art, mere instrumental tangents to true aesthetic "nourishment"; merely momentary distractions with whom to "fornicate under pictures by Matisse and Picasso" (25). Unlike art, the girls cannot keep him alive:

> "Art! Be an artist or a writer. When you are cold, warm yourself before the flaming tints of Titian, when you are hungry, nourish yourself with great spiritual foods by listening to the noble periods of Bach, the harmonies of Brahms and the thunder of Beethoven. . . . Tell them to keep their society whores and pressed duck with oranges. For you *l'art vivant*, the living art, as you call it. Tell them that you know your shoes are broken and that there are pimples on your face, yes and that you have buck teeth and a club foot, but that you don't care, for to-morrow they are playing Beethoven's last quartets in Carnegie Hall and at home you have Shakespeare's plays in one volume."
> After art, Shrike described suicide and drugs. (35)

Shrike advocates a positive withdrawal from the vulgar ugliness of contemporary culture, urging an ever-vampiristic "nourishing" on the aesthetic products of the past as a way to escape a meaningless, acquisitive present. This necessitates an equally violent repudiation of the body, its cold to be warmed by the momentary heat of a painting's false flame, its hunger to be fed "spiritually" by something as defiantly insubstantial and nonutilitarian as the sound of music. The reality of suffering and deprivation is to be overcome by the intellectual and sensory satiety provided by art, as the material abjection of pimples, broken shoes, and buck teeth is rendered irrelevant by its aesthetic other. This fetishization of art entrenches it, alongside Lonelyhearts's Christianity, as a strategy of fixity in a world of flux and differentiality. It thereby undermines art's very operations by ignoring the movement of its necessary generation on the materiality that both men eschew. In his valorization of the dead and intangible above the temporality on which art vitally depends for its critical life, Shrike strips it of its constitutive dynamism, thereby transforming it into an agent of the same kinds of stability, law and order that Miss Lonelyhearts espouses in slavish repetition of the daily death sentences in which he so earnestly believes.

Part III

Blackness (In)Visible

5

Chaos and Surface
in Invisible Man

*Historically, the Negro steeped in the inessentiality of
servitude was set free by his master. He did not fight for
his freedom.*

—Frantz Fanon, "The Negro and Recognition," in *Black
Skin, White Masks,* 1952

If notions of selfhood originate, as do Paul de Man's categories of
knowledge and virtue, out of lies institutionalized and replayed as
foundational truths, then constructions of meaningfully "black"
identity must take on a doubly deceptive resonance in Western sociality and representation. Untroubled linguistic conversions of experimental life into atrophied, abstracted performances of racial being
manage, with each successive repetition of the designations "black"
or "white," to submerge more deeply the primary anxieties and potentialities of self within beings freshly ossified by ideology and language. For Diana Fuss, following Fanon in her *Identification Papers,*
"white draws its ideological power from its proclaimed transparency,
from its self-elevation over the very category of 'race,'" a category that
from this perspective can be seen to embody and define *completely*
the social practice of "whiteness" itself.[1] For Slavoj Žižek, the racialized Other (in an example apparently borrowed from Lyotard, designated as "the Jew") functions strictly as a symbolic strategy of suture,
an "ideological figure . . . a way to stitch up the inconsistency of our

own ideological system."[2] Fanon perhaps puts it most succinctly in the same chapter from *Black Skin, White Masks* when he writes, "The Negro is comparison."[3]

Displacing its own void of self-certitude as it issues the positive character of its Other, "white" grants itself the reality of its "whiteness," tautologically finding its own potency through its fabrication of an Other from whom it can measure its tangible difference. This racialized Other is at all times posited as an entirely separate unity in itself; the Negro, the black, the nigger, as its many designations, despite their very number, all proclaim its monadic status as something unitary, something absolutely apart from that which names it into existence. Yet it is the very urgency demanding that these names be named, demanding that the firm classification of an Other be enunciated and instituted publicly, that also confirms the interpellating governance of the subject of the Same. The reference toward the Negro as an absolutely unconditional reality must also at all times directly reflect back toward the place of its birth, since the designation of "Negro" also establishes negatively and silently, but all the more powerfully for that silence, the unconditional difference and unity of "whiteness," born of course, in the same moment.

The variant of modernism explored in this section is unsparing in its examinations of a blackness that has necessarily and reflexively incorporated into its own programs of play and critique the logic and the terminology of its own absolute deficiency before an equally fictive, self-ordained "whiteness." The power of this whiteness is at once concretized and compromised by the fact of "the nigger" stationed beneath it. For "whiteness" recognizes itself as such only through its domination of "the nigger " it creates, and is privately nothing without this public object of abjection that substantiates "white's" self-conferred authority. This mutual interdependence for the meaningful existence of "the one" sphere upon the fact of "the other" is complicated paradoxically for such thinkers as W. E. B. Du Bois because of these spheres' inability to intersect as equal, if separate forces in real time. In other words, "the nigger" of traditional American literature is not permitted to outlive its slavish status as a mere racialized thing, but is instead liquidated in the moment that it begins to assert its singularity as a thinking, speaking subject.

But Ralph Ellison's *Invisible Man* (1952) finally forces a confrontation with the illusion of this oppositional duality, exploding Du Bois's famous formulation of "twoness" in *The Souls of Black Folk* by tracing the material and noumenal intertwinings of "one" sphere's destiny with "the other's." In the futuristic binding of these destinies, which is, for Ellison, in no way a peaceful "reconciliation," the text must also continually return to that originary, individual space of aporetic wonder and void, one solved only momentarily by the logic of race specifically or by that of identity generally. In so doing, it shatters the mirage of a unitary oneness that any proper twoness necessarily presumes, and dismantles the dialectical underpinnings of other such binaries as the visible and the invisible, opening a literary terrain that maps zones of experience outside accepted registers of history. By way of its circular or "boomeranging" narrative temporality, its insistent slippages between reportage and interior monologue, and its figures of liminality (Rinehart, Bledsoe, the grandfather, and ultimately the Invisible Man himself), the text illuminates the multiplicity and nothingness of appearances and tropes that alone provide culture and, indeed, cultural "blackness" any sense of self-reality.[4]

> "And my problem was that I always tried to go in everyone's way but my own. I have also been called one thing and then another while no one really wished to hear what I called myself. So after years of trying to adopt the opinions of others I finally rebelled. I am an *invisible* man. Thus I have come a long way and returned and boomeranged a long way from the point in society toward which I originally aspired." (573)

The "I" to which the Invisible Man refers is a figure that is vaporized in the moment it discloses itself, subject as that self has been, to the interpellative force of the social. This is a generalized pressure mandating the performance of an identity that signifies not the fluid specificity or grace of a being's unique expressionism, but only one's slavelike adherence to a prefabricated register of typology. This pressure is manifest in the sounding of an interpellative call into identity that disrupts his hearing of another "myself": a self that if not the occupant of a stable, referential classification, must necessarily be a more liquid movement of being and experience. The "I" by which the Invisible Man communicates the idea of himself is only the voicing of a preexisting unrest, a verbal enactment of an attachment to that matrix of designations and determinations to which its singularly distinct multiplicity is always radically other—but at no time distant. The verbal "I" is no more than a strategy of self-implication into that legislative configuration of power, whose force inheres primarily in its ability to determine and to place; is only the verbal reconstitution of an idealized self-coherence that is already shattered by the mobile experience of living thought; thought that materializes only in its transit from indecision to decision, from possibility to identity. And back again. A continual migration that, as the Invisible Man recognizes in the stolen light of his stolen cellar, can never identify any proper destination or way as being one's "own." Having "come a long way and returned and boomeranged a long way from the point in society toward which I originally aspired," he realizes that all origins and ends are strictly discursive sites, no more than verbal strategies elaborated to organize the ongoing experimentation that constitutes experience into manageable scenes of referentiality, meaning, and valuation.

They are mere locales that, like the University of his youth, in the mouths of Dr. Bledsoe or Mr. Norton, or like the Brotherhood in that of Brother Jack, can be subjected to the unifying force of a mythifying narrative. Such narrative, in establishing itself as historical authority, wields the power to exclude from its self-legitimating boundaries any thinking that exceeds linguistic province. Issuing from the destituted space of his subterranean stolen hole, the very words from the cited passage are spoken from precisely such an excluded region of void, or indeed its ocular analogue, blackness—in his own words, from "outside history." This, of course, is the phrase that he uses to describe the final destiny of Tod Clifton, his former Brotherhood comrade, who, in abandoning the haven of institutional designation, plunges into what the Invisible Man can only conceive as the blackness of ontological abyss. He describes Clifton's departure from the Brotherhood as the abandonment of his own "voice," locating the agency of the would-be subject solely within that being's ability to be recognized publicly, and thereby implicated within systems of social power—

which, bringing this Hegelian logic to its Fanonian conclusion, amounts only to a new incarnation of nonsubjectivity for racialized pawns of whiteness, liquidated in their very reliance on that whiteness for a sense of public legitimacy.

But what is even more interesting to this investigation is the protagonist's conflation of "voice" with "identity." This move renews Ellison's rigorous and reflexive theorizing of the distinction between expressivity and signification, or what plays out in literature as the distance between idiom and identity, between the incessant transmutability of style and the linguistic stasis of referentiality. The "I" that supposedly speaks or denotes a self is but a linguistic arrest of the boomeranging flight that is the nondevelopmental and perpetual movement of subjectivity. The "I" marks only the verbal form of a mythic agency that is necessarily absent to itself, as evinced in the moment that it is uttered. The self it signifies in the novel is absent. By this I mean that it is present only in what is still silenced within the novel—this name that is never named, this nondisclosure of a selfhood that the protagonist positivizes only in forms of anonymity, experimentation, and change.

The Invisible Man's voicing is never a mere vehicle by which an interiorized region of "content" or "substance" is made public. It is never simply an instrument of revelatory transmission but is instead an auditory order of experience whose material reality exceeds the bounds of its coding. Not for nothing is the only "true" calling of the Invisible Man his summoning into oratory. For at no point in this purported narrative of "development" is he so naively bound to a particular discourse of meaning, message, or identity that he loses himself totally in the ideological imperatives of whatever institutional structure he is attached to. He admits as much in recalling his first public oration, a graduation day lecture that will later be replayed with heavily ironic reverberations after the battle royal. Of the moral content of his own paper he says, "Not that I believed this . . . I only believed that it worked." The measure of whether it "works" has nothing to do with the imagination or logic of the speech but only with the extent of its public approbation. Its success is determined by the degree of its regurgitative force in reaffirming this culture's values to itself as well as in the execution of its style.[5]

During his first meeting with Brother Jack, following his im-
promptu street speech protesting the eviction of an elderly Harlem
couple, the speaker's detachment from the spoken exposes itself more
baldly. He resists Jack's imposition of motive onto something that the
protagonist believes is more precisely a question of performance and
its improvisation: "Look, my friend, thanks for the coffee and cake. I
have no more interest in those old folks than I have in your job. I
wanted to make a speech. I *like* to make speeches" (293). The very fact
of his "calling" into the practice of oratory itself bespeaks the totality
of his envelopment not in the teleologies of signifying and signification but rather in the idiomatic movements, sounds, and textures of a
singular expressionism. The distance that he remarks on repeatedly
between the meaning or content of his speeches and the materiality
of their utterance indicates that for him, as for Blanchot, his words
"say" nothing, except in the very figurality of their *saying*, their meaning obtaining in the particularity of his verbal style or idiom. This enables him an ironic, which is to say an aesthetic, which is to say a
profoundly political, line of flight beyond the narrowly telic discourses of "racial uplift" organizing and legitimating the hierarchy of
the University, or of totalitarian advocacy for "the people," that justifies the Brotherhood to itself. Discovering that the particularities of
style, sound, and cadence work independently of the codes of reference to which they are assigned and subordinated, he is surprised to
find his deepest discovery of radical selfhood within a moment of
sensorial "*non*-sense," in which the seemingly banal experimentation
with a sweet potato bought on the street channels the gushing experience of liberation from every mundane logic of propriety and identity to which he has ever been compliantly subject.

> I took a bite, finding it as sweet and hot as any I'd ever had, and
> was overcome with such a surge of homesickness that I turned
> away to keep my control. I walked along, munching the yam,
> just as suddenly overcome by an intense feeling of freedom—
> simply because I was eating while walking along the street. It
> was exhilarating. I no longer had to worry about who saw me or
> what was proper. To hell with all that. . . . If only someone who
> had known me at school or at home would come along and see

me now. . . . I'd push them into a side street and smear their faces with the peel. . . .

This is all very wild and childish, I thought, but to hell with being ashamed of what you liked. No more of that for me. I am what I am!

. . . "I yam what I am! What and how much had I lost by trying to do only what was expected of me instead of what I myself had wished to do? (264–66)

Preceding every principle of designation and identity, naming and placement, is the "wild" absence that social agents of order seek to repress through the summoning and activation of such principles. Divorcing himself from what he now sees as the policing function of prefabricated or responsibly typological selfhood, the Invisible Man embraces the irresponsible, childlike joy so long displaced by the restrictive performance of a proper black identity. The sweetness of the yam returns the Invisible Man to the molecular experience and engagement of his senses, to the living of a bodily selfhood that can now feel shame only for having felt shame of itself for so long. The taste and texture of the yam emancipates him from the ontological lockdown of cultural expectation attendant to his "station." Charging a self that no longer thinks in terms of its immobilized representation but only in terms of reaching and surpassing its own experiential/experimental borders, of imagining and satisfying its own aesthetic contours. No longer concerned with his place as a subject within someone else's frame of hierarchical sociality, his exclamation "I am what I am! . . . I yam what I am!" is no claim to the clone status of mere "subject" in any slavish reproduction of ideology. It is rather the "wild and childish" precondition of his becoming. "I yam what I am" improvises the motion of idiosyncratic self-stylization and signifies nothing, repeats nothing, identifies with nothing—other than the freeing movement and tonality of its own expressionism. Its voicing is not the externalizing of any embedded inner essence of true self but is only the sounding of the idea of its own sound, and the distancing it enunciates from the inhibitions that precede it.

In this particular mode of entropic understanding, the Invisible Man anticipates the (non)figure of the Harlem hustler Rinehart.

Beholden to no principle and no cause, this apotheosis of the non-identitarian moves darkly through Harlem like an anthropomorphic unit of chaos; his look, his voice, his stride, his clothing, his identity absolutely improvisational and exchangeable, Rinehart embodies the thinking fugitivity of philosophical expressionism. In his inability to be identified under a stable code of referentiality, he performs the substance of movement, recognizable only by fragmentary accoutrements such as dark, green-lensed sunglasses, knob-toed shoes, and a Cadillac that rolls only by night—these, in addition to slightly more personal indicators, such as "a smooth tongue, a heartless heart," and, indeed, a readiness "to do anything" (493). Such attributes coalesce to form a radical singularity whose only signature is its radical *plurality*, whose differentiated modes of speaking, walking, lying, loving constitute an absolutely sovereign way of being.

> Can it be, I thought, can it actually be? And I knew that it was. I had heard of it before but I'd never come so close. Still, could he be all of them: Rine the runner and Rine the gambler and Rine the briber and Rine the lover and Rinehart the Reverend? Could he himself be both rind and heart? What is real anyway? But how could I doubt it? He was a broad man, a man of parts who got around. Rinehart the rounder. It was true as I was true. His world was possibility and he knew it. . . . The world in which we lived was without boundaries. A vast seething, hot world of fluidity, and Rine the rascal was at home. . . . It was unbelievable, but perhaps only the unbelievable could be believed. Perhaps the truth was always a lie. (498)

Identifiable with no institutional quarter or party, Rinehart works the illicit, voided zone, or "rind," designated as "outside history" by those who claim its inside, or its "heart." In this way, he reveals himself to be at the center of their concern. Irreducible to any single role, or to any identifiable motives such as money, power, or sex, in his embrace of multiple modes of identification, he abandons all, freeing himself to align with the fluid and shifting forces of life "underground" in plain sight. His objectives are never identified—unless they obtain, as they must, in his liquidity. Rinehart embodies multiplicity in ceaseless motion, undermining every certitude, destabilizing every authority, *concealing* the truth of his character by *performing* its proliferation in public.

Suspending the "subject/object" humanistic imperatives by which he would except himself from his surroundings and categorize all before him, Rinehart recognizes the fact of his ongoing implication in the urban landscape. At once predatory and escapist in his relation to Harlem, he embodies the hardness, caprice, and protean becoming that constitute any urban complex of sensations and circumstances. Utterly indifferent to every question of personality, character, or subjecthood, he is one with the movement and flux of the city, glimpsed *only* in transit, *only* as he vanishes into the terrain of Harlem night, never stopping to explain or to telegraph his destinations. His is a chaos that, like any other, is contagion, and haltingly the Invisible Man follows Rinehart's pathless lead into the voided black zone of nonhistory and nonidentity.

> . . . after first being "for" society and then "against" it, I assign myself no rank or any limit, and such an attitude is very much against the trend of the times. But my world has become one of infinite possibilities. . . . Until some gang succeeds in putting the world in a strait jacket, its definition is possibility. Step outside the narrow borders of what men call reality and you step into chaos—ask Rinehart, he's a master of it—or imagination. That too I've learned in the cellar, and not by deadening my sense of perception; I'm invisible, not blind. (576)

Stripped by experience of every designating and confining "rank," the Invisible Man now rejects the logic of designation as a bad faith strategy against the cultural entropy that alone lends naming its meaning, that alone enables the thinking of identity its elevation above the nothingness it combats. Suggesting instead that along the fictive path of linearity that has led the protagonist from one mask to the next in his odyssey through a taxonomic museum of institutional designations, he is accompanied by a radical alterity. It is the ironic filter by which the experience of this vast room full of socially prescribed mirrors is organized and narrated at a critical distance. The Invisible

Man is always already exterior to a room in which all he can see is one
prefigured code for one proper selfhood after another, without any
recognition of the radical singularity that is his polyglot of aesthetico-
political inclinations. For no single name or cultural designation can
account for the always mobile reflexiveness that characterizes his
thinking and speech, reflexiveness that always keeps him at a critical,
ironic distance from total implication in whatever ideological imperatives supposedly provide him identity and voice. Escaping what
Amiri Baraka identifies as "an area of act that is hell . . . a place of
naming."[6]

The imperative of proper naming would shield the notion of solid
identity from the alterity that anticipates and demands the strategy of
closure that is that name. Ideologically instituted identity is dependent on the cleanliness of its exclusions, be they political or sensorial,
and is undermined in the moment that these negativities resurface.

On one of those post-University, pre-Invisible days, Ellison's protagonist is overtaken precisely by the reality of this return.

> One moment I believed, I was dedicated, willing to lie on the
> blazing coals, do anything to attain a position on the campus—
> then snap! It was done with, finished, through. Now there was
> only the problem of forgetting it. If only all the contradictory
> voices shouting inside my head would calm down and sing
> a song in unison, whatever it was I wouldn't care as long as
> they sang without dissonance; yes and avoided the uncertain
> extremes of the scale. But there was no relief. I was wild with
> resentment but too much under "self-control," that frozen virtue,
> that freezing vice. And the more resentful I became, the more my
> old urge to make speeches returned. While walking along the
> streets words would spill from my lips in a mumble over which
> I had little control. I became afraid of what I might do. All things
> were indeed awash in my mind. I longed for home. (259)

The words that issue from his lips are themselves a double reverberation, and not only of the excluded anguish of a sharply detoured desire for a satisfactory ideological destination in the lockdown of
cultural identity. They are also incoherent testimony to the aporia

from which language itself emerges in its urgency to reconstitute the objects for which it now substitutes. The entropy of the discordant material in his mind demands a solidification into an identical presence that would form the basis of a unitary and acutely visible self, excepted from the numerous undifferentiated crowds on which his subsequent career as a speaker ignites. This anxiety materializes in the protagonist/orator's frequent references to the masses before which he speaks as anonymous, collective shadows, a "blurred audience," a shapeless amalgam of "faces becom[ing] vaguer and vaguer," against which he speaks himself into what he imagines as a sharply distinct presence (340–53). The urgency for sameness disclosed in the cited passage, the veritable mania for consistency and consonance, is only the outcome of language's metaphoric fiction revealed, in that no verbal designation of social identity can make one identical with it. The word does not ever collapse that originary gap but is at best a momentary strategy against that chaotic void.

This void is viciously ironized throughout the body of the work, as when the paternal white benefactor of the University, Mr. Norton, traumatized by his encounter with the incestuous black sharecropper, Jim Trueblood, blurts and stammers his astonishment at Trueblood's survival of his personal horror. The shocked Norton can shout his incredulity at Trueblood only with what the Invisible Man describes as a look of both "envy and indignation," exclaiming, "You have survived . . . and are unharmed! . . . You have looked upon chaos and are not destroyed!" To which the bewildered Trueblood replies, "No suh! I feels all right" (51). Trueblood's complete externality to the white man's shock, and his concurrent inability to assimilate that shock, makes concrete the distance between those who would abjure chaos and those who are consigned *to live it* in the presumed abyss of ocular and cultural blackness. For this is also the distance between those who write "history" and those who are excluded from it. The fundamental incompatibility between these two zones activates the wishful inversion of incomprehension sputtered by Norton.

At the same time, it localizes, in the form of Trueblood's utterance—"I feels all right"—the ongoing relinquishment of comprehension, the embrace of understanding's opposite, supposed by Enlightenment discourse from Kant to Hegel to Hume to characterize the presumed

subhumanity of black existence. No rhetoric of mere marginaliza-
tion, no vocabulary of simple exclusionary practice, begins to address
the problematic of blackness's pure externality to the categories of
modernity that Ellison theorizes in this novel. He investigates this
problematic not simply as the labor of existing within a social void of
abjection and repudiation but of *living* that experiential/experimen-
tal void of "nonknowledge" itself. Of the ongoing work and play of
embodying, performing, and *improvising* life that is culturally designated as outside or beneath any self-legitimated human register of
thought, identity, or propriety.

In its utter unresponsiveness to social imperatives of identity and
classification, the questioning cut of such chaos sounded by Louis
Armstrong's first experiments corresponds exactly to the discordant
irruptiveness that the Invisible Man tries to repress in his head. The
abdication of the idea of mastery and personal sovereignty that Armstrong performs in his identification—not with any social typology
but rather with sound, movement, and rhythm—eviscerates the messianic impulse to reduce the sonic experimentalism of improvisational
music to the willed and perfected product of any anthropomorphic
subject. The "home" for which the Invisible Man longs is a fantasy of
smoothness and order that would contain and arrange the discordant
voices in his head into a monadic fusion of unruly particularities,
creating a sameness that elsewhere in the novel he takes pains to escape. The effacement of difference he craves in this instance counters
the intensely egoistic insistence on cultural recognition of his intellectual and stylistic exceptionality that motivates the narrative.

From within the density of absolute social void, from within that
black hole of stolen light, the protagonist must discern an entire negative constellation of possibility. Ellison's working of the play between the visible and the invisible resonates darkly at the differential
boundary of the abject. Proceeding from the notion that the field of
the visible, the legitimate world of "light," is always already governed
by its other, the invisible and delegitimated, Ellison deconstructs the
distance between the seer and the seen, inside and out, in a space circumscribed by transcendental imperatives of identity and race, forging a new nonspace, in which the Hegelian pressure of finding
self-confirmation through the recognition of another is utterly sus-

pended. The dialectic broken, each step further into this black hole of nonidentity is a step into the terror and ecstasy of nonrecognition. By this I mean not simply the centripetal destruction that attends any withholding of recognition of self from without; I mean the improvisational possibility of working or *playing* oneself into the semblance of a self, a self that becomes a self only in the performative materiality *of* its playing, not in any constative assertion of its substance. It is the improvising of what the Invisible Man calls in the prologue "the invisible music of my isolation." It is the experimental playing of the void, of both purely visual and culturally inscribed blackness as the embodiment of epistemological absence—as if this abyss of solid identity were a musical chord or tone to strike.

> Before that I lived in the darkness into which I was chased, but now I see. I've illuminated the blackness of my invisibility—and vice versa. And so I play the invisible music of my isolation. The last statement doesn't seem just right does it? But it is; you hear this music simply because music is heard and seldom seen, except by musicians. Could this compulsion to put invisibility down in black and white be thus an urge to make music of invisibility? But I am an orator, a rabble rouser—Am? I *was*, and perhaps shall be again. Who knows? All sickness is not unto death, neither is invisibility. (14)

The pivot that Ellison actually puts into motion is hardly represented as a pivot, or a nonlinear "break" at all by his narrator, but is rather embedded as a purely temporal movement of development, or straight-ahead evolution. "Before that I lived in the darkness . . . but now I see" is no more than a formula for a transparent kind of redemption that stitches over the rupture or traumatic violence that any moment of correction, any conversion of nonknowledge to comprehension, necessarily constitutes. This fiction of firm channels bridging the aporetic and the comprehensible, of smooth, noncircuitous travel between blindness and insight, nonknowing and knowing, is itself a nearly indiscernible device of narrative dislocation, programming us into a certain readerly faith—a faith in the temporal premise of full understanding or closure that makes even the entropic point of finitude that is "playing invisibility" a reassuring notion because of its temporal status *as* an endpoint, as a destination, an outcome preceded by something else that is escaped. Invisibility, or nonidentity, is a break made soothing by the familiarity, or what Lyotard would call the "good form," of the linear structure in which it reveals itself as such.

The precise moment of transmission of transformative information is necessarily obscured. At what point is nonunderstanding converted into understanding? This is a point about which it should be impossible to generalize, and yet it can never fully be made to materialize. For Ellison, articulating the thematic of invisibility is the device of invisibility itself. He works a narrative strategy whereby the very idea of the narrator is enabled to survive only by the subtle dissembling that momentarily excludes the memory of his various traumatic shocks or rude "awakenings." These might include his expulsion from the University, the explosion at Liberty Paints, and his subsequent electric shock therapy; for his narration of these awakenings can be only a belated epistemological schema, which is to say, an absolute effect of his devastation. This evolutionary tale at once allows the illusion of the narrator's totality and performs the self-deconstructive drive of a narrative organized by endlessly circular, self-referential principles. What is momentarily excluded is the event upon which the system is built; but this event resurfaces later, as something like revelation or content. By the time it does return as "something" to be narrated, as an object to be communicated, the solidity of the frame—this being the narrator himself—has been established, despite the crushing damage it has endured in the moments it now objectifies as a distant, survived past. The frame speaks from the presumed stability of an outside that is but a standing ruin of a never distant inside. The frame relates the interiority that would have destroyed it; the interiority conditions and traumatizes the frame that now assigns it its proper definition and place. For Ellison, it is precisely, indeed only, this necessary "step into chaos" that actuates the fluidity of *possibility*.

Heard in a different key, Ellison's plunging of his readers back into the chaos—by way of a chiasmatic irony that participates within the classificatory frames of social reality even as it ridicules those frames as only makeshift strategies against chaos—can be read as a sharp antecedent and embodiment of some of the most provocative movements in literary deconstruction. Examples are found in a few formulations from Paul de Man. For as quickly as de Man isolates the inadequacy of self-posited metaphysical truth through deconstruction of that truth's rhetorical figure, he turns deconstruction on itself. He argues that for any theory of difference to be satisfied with merely dethroning false idols of metaphysical value and identity, would simply be a fresh repetition of the logic of truth.

> What was originally a simply referential text now becomes the text of a text, the figure of a figure. The deconstruction of the self as a metaphor does not end in the rigorous separation of the two categories (self and figure) from each other but ends instead in an exchange of properties that allows for their mutual persistence at the expense of literal truth. . . . The lie is raised to a new figural power, but it is nonetheless a lie. By asserting in the mode of truth that the self is a lie we have not escaped from deception. The pattern is perhaps clearest in the reversal of the categories of good and evil as they combine with those of truth and lie. The usual scheme derives good from truth and evil from falsehood. But Nietzsche tells the tale of the reversed pattern: in order to survive in society, man began by lying. . . . But the text cannot go to rest in this deconstruction that would justify, to some extent, the morality of deceit (as we find it, for example, in a political context, in Machiavelli or in Rousseau). For if we believe in the morality of deceit, we also have to believe in the evil of truth, and to the extent that the society is held together by means of deceit, the open assertion of this fact will also destroy the moral order. . . . Once again the reversal of polarities has not led to a restoration of literal truth . . . but has driven us further into the complications of rhetorical delusion.[7]

For de Man, the justificatory gesture of revealing the ideological emperor's nakedness extinguishes its own power in the moment of its realization. To assert a new sense of propriety or coherence that proceeds from the negative act of revealing the nothingness that structures every ideological truth, is, for de Man, to fall prey to that same primary need for truth. It is to capitulate to that same primary egoistic drive, to demonstrate in the act of dethroning ideology that even a logic of deconstructive nonidentity can function as a new metanarrative, as a new replacement truth.

But as Nietzsche's strategy of survival through deception is deployed closely by Ellison in the opening chapter of *Invisible Man* in the grandfather's dying scene, we observe that this deceptive practice, if lived strictly according to its own internal logic, can safeguard itself somewhat against the moralistic temptation to justify itself politically before any other authority. It can free itself of every political responsibility except its formal allegiance to itself as a strong practice of figuration. For the grandfather articulates in his final "confession" that his "treacherous" tactics in what he identifies as an ideological war between marginalized black Americans and oppressive white racism, are nothing more than sharply disingenuous gestures of concord with the values and representations issued from that "whiteness."

These gestures of ironic signification need not bear any corresponding internal truth content or genuine belief therein, but must at all times indicate and perform such belief. The grandfather's vision is a profoundly negative one in itself, as he never affirms any idealistic outcome of this battle, never proposes any proper end or closure to this process of deception, such as a replacement of "white" hegemony with "black." The grandfather stresses instead only the material means and terms of that deception of "whiteness," locating the political reward of this deception within its own aesthetic practice, finding its social victory in the fleeting moment of its formal execution, one that, if carried out successfully, will never be acknowledged for what it is. It is an invisible, self-negating triumph without celebration or logical conclusion. The grandfather's strategy of Tomming is predicated on an internal fissure that subordinates the idea or image of an autonomous self to the material practice of artifice before a structure of political power, a practice by which actual life and thought may persist. This personal sublimation duplicates, in its attentiveness to form rather than immediate self-gratification, the strongest or toughest impulses of individuated art production and ascesis.

Recognizing that American society is united largely by the fiction of black subhumanity, the grandfather scandalizes his family by bequeathing a deathbed imperative advocating the deception *of* deception, elaborating a plea for the sustained practice of lying and dissemblage before the grand lie of whiteness.[8] He does not attempt to justify this practice by framing it as an oppositional, heroic logic of resistance, even as he refers to his subversive habit as "the good fight." For his opponents are manifold; they are not merely structures of legislated African American objectification and degradation, but are more pervasive cultural habits of literal engagement with ideological fictions posited as social truths, impervious to irony. The magnitude of his struggle is made plain by the horror with which his family greets his final words.

So completely transparent is the degree of their engagement with social doctrines of "race" division and "black" subservience that his admission to having waged acquiescent war against these all his life necessitates for them its immediate foreclosure, its absolute effacement from memory and knowledge. In their commitment to the Booker T. Washington ideal (quoted partially by Ellison in the italicized part of the passage below) of slavishly materialistic unity with their masters, as "cogs" in the Southern economy, and social separation from those same masters, they "exult" in the notion of their own inadequacy. The dying imperative of the grandfather alone suggests the recalcitrant alternative of a slavish freedom with limits, an existential dialectic with one's own abjection—a dialectic whose very structure confers on its subject a secret and profoundly singular or nondialectical autonomy—which itself is just as profoundly compromised by its strategic inability to ever announce itself. His dying words provide his unwitting grandson the model of ironic "invisibility" to which he will later "aspire."

I am not ashamed of my grandparents for having been slaves. I am only ashamed of myself for having at one time been ashamed. About eighty-five years ago they were told that they were free, *united with others of our country in everything pertaining to the common good, and, in everything social, separate like the fingers of the hand.* And they believed it. They exulted in it. They stayed in their place, worked hard, and brought up my father to do the same. But my grandfather is the one. He was an odd old guy, my grandfather, and I am told I take after him. It was he who caused the trouble. On his deathbed he called my father to him and said, "Son, after I'm gone I want you to keep up the good fight. I never told you, but our life is a war and I have been a traitor all my born days, a spy in the enemy's country ever since I give up my gun back in the Reconstruction. Live with your head in the lion's mouth. I want you to overcome 'em with yeses, undermine 'em with grins, agree 'em to death and destruction, let 'em swoller you till they vomit or bust wide open." They thought the old man had gone out of his mind. He had been the meekest of men. The younger children were rushed from the room, the shades drawn, and the flame of the lamp turned so low that it sputtered on the wick like the old man's breathing. "Learn it to the younguns," he whispered fiercely; then he died.

But my folks were more alarmed over his last words than over his dying. It was as though he had not died at all, his words caused so much anxiety. (15–16, my emphasis)

The grandfather's affirmations of white "mastery" enact de Man's "morality of deceit," in this instance, a private practice of self-recognition through the public, grinning subversion of another's sense of self. Drawing his power from the absolute necessity of performing mindlessness and servitude before whiteness, the old man preserves himself by muting his own hatred and relocating it in an ongoing dance of perpetual irony, absenting himself from his own triumphs. However, it is the necessarily sequestered nature of this pleasure that undermines its deceit as a workable strategy of self-invention and that typifies the constant, critical admission into Ellison's own work, of the insistent negativity presented by material reality's refusal of even imaginary reconciliations.

For while the grandfather's accommodation of racism is a concentrated pretense and performance, it is nonetheless an actual accommodation as well, serving the material imperative of white supremacy. While the old man feigns goodwill toward white people, his inability or refusal to contest their hegemony on any front amounts to a reinforcement of that power in the real. It is crucial, to the interpretation of this scene in particular and of literary modernism in general, to realize that the limitations of his stance emerge from within the structure of their enunciation, and not only topically from an external antagonist without. Sedimented finely within ironic exercise itself is the negativity of its own frustration, is the promise of its own failure or thwarting that necessitates it as an aesthetic form and a subjective practice in the first place. Its primary inability to make itself concrete, to make itself heard in the motivated totality of its content, is central to its own logic. Following Schlegel's supremely generative essay "On Incomprehensibility," Hamacher writes that irony is at all times:

> making language possible and making it impossible. . . . Irony is not a position but an excess beyond the form of subjectivity, and it thus cannot be reduced to a comprehensible thing: it is the incomprehensible, the "impossibility . . . of a complete communication." But it is just as much the necessity of this impossibility, for only in this excess—only by acceding to another— does the subject have the chance to constitute itself.[9]

De Man himself, also proceeding from Schlegel's investigations, underscores Ellison's denial of simplistic social concords, political justifications, and claims of final truth. For de Man, the tendency to read irony in such tightly piloted fashion is to miss its function.

> [T]he error in seeing irony as a preliminary movement toward a recovered unity, as a reconciliation of the self with the world by means of art, is a common (and morally admirable) mistake. In temporal terms it makes irony into the prefiguration of a future recovery, fiction into the promise of a future happiness that, for the time being, exists only ideally. . . . *The dialectic of the self-destruction and self-invention which for him (Schlegel), as for Baudelaire, characterizes the ironic mind is an endless process that leads to no synthesis. The positive name he gives to the infinity of this process is freedom,* the unwillingness of the mind to accept any stage in its progression as definitive, since this would stop what he calls its "infinite agility . . ." (I)rony is not temporary (*vorlaufig*) but repetitive, the recurrence of a self-escalating act of consciousness. Schlegel at times speaks of this endless

process in exhilarating terms, understandably enough, since he
is describing the freedom of a self-engendering invention.[10]

The self-denial inherent in ironic practice generates and sustains the
continual self-discovery of the ironist, going a long way toward explaining the grandfather's lifetime refusal to posit an idealized end to
his lifelong dissembling and lying to "white" people. It helps contex-
tualize instead his continued exhortations to simply carry it on, to
"keep up the good fight" without so much as the image of a discrete
object of victory or reward in sight, because that sense of victory
inheres in the very fluidity of his lies, repeated so incessantly and con-
vincingly over years that they completely annex his character. His insistent lying is for him the most intense mode of self-experimentation,
originating as it does in a Southern context of codified "black" nonsubjectivity.

   "Whiteness" is the specified other necessary to his performance,
the audience before which this existential pattern will give itself its
own private shape and resonance. The figure and form of his irony
nullifies his personality while at the same time providing it perhaps
its strongest, most effortless expression. Even its presumed undoing
during the moment of its "truthful confession" marks him further
not as the man of quiet humility and meekness he had been thought
to be for decades, but rather as an insubordinate, even ornery and
disruptive figure of contradiction and paradox. He embodies the
chaos of lived *non*identity—and is there at home, a textual signpost
toward the entropy of the unfolding narrative.

   It is from within this field of public and private contradictions that
his grandson, the Invisible Man, must forge himself. Unspoken until
the moment of the old man's death is the impossibly vast distance between the fictive congeniality and timidity that he affects and the
earnest acquiescence and goodwill unto whiteness that his family
members genuinely avow. Stranded in this divide, an ideological
no-man's land that forces a choice between material survival and personal self-respect, between the hard-won satisfaction of acute reflectivity and the ignorant bliss of unmediated agreement with racist
convention and freedom from thought, is the boy, for whom the
grandfather's imperative is an augur. "It became a constant puzzle in
the back of my mind," he says of the old man's final admonition.

Speaking in his adult voice in the novel's Prologue, the narrative space from which he commences his vertiginous journey, he entertains embracing the old man's renunciation of conventional virtue and subjective solidity, speculating on the possibilities opened up by his peculiar experience of multiform alienation.[11] His sense of personal liminality and indeterminate belonging becomes in itself a ground for a private celebration, and not only of a certain freedom from ideological confinement. But this is preceded by a "darkness" in which the hole he occupies is not literally underground but in plain sight, a period in which he longs only to belong. This desire to submerge the self before the mere image of another ideal is itself an ideological outcome of the pressures of racist convention, which immediately establish themselves as truth in his mind, displacing the profound confusion he feels after his grandfather's dying statement:

And whenever things went well for me I remembered my grandfather and felt guilty and uncomfortable. It was as though I was carrying out his advice in spite of myself. And to make it worse, everyone loved me for it. I was praised by the most lily-white men of the town. I was considered an example of desirable conduct—just as my grandfather had been. And what puzzled me was that the old man had defined it as *treachery*. When I was praised for my conduct I felt a guilt that in some way I was doing something that really was against the wishes of the white folks. . . . Still I was more afraid to act any other way because they didn't like that at all. The old man's words were like a curse. On graduation day I delivered an oration in which I showed that humility was the secret, indeed, the very essence of progress. (Not that I believed this—how could I, remembering my grandfather—I only believed that it worked.) It was a great success. Everyone praised me and I was invited to give the speech at a gathering of the town's leading white citizens. It was a triumph for our whole community. (17)

The Invisible Man gathers himself into a prescribed being, configuring himself into a shape desired by others, without questioning his own desire, without investigating the nagging remainder of difference that prevents his total conversion into a conformist effect of "race" prefabricated by "white" society and joyously incorporated by "black." The only truth of this identity lies in the Invisible Man's libidinal attachment to his cultural "being," to a socially projected frame that denies its own essential anxiety and insubstantiality. Likened to the figure of Booker T. Washington, he fails to see that this gesture itself is a reference to a certain, numbed cultural conventionality. The materialism of the Tuskegee model of "blackness" accommodates Southern racist stricture in a manner of "dignified" quietude and economically driven subservience practiced most famously by Washington himself, in an obsequious counter to the critical antagonism of Du Bois in the early twentieth century. Plagued by the haunting sense left by his grandfather, that both acquiescence and hostility are forms of betrayal, either of self or other, the Invisible Man cynically follows the path of least resistance, abdicating the notion of truth in his own work for the easy rewards of public affirmation.[12] The "love" he receives comes in return for his affirmation of public ideology—not for nothing is his paper on "humility" adjudged so favorably.

In this instance, the Invisible Man exemplifies the inherently slavish "freedom" that Fanon argues can only condemn the Negro to perpetual subjection, the eternal punishment of having his freedom bestowed upon him by another. The fact that this freedom, this "great success," this "triumph" is conferred openly by "white" people without having been asserted by the Negro in the violence and absolute self-risk that separates mastery from servitude, means that it is not a freedom at all but only an embrace of one's own nonagency. In this way, the Invisible Man's "triumph" is more accurately a larger victory for the town's white people, who further cement and confirm the powers of subjectification and interpellation that their Negro counterparts content themselves without. Such a "success" for Fanon is only a parasitic feast, a celebration of one's own personal disaster and distance from autonomy, sold to him, expensively, as "victory":

> But the Negro knows nothing of the cost of freedom, for he has not fought for it. From time to time he has fought for Liberty and Justice, but these were always white liberty and white justice; that is, values secreted by his masters. The former slave, who can find in his memory no trace of the struggle for liberty

or of that anguish of liberty of which Kierkegaard speaks, sits unmoved before the young white man singing and dancing on the tightrope of existence. . . . For Hegel there is reciprocity; here the master laughs at the consciousness of the slave.[13]

During his fateful drive across the University with Norton, the Invisible Man derives from his "benefactor" a picture of perpetual self dissolve within a shapeless vortex of race ideology, a disappearance of singularity into abstraction. In his remembrance, he sketches out the false topography of autonomous mastery and the necessity of its tight relation to its slavish, eviscerated other in this passage:

> As I drove, faded and yellowed pictures of the school's early days displayed in the library flashed across the screen of my mind, coming fitfully and fragmentarily to life—photographs of men and women in wagons drawn by mule teams and oxen, dressed in black, dusty clothing, people who seemed almost without individuality, a black mob that seemed to be waiting, looking with blank faces, and among them the inevitable collection of white men and women in smiles, clear of features, striking, elegant and confident . . . now I felt that I was sharing in a great work and, with the car leaping leisurely beneath the pressure of my foot, I identified with the rich man reminiscing on the rear seat. (39)

Propelled by his effortless mastery over the expensive automobile that rolls with such "leisurely" grace beneath him, the protagonist senses a oneness of regency between himself and Norton. This is enabled by his simplistic specularization of autosovereignty, reflected by the photographic image of amorphous, abject otherness, the otherness of a holocausted Southern black mass lending background to the comparative shapeliness of its paternalizing benefactors. His own sense of power and identity is formed not out of a conscious working-through, or overcoming of such abjection on his own part, but only through a wishful, superficial identification with the stylization of a "white" mastery that prohibits it. Norton's "wafer thin watch," soft silk shirt, and "aristocratic" bearing accomplish the same posture of easy hegemony as do the serene expressions of confidence smiled by the white people in the photograph.

Buoyed by a similar sense of confidence as he handles the luxuri-
ous car, the Invisible Man feels himself utterly disconnected from the
material and subjective impoverishment of the black people in the
same photograph, who communicate no such enjoyment of singular
selfhood, let alone any sense of untroubled mastery alongside "elegant" white people. Yet, in this dreamy identification, the protagonist
overlooks the central fact that neither the automobile nor any of
these expensive trinkets are his own. He deflects the pivotal fact of his
own peripherality in this fantastic, fleeting semblance of sovereignty.
He sidesteps the fact that he is materially bereft in such a comparison,
that his momentary sense of completion is only the imaginary effect
of a process that to this point he has carefully avoided. This process is,
of course, the rigorous fight for self-emergence that Fanon accuses
the black man of having escaped.[14] The protagonist's idealization of
white privilege corresponds to an equally sincere refusal of admit-
tance into his conception of self, the pure longing, desperation, and
nothingness represented to him by the images of impoverished black
people trudging on without individuality.

Ellison foregrounds the rivalry between the contrarian, resistant
singularity of divergent selfhood and its simultaneous lawlike tendency toward blanket repression of that divergence. It is precisely this
sense of constitutive internal division, of self-recognition from a distance, of witnessing and *enjoying* his own depersonalization that
complicates the protagonist's tenure within the Brotherhood.

The Invisible Man senses immediately that his thinking originality
is once again being converted into a rank objecthood for someone
else's ideological purposes. This is clear not only from Jack's appropriation of the sidewalk speech, but also in his reduction of the
people at its center, the elderly couple and the angry Harlem residents
around them, to lifeless dimensions of strictly political obsolescence.
Crucially, the problem of distinction within and from a collectivity
emerges again in plainest terms:

"[Y]ou mustn't waste your emotions on individuals, they don't
count. . . . Those old ones," he said grimly. "It's sad, yes. But
they're already dead, defunct. History has passed them by. Un-
fortunate, but there's nothing to do about them, They're like

dead limbs that must be pruned away so that the tree may bear young fruit or the storms of history will blow them down anyway. Better the storm should hit them . . ." (291)

With hesitation, the Invisible Man now repeats the progression of Bledsoe, willfully exchanging his own subjective anxiety for the promise of identity's certitude. Before taking the stage in his first speech for the Brotherhood, the Invisible Man returns dreamily to this inchoate, aporetic state of self-insubstantiality, trying to arrange a self out of its fabric of anxious affects:

I seemed to view myself from the distance of the campus while yet sitting there on a bench in the old arena . . . yet there was a disturbing vagueness about what I saw, a disturbing unformed quality, as when you see yourself in a photo exposed during adolescence; the expression empty, the grin without character, the ears too large, the pimples, "courage bumps," too many and too well-defined. This was a new phase, I realized a new beginning, and I would have to take that part of myself that looked on with remote eyes and keep it always at the distance of the campus, the hospital machine, the battle royal—all now far behind. Perhaps the part of me that observed listlessly but saw all, missing nothing, was still the malicious, arguing part; the dissenting voice, my grandfather part; the cynical, disbelieving part—the traitor self that always threatened internal discord. Whatever it was, I knew that I'd have to keep it pressed down. I had to. For if I were successful tonight, I'd be on the road to something big. No more flying apart at the seams, no more remembering forgotten pains. . . . No I thought, shifting my body, they're the same legs on which I've come so far from home, And yet they were somehow new. The new suit imparted a newness to me. It was the clothes and the new name and the circumstances. It was a newness too subtle to put into thought, but there it was. I was becoming someone else. (335)

The coherence provided by the new suit is the effective cancellation of the former "emptiness" and incongruency of expression; the frank self-evidence provided by the new name is the new code of solidity and substance that replaces the "unformed" character of a being formerly "without character." The contradictions and "vaguenesses" of the past are erased completely in the newness of the well-tailored "someone else" brought into being by the Brotherhood. The vision of unity confirmed by the new suit is the spectral embodiment of Jack's admonition that the old self of the protagonist is dead, the visual signification of this specter all the validation necessary to prove its truth as a consistent unity. The newness of his clothes and name confer on the Invisible Man an autosynthesis of subjectivity and public identity that all but displaces every trace of its former nothingness. For while the newness conceals its former degradation, in so doing it also testifies to it, and in its very presentation perpetuates the abject life that this new image is organized to refute.

Thus the ghostly remainder of insurgent singularity that enables the Invisible Man to detach himself from this "newness" and to envision the aporia from which it emerged; thus the "traitor self," the "dissenting grandfather part," the disruptive remainder that cannot obliterate itself in capitulation to the call of belonging. It is this nagging, disruptive will to maintain an originary, if uncertain character that resists ideological pressure, even as it is necessarily informed and contaminated by such pressure. The "internal discord" it generates antagonizes every representational semblance of unity imposed on it—resulting in the continual prospect of "flying apart at the seams" the protagonist believes to threaten his public image. His task now is to conquer the anxiety of how to repress this unruly singularity.

Its threat is successfully "pressed down" in the Invisible Man's renewed effort to become "something big," perhaps as overt a statement of the crassly egoistic cynicism driving cultural identity as will be found in this study of its procedures. Such repression is enabled not only by the promise of prestige in return, but also by the actual enjoyment of that prestige. Again, for the protagonist, this is a function of the differentiation of self from the amorphous mob; continually he notices how his audiences "become one, its breathing and articulation synchronized" (340), how he is "looked upon by so many people . . . the focal point of so many concentrating eyes" (336). The necessity of self-exception reverberates with acutely reflexive modernist irony, as his studies in Brotherhood "ideology" under Brother Hambro lead to his daydreaming of old lectures on literature at the university. In one scene the protagonist remembers a lecture from an old professor on Joyce:

> I could hear him: "Stephen's problem, like ours, was not actually one of creating the uncreated conscience of his race, but of creating the uncreated features of his face. Our task is that of making ourselves individuals. The conscience of a race is the gift of its individuals who see, evaluate, record. . . . We create the race by creating ourselves and then to our great astonishment we will have created something far more important: we will have created a culture. (354)

In this schematic rendering of the rupture of the new, the notion of tradition that amounts to no more than a series of breaks and interruptions is institutionalized and reified, as the materiality of creation's cut is made subordinate to the "far more important" task of establishing "a culture." Even in the rescue of the individual, the ultimate aim is the life of the collective for which the individual exists. There is no question of differentiation outside the legitimating purview of collective "culture." The supreme example of this cynical disposability is the case of Clifton himself, a sharply skilled and attractive member who soon finds himself shunned on the streets of Harlem for selling out to this organization of callous white leftists and allowing himself to be used as a political pawn. As he begins to show signs of self-doubt in his private wonder about the efficacy of the Brotherhood, he suddenly disappears without explanation, and the absence of worry or even curiosity about his whereabouts increases the Invisible Man's suspicions about the group. Only in the aftermath of Clifton's death does the Invisible Man begin to conceive of Clifton's renunciation of "history" and ideology as the only logical rejoinder to ideology's absolute refusal to see him as more than simply "a cog in a machine," to its inability to register his as a stunningly unique personality and image with singular talents and faults. Clifton's murder is the thematic pivot for the protagonist's numbed entry into the life of liminality and nonidentity, the invitation into his abandonment of recognition on ideology's terms.

Why should a man deliberately plunge outside of history and peddle an obscenity, my mind went on abstractedly. Why should he choose to disarm himself, give up his voice and leave the only organization offering him a chance to "define" himself.... Why did he choose to plunge into nothingness, into the void of faceless faces, of soundless voices, lying outside history ... the cop would be Clifton's historian, his judge, his witness, and his executioner, and I was the only brother in the watching crowd. And I, the only witness for the defense, knew neither the extent of his guilt nor the nature of his crime. Where were the historians today? And how would they put it down? ... What did they ever think of us transitory ones? Ones such as I had been before I found Brotherhood—birds of passage who were too obscure for learned classification.... We who write no novels, histories or other books. What about us, I thought, seeing Clifton again in my mind and going to sit on a bench as a cool gust of air rolled up the tunnel. (439)[15]

In the moment he discovers that only a new blast of light and sound is capable of rendering the history of Clifton and the other "invisible ones," a Benjaminian blast of a different materiality that will pierce and deflate the accepted practices of mimetic, official history, so too does the protagonist realize for the first time the depths of his implication within the legions of the faceless and voiceless he has insisted for so long on *not* seeing or hearing. The Invisible Man emotionally collapses himself back into the collective "we" from which he had struggled so long to emerge, recognizing that his meaninglessness before a racist "power set-up" of ideology and culture is a shared condition of disappointed avarice and ambition for distinction. He begins, however unwittingly, to realize that Clifton's decision to "give up his voice" by leaving the Brotherhood is actually one of the strongest demonstrations of Clifton's recommitment to a self he had abdicated years before in joining the group. In relinquishing the voice through which he was allowed to speak only programmed words, thereby gaining notoriety in the role of a fiery member of a larger collective, he actually reclaims an anterior voice, with all of its contradictions and thwarted frustrations, but with none of its former restrictions. In forfeiting his "chance to 'define' himself," he stamps his own invisible signature on an existence that had previously depended upon a defining externality to distinguish its "obscure, ambiguous, distant" nature—and thereby alienate it from itself. Returning to the "void of faceless faces" from which all identities must necessarily originate in the time before a differentiated name is conferred and recognized, Clifton is able to reconcile nothing, to establish nothing, other than his unharnessing from a tether of ideology meant to define and, therefore, annihilate him.

The anonymity of his death is the signature of a life given over to its ideological master; the anonymity is the consequence of removing the ideological consistency from one's sense of difference. His plunge outside history transports him beyond conversational reach and interrogation, dependent as verbal exchange is on a presumed mutuality of values shared and understood. His very move to the outside precludes this possibility, as the decision to plunge, by itself, places him at a remove from cultural comprehension, his willful renunciation of recognition and prestige not only a repudiation of the mastery so desperately craved in sociality but also an escape from the slavery it helps define. His refusal of the entire ideological economy of social exchange frees him from the master's possession and the slave's aspirant desire, leaving him the paradoxical realization of a strangely sovereign existence within the black void of nonidentity from which he once tried to break.

Emboldened by Clifton's plunge, the Invisible Man acts with increasing self-commitment, speaking his own words at the funeral he arranges independently for the former "Brother." His numbed, angry assessment of the futility and waste of Clifton's efforts runs a nihilistic counter to the pointed enthusiasm that his Brotherhood-programmed speeches are supposed to inspire. "He's dead, uninterested, and except to a few young girls, it doesn't matter," he says bitterly of his butchered friend and mentor. "When he was alive he was our hope, but why worry over a hope that's dead?" (455, 459) But his own sense of hope reawakens when, for the first time during one of his performances, he gazes out into the crowd, where "I saw not a crowd but the set faces of individual men and women" (459). The moment signals his recognition of his own prior blindness to the particularity of subjectivity, which has always surrounded him but has appeared to him as an undifferentiated mass.

Such blindness obliterates from view precisely the contours of distinction that he desires others to see in him. It is such blindness, literalized by the glass eye with which Brother Jack conceals the gaping loss of his own organic eye, that confirms for the protagonist his utter invisibility. The Brotherhood leadership is angered by the protagonist's independent organization of the Clifton funeral, viewing it as further evidence of his individualistic opportunism and treachery to the totalitarian rule of the collective hierarchy. As the leadership committee interrogates him harshly, forcing him to account for this "affront," he is at first bewildered, wondering of the formerly supportive Jack, "Doesn't he see how I feel, I thought, Can't he see why I did it?" (464) But Jack and the rest of his "brethren" are not able to see anything that is not first framed within a rigidly ideological scope that divides the world into objects of immediate utility or frivolous waste—of absolute conformity to doctrine or absolute treachery.

"You were not hired to think," Jack informs him. "[T]he committee does the thinking . . . you were hired to talk. . . . We furnish all ideas. . . . Let *us* handle the theory and the business of strategy" (469–70). When he resists this coercion, Jack becomes enraged, compelled now to make concrete the necessity of this principle of self-reduction:

[S]uddenly something seemed to erupt out of his face. You're seeing things, I thought, hearing it strike sharply against the table and roll as his arm shot out and snatched an object the size of a large marble and dropped it, plop! into his glass, and I could see the water shooting up in a ragged, light-breaking pattern to spring in swift droplets across the oiled table top . . . there on the bottom of the glass lay an eye. A glass eye. A buttermilk white eye distorted by the light rays. An eye staring at me as from the dark waters of a well. . . . I stared into his face, feeling a sense of outrage. His left eye had collapsed, a line of raw redness showing where the lid refused to close, and his gaze had lost its command. (474)

The outcome of this unseeing gaze is the plasticized, mechanical reproduction of a monodimensional (non)subject, whose public usefulness hinges completely on the repression of those remainders of excessive difference that mold it into more than the "one thing" it is required to be politically. Its inherent ambiguities, contradictions, and incongruities are evened out beneath the equalizing gaze of this sightless, nonpenetrating eye, flattened by the very terms of its public visibility. In short, the false eye of I-deology can produce only a secondary false eye of I-dentity, the smooth, plastic evenness of the unity identical with its representational apparatus and terminology.

Without such a prosthetic, the eye wound now "loses its gaze," and its object assumes the same shapelessness as the empty, raw socket, now powerless to either project a firm picture of a solid, external identity or to maintain for itself a stable appearance of totality and cohesion. Under the false gaze of its prosthetic interpellation into "one thing," the heterogeneous subject sacrifices its diversity to become a strictly representational figure, an "I" reprojected by the synthetic, reductive eye of ideology. The glass eye restores to Jack's face the fiction of its wholeness and the image of its symmetry and balance, closing the raw, open wound that hopelessly forfeits its gaze, allowing its object to escape definition. Ideological frameworks of identity operate in exactly such a way, emerging as effective strategies by which to solve the primary, chaotic anxiety of subjectivity. This is the problem of how to solidly translate the self *to another,* of how to convert a porous multiplicity of disconnected sensations, thoughts and impulses, into a single, firm and positive representation. Identity, in other words, is a response to an earlier enigma of selfhood that demands a resolution, or a name that will close this epistemological void within the self. The sense of self-certitude provided by illusory categories of social identity (such as "whiteness") transforms the former space of raw, shapeless anxiety into a unit of concrete determination, erasing all memory of the vacuum from which it takes flight and issues itself whole.

6

Assuming the Position: Fugitivity and Futurity in the Work of Chester Himes

But there exist other values that fit only my forms.
—Frantz Fanon, *Black Skin, White Masks*

In the disappeared third side of a Parisian triangle he draws between Richard Wright, James Baldwin, and Chester Himes, drinking and fighting, advancing and recoiling, all on the terrace of Les Deux Magots on a spring evening in 1953, *New Yorker* writer Hilton Als, describing the scene nearly fifty years later in a profile on Himes, detects the betrayal of an unspoken ideological mandate presumably governing the field of black American literature after World War II.

The alcohol consumed by the three writers that evening loosens the boundaries of a hazardous zone of dense interpersonal tension, already laced by an ancient intertwining of fiction's force and ideology's racialist insistence. The primary fabric of this tension is a ruptural, sarcastic *wordplay* that, without drink, might have remained soberly submerged, repressed within a public sphere essentially tone-deaf to the agonistic gestures of an inchoate, expatriate black literature, defined from its very beginnings by the paradoxical task of making poetic sense of the multiply dislocated conditions of its own expression. What results that evening is a conversation between Wright and Baldwin that is as sharp in its mutually contemptuous edges as it is pointedly free in its accusatorial range.

The freedom of the dialogue's violence, however, is silently enframed and brutally circumscribed throughout by the American literary rules of professionalized "blackness." The rigors of such rules—policed as they are within the self-reproductive regimes of the publishing arm of the American culture industry—are amplified even as they are reconfigured by this interplay among artists who are rivals and, in the sharedness of the ground each seeks, also brothers—writers who will never form an ideological or creative unit, yet who will ever be viewed within a certain unitary fusion.

The scene at Les Deux Magots in 1953 is originally recorded by Himes himself in the first volume of his memoir *The Quality of Hurt* (1972). By Himes's account, its very arrangement is born in an antagonistic swirl of egoism, betrayal, voyeurism, and perhaps, not so surprisingly, fraternity:

> Later, as we were preparing to leave for the party, the telephone rang. When Dick returned from answering it, he wore that look of malicious satisfaction which his close friends knew so well. He asked if I knew James Baldwin. I said no, but I had heard a great deal about him . . . I had read a review of *Lonely Crusade* that Baldwin had published in the Socialist Party's newspaper, the *New Leader,* but I had never met him.
>
> Dick said that he had been instrumental in getting Baldwin an award for eighteen hundred dollars and a renewal for nine hundred from Harper & Brothers to enable him to write his first novel. . . . He said Baldwin had "repaid his generosity" by "attacking him" in a number of published articles. . . . "Now Baldwin has the nerve to call me to borrow five thousand francs (ten dollars)," he said gleefully.
>
> He had made an appointment to meet him at the Deux Magots, and insisted that I go with him. I remember thinking at the time that he sounded as though he wanted a witness. . . .
>
> Then we hurried to the Deux Magots and found Baldwin waiting for us at a table on the terrace across from the Eglise Saint-Germain. I was somewhat surprised to find Baldwin a small, intense young man of great excitability. Dick sat down in lordly fashion and started right off needling Baldwin, who defended

himself with such intensity that he stammered, his body trembled and his face quivered. I sat and looked from one to the other, Dick playing the fat cat and forcing Baldwin into the role of the quivering mouse. It wasn't particularly funny, but then Dick wasn't a funny man. I never found it easy to laugh with Dick; it was far easier to laugh at him on occasion. Dick accused Baldwin of showing his gratitude for all he had done for him by his scurrilous attacks. Baldwin defended himself by saying that Dick had written his story and hadn't left him, or any other black writer, anything to write about. I confess at this point they lost me.[1]

Somewhere within the sudden relocation of a conflict from the sphere of the personal and its competing narcissisms, to the more abstracted planes of the political and the aesthetic, Chester Himes becomes unmoored from the contest's stakes. Where he becomes "lost" is on the idea of a somehow "proper" program by which to write or re-present the linguistic, aural, and textu(r)al fluidity of an immanent blackness that, in Himes's own work, is *always* antecedent to the local act of closure and exclusion that is racialization. Much of the cited passage gestures toward that realm of strangeness—that fevered, often ecstatic and megalomanic blindness to the limits of one's "own" position in space; that blackness, which is prior to and always outside social orders of propriety, designation, and tradition. It is a plateau of nonidentity and ongoing incomprehensibility that, for Himes, designates the actual point of writing's commencement.

Stage directions toward this zone of private abandon gone public abound in Himes's account: the silent self-satisfaction with which Himes notes Wright's curiously "malicious" pleasure at Baldwin's embarrassing need for money; the more conspicuous editorial silence about what Himes thought of Baldwin's review of Himes's second novel; the wicked suggestiveness of the thought that Wright may have wanted and even needed "a witness" before his dealings with the suddenly suspect Baldwin; the studied attunement to Wright's supposedly defunct humor; the sharply critical opposition of Wright's "lordly" "fat cat" to Baldwin's effeminized, nearly infantilized "stammering," "trembling," "quivering mouse." Each of these characterizations transmits an enmity born of intimacy that disrupts the scene's reportage even as it reconstitutes it, and by way of caricature in the last instance, points toward the textures of the tragicomic *absurd* that Wright and Baldwin tend to abjure in their own work. But at the same time, these are the vertiginous textures of self-abyss and self-contradiction within which Himes's writing finds itself very much "at home."[2]

In his reconstruction of the conversation, Als notes with a momentary prescience that is nearly fatally compromised by a characteristic glibness, that Himes's quiet disidentification that evening is at least partially a function of his aesthetic comportment, a salient feature of the singular philosophical freedom that enables his indifference to the personal and political rewards over which Wright and Baldwin now carp. As Als writes:

> He was not a skilled literary politician nor was he as adept as Baldwin or Wright at self-promotion. He had never been hungry enough or insecure enough to learn the game. So, on that Paris evening, he failed to recognize that his compatriots weren't discussing the finer points of *literature*—that, unlike the former college boy sharing their table, Wright and Baldwin were gladiators by necessity, fighting, at Les Deux and in parlors around the Faubourg Saint-Germain, to establish whose spear was long enough to pierce their largely white audience's consciousness, and anoint its wielder head literary Negro.[3]

As we observe, the vanishing side of this would-be triangle is more cutting in the totality of its self-effacing, its disappearance more playfully and, indeed, drunkenly free in its withdrawal than is the hyperdefensive aggression of either of the anxiously narcissistic combatants. Which is only to say that in the absence of anything for which to compete against either Wright or Baldwin this particular evening, Himes dissolves into the unheard contouring of another articulation—into the soundless articulation of an altogether different mode of critical presence, belonging to a completely other set of critical imperatives. He abandons, or more precisely, is abandoned by what he imagines as a literary zone of social realist pathos, now demanding and regulating the aesthetic representation of a black masculinity whose continual estrangement from any hope of self-possession would allegorize the entirety of twentieth century black thought and experience in the United States.

In his disengagement from the performative protocols of such conventionality, Himes opens a silent investigation into the deeper implications of Als's journalistic reduction of the encounter's stakes. But the theoretical space cleared by Himes's silence extends also into the darkly vast otherness of an ongoing history of abjections and abolishings, whose energies and afterlives cannot be managed or accounted for by reigning academic practices of historicism, and whose extradocumentary realities are only marginally available to any representational aesthetic logic of realism. The question at Les Deux Magots that evening, while clearly inflected with the kinds of careerist gamesmanship foregrounded in Als's snapshot, has more to do with how to animate novelistically these ancient and future realities of black survival and black creativity. The question is complicated in Himes's case because his literary project seeks to activate an aesthetico-political engagement of a delegitimated and outcast sensibility, whose ineffable and ineradicable *blackness* is at once anterior to the logic of racialization and, at the same time, augmented, reshaped and intensified exactly by those dimensions of lived experience unique to the scene of public fascination and public abjection (or exclusion from the zones of thought, value, and history) that is cultural blackness.

Himes's critical tendency toward the necessarily highly reflective figurality of this discarded life and thought has something vital to do with what Theodor Adorno sees as radical in all "dark" art of the post-1945 twentieth century: its reopening of an abyssal "speechlessness" that accompanies and critiques the banalities and horrors of everyday consumerism, administered sameness of social and commercial forms, and the nonstop atrocities on which such art obsessively ignites.[4] It is an art whose blackness inheres in its open inability to console or to reconcile its auditor or spectator with such realities, produced and intensified as these realities are by the hypercapitalism to which they are attendant, and by which its spectators are compliantly conditioned. In Himes, however, this immanent blackness moves beyond what might seem the strictly dialectical terrain of Adorno's model, and into the question of what Jean-François Lyotard later calls the impenetrable "time, space and matter" of language in the moment of working within literature.[5] This question forms a great part of the basis of Himes's most incendiary work, and severely complicates, if it does not entirely explode, the customary critical logic by which his work is disposed of as strictly "oppositional." Such a logic presumes Himes's work to be yet only another sounding of the "anguished cry" of social realism or naturalism that Robert Bone pronounced it to be in 1965.[6] It is suggested here that in both his detective fiction and what he called his "serious" novelistic meditations, Himes's work actually produces something much closer to the cry of "the real" that by necessity escapes every symbolic coding and classification, that breaks every contract of transparent meaning or valuation and undoes every uninterrogated "law of the named."[7]

Not attuned to the radical nonpositionality of this kind of figural irruptivity, Als, throughout his *New Yorker* piece, conflates author and literature. He continually attempts to sketch Himes biographically by way of presumably explanatory narratives of class warfare, threatened masculinity, and, most predictably, "black authenticity," ultimately collapsing these speculative figurations into the journalistic conjuring of a one-man Negro Problem—the very ethos that Himes himself weaves and *unweaves* so athletically throughout each of his novels. It is the literary *unweaving* of this ethos in Himes's work that most of his commentators, like Als, leave almost entirely unattended, focusing instead on what seems the "hardness" of the "hardboiled" cadence that characterizes the speech of many of Himes's protagonists and the general style of his narratives themselves, What customarily eludes analysis is the equally palpable parallel track of Himes's style—an imperative of incessant and fluid *movement*, the continually transformative upheaval of internal vision and thinking by which those same protagonists *become* more sharply defined in the first place. It is a fluidity within which what is *hard* is made to *boil* and dissolve; a technical principle of liquidity by which these characters' masculinist stances and postures are constantly exposed as nothing more than identificatory stops between situational and conceptual crises—which themselves turn out to be as foundational to the stylistic figuration of the novels as they are to the works' thematic premises. As Als claims:

Himes produced male characters who really were *noir*—in fact and in sensibility. Unapologetic and testosterone-driven, they weren't hard-done-by; they were in love with having done wrong. Turned on by their own bravado, they claimed entitlement and viewed sex as a struggle for power—the only form of intimacy that engaged them. "Race was a handicap, sure . . . but hell, I didn't have to marry it," says Bob Jones, one of Himes's narrators, before describing how he has used his skin color for financial gain. . . .

Undoubtedly, Himes's detachment from the forces that shaped his fellow writers had much to do with his own social entitlement. Unlike Wright or Baldwin, he was a child of the middle class. Privilege doesn't always cushion you from the sting of the lash, but it can act as a balm. Still, Himes was in constant rebellion against his background. . . . In a sense, Himes's entire oeuvre can be read as an attempt to prove how black he really was, and to authenticate, de facto, that abstraction.[8]

Just now, it does not seem advantageous to send those stranger effects of Himes's *writing* into the conceptual lockdown of a merely strategic move of defense against such a psychologizing, even pathologizing account as Als has provided us—though, among other things, the totality of Als's misreading of the cited lines from *If He Hollers* may appear to demand exactly such a direct and immediate rejoinder. For what eludes Als is the radical hollowness at the center of each example of "hard-boiled" Himesian positivity he enumerates; the acutely reflexive and ever-present *absence* of the kinds of self-certitude and self-consistency that such "testosterone-driven" "bravado" as that found in Himes's protagonists would depend upon for all psychic support. Such internal absence characterizes the very first image that Als presents—Himes's own silence before Wright and Baldwin at Les Deux Magots.

Himes's quiet withdrawal from the triangle Als imagines is not an act of aggression or repudiation but is something far less volitional. His concluding line, "they lost me," is in the lexicon of a certain incompetence. It testifies to a frank inability to participate in the exchange as an equal on the field of assertive positing and combat.

However, its passivity registers not as a withered impotence but as an educated hesitancy to step into any line of argumentation that might validate primary presumptions of cultural "blackness" or the stasis of subject positionality or identity of any kind. His identification is not with the professional "race-men" that Als all too blithely and reductively suggests Wright and Baldwin to be; nor is it with any flattened, commercial image of "the writer" by which Als can be said to frame the café exchange itself. The signature shifting speeds and intensities of Himes's writerly style, its organizational liquidity and constant transfigurality, all seem to channel Blanchot's channeling of Schlegel: "you can only *become* a writer, you can never *be* one; no sooner are you, than you are no longer, a writer."[9]

Himesian *becoming* permanently disables and scatters the notion of "Himesian" being, and is, for this reason, largely unavailable to instrumentalist or identitarian/ideological concerns of how "black," how "middle class," or how "rebellious" he "was" or "was not." Such typology marginalizes the strangeness to which Himes is attuned, converting the play of his poetics into the flat realism he molecularizes—and thereby reverses. It freezes the divergent energies, tensions, contradictions, colors, and tones that constitute thinking/writing life into a uniform set of narrative ordinances that would choreograph the scripted gestures of some such novelistic "black" "subject" in the American textual marketplace. Himes's reticence is thus only a withdrawal from the assertive furor of transparency and certitude that is taken so frequently and unironically to mark his own highly reflexive writing.

For Himes, the only reality of noir is its dissonant, discordant, always jarring sensibility. What Als puns as noir's social "fact"—the cultural imposition of anthropomorphic "blackness"—for Himes is only one more bizarre code inscribing the matrix of constructed social boundaries, identities, and binaries—top/bottom; in/out; black/white—that alienate thinking life from itself and constitute what Himes views as the absurd aspiration of "locating one's place" in American culture.

In such work, the question of literature's time, space and matter, or its figural materiality, as heard and felt within its American twentieth century anyway, is always already cut by the urban sonorities, colors,

and movements that, in most of his American literary contemporaries, constitute little more than added flavorings, punctuations, and
accents by which to augment an already-established, normative
"white" interiority. That is to say, that for most of Himes's contemporaries, forms of vernacular blackness are reduced to modes of black
affectivity that are depreciated into the mere instrumentality of
seasoning, distorted, and imported for the purpose of stereotypic
ridicule. What Himes realizes and reworks is the inexhaustible force
of this figurality's darkness to itself: the aesthetic shock, to itself, of its
very becoming, the ongoing event of its necessary regeneration
within the discarded districts of his Harlem, his South Central Los
Angeles, his Cleveland, his Jersey City. This figurality's own time,
space, and matter, its duration, movement, sound, and color, is the
surface expressivity of *thinking's* motion. It is a membrane of expressivity as impenetrable as any other—indeed, more so, owing to the
thick wall of mythology constructed around its meanings. It is the
criminally resistant idiom of an abjected and discarded urban blackness, defined primarily by its being subject to discourses of its utter
*non*subjectivity.

While the gestures of such an idiomatic opacity work in part to
subvert the "rational" arresting procedures of ideological machiner-
ies of comprehension and mastery, in Himes's fiction they also haul
themselves in for routine questioning, exposing a reflexive inclination toward self-suspension and self-dissolve in his art that is fundamentally at odds with the conventions of the "hard-boiled" tradition
within which his work is slotted critically and flattened. The dark
sensibility that informs the singularities of his work by 1953 is
sharply differentiated from the by-then normative protest routes of
resistance and advocacy made so pristinely and programmatically
"respectable" and devoid of risk or even surprise as to be nearly impotent by the midst of the civil rights movement (indeed, so predictably respectable that in novels from *If He Hollers Let Him Go*
[1945] and *Lonely Crusade* [1947] to the delirious satire *Pinktoes*
[1961], Himes makes a concentrated point of holding what he views
as the paralytic middle-class liberalism of the movement up to sustained ridicule, as only another "hustle" in an American matrix of
endless con games).

In other words, the silence that is the breaking of the triad at Les

Deux Magots is only another moment of a critique immanent to a wave of untimely and often unknown black artists that includes such figures as Himes and, before him, George Schuyler, as well as younger contemporaries such as Charles Wright, William M. Kelley, the film-maker Melvin Van Peebles, and Ishmael Reed. Their work, in its radical obsession with the fullness of its own poetic effects and with the rupture of ideological continuum constituted *by the very fact of such figural obsession,* shows the degree to which it is also calculated to expose the hollowness of the social equilibrium from which it emerges.

Disappearance, taking the affective form of reticence during the meeting at Les Deux Magots, is Himes's only logical response to cryptic chords sounded by Wright and Baldwin. Himes hears these chords as part of a "pathetic" and premodern song demanding the novelistic rehearsal and reprojecting of an essential black humanity and even nobility. The entire life project of such a humanity, as Himes hears it, would be to demonstrate the truth of its claims to the very structure of power and exclusivity that has made the performance of such a plea necessary. In a word, perhaps Himes's favorite, such a project is essentially absurd. That Himes's social nonengagement of this demand might blithely undermine a cultural metanarrative of American "blackness" that his *art* undertakes to shatter, rather than to exploit, is theoretically consistent, if affectively incongruous, with the more overtly noisy and aggressive ruthlessness of his writerly aesthetic. As Himes writes in *If He Hollers*:

> The alarm went off again; I knew then that it had been the alarm that had awakened me. I groped for it blindly, shut it off; I kept my eyes shut tight. But I began feeling scared in spite of hiding from the day. It came along with consciousness. It came into my head first, somewhere back of my closed eyes, cold and hollow. It seeped down my spine, into my arms, spread through my groin with an almost sexual torture, settled in my stomach like butterfly wings. For a moment I felt torn all loose inside, shriveled, paralysed, as if after a while I'd have to get up and die.[10]

Abandoned here is the calm self-mastery and effortless resourcefulness of the traditional "hard-boiled" hero, now collapsed into the involuntary shudders and spasms of a body at the mercy of the unconscious's submerged frequencies. Self-mastery is inverted, self-estrangement is intensified as Bob Jones, protagonist of the first Himes novel, *If He Hollers Let Him Go,* begins to sense, long after the fact, that he is caught up in what Avital Ronell would call an "exploration of the limits of *interiorizing violence.*"[11] What "comes with consciousness" is the noxious return of ideological matter ingested from without. He finds his body to have been no more than a false boundary, powerless to exclude the toxins that so organize and paralyze "his" movements. He finds, with repeated surprise, that if ideology is indeed ingested like the air we breathe, the racialism that it plugs into is necessarily and incessantly breathed back into the atmosphere with the vengeance of an internally eviscerating virus, returned to the zone of its origin. Himes writes:

> It was the look in the white people's faces when I walked down the streets. It was that crazy, wild-eyed unleashed hatred that the first Jap bomb on Pearl Harbour let loose in a flood. All that tight, crazy feeling of race as thick in the street as gas fumes. Every time I stepped outside I saw a challenge I had to accept or ignore. Every day I had to make one decision a thousand times: *Is it now? Is now the time?* . . .
>
> I carried it as long as I could. I carried my muscle as high as my ears. But I couldn't keep on carrying it. I lost twenty pounds in two weeks and my hands got to trembling. I was working at the yard then as a mechanic and every time my white leaderman started over toward me I drew up tight inside. I got so the only place I felt safe was in bed asleep.
>
> I was scared to tell anybody. If I'd gone to a psychiatrist he'd have put me away. Living everyday scared, walled in, locked up. I didn't feel like fighting anymore. I'd take a second thought before I hit a paddy now. I was tired of keeping ready to die every minute.[12]

The detached perspective of the knowing hard-boiled hero is here broken up, folded into a scene that heretofore, it would have described and managed as if from a clear-eyed distance. Jones finds himself possessed within the field of social vision, his claustrophobic view limited *only* to the immediate scene of the affective movements before him, his thinking now organized *not* by the social premapping of any given situation, but strictly in terms of his internal responsiveness to the image of "the look;" to the suffocating "thickness" of a "crazy, wild-eyed" "feeling," whose reality corresponds to its total inability to articulate itself into anything as reassuringly direct as an actual "challenge"; a feeling, whose force is made more palpable and tyrannical by its failure to cohere itself into something like a position; by its utter difference from anything resembling a discourse. Negotiating this passage, like so many in Himes, means abandoning the presumptively given scene of "the racial" and radically rethinking the contours of "the social." For what we observe in Jones are the gradual movements of the opening of an internal vision—not as it reacts to the practical ordering of a situation within culture—as in the narrative progression of a workday or a trip to the grocery store—but as it reacts to the unfoldings of singularized images, sounds, movements, and textures momentarily disconnected from the principles of "situation." In its dislocation from situational continuity, the fluidity of Himesian scenography transmaterializes the defining lines of identity. Jones's sense of a recognizable self-shape is sharply compromised by the fact of his hyperresponsiveness not to "selves" or to types, but to glances, blinks, and stares, tonalities and cadences of voice, speeds and arcs of movement. Such fragmentary agents orbit around him as a constellation of blindnesses and deafnesses, insensate and indifferent to any analytic of control or identity, forcing him into an excruciatingly liberatory zone of what Nathaniel Mackey might term a postexpectant futurity, within which the redemptive promise of "the human" and its hierarchies of rights and values are abandoned in the experimental practice of life continually exposed to the impossibility of finally determining its own meaning.[13]

What is required is the movement of life into the continual opening of such internal vision and hearing, unburdened from the weight or preemptive conditioning of the baggage of former hope or expectation, of any specific circumstance, disposition, or ending. In this way we observe that Himes's thematizations of racialist American antagonisms function as conceptual vehicles by which not merely to describe, but to *detonate* and destructure as radically absurd the American ideological nexus of "race," consumerism, and anti-intellectualism that so completely warps his swarming cityscapes. It is in this sense that Himes's fiction, and, perhaps more devastatingly, the series of detective novels for which he is best known and most popular, does more than eviscerate the "high/low" ideological dynamics that separate such writing from the "proper" novel. It also disrupts the troglodytic political drives that prop up mythologies of racialism, and that also support humanist notions of canonicity, literary modernism, and even postmodernism that are formed nowhere near so rigorously as the unsparingly ironic writing that exposes their contradictions and absences. The sudden popular resurgence of the long-obscured Himes as the grand documentarian of all things "street"—whose customary invocation itself forms only another static substitution for actual engagement of his writing—displaces with the frozenness of journalistic image the aporetic fields of sonic and chromatic *breakage and duration* that are the real object of Himes's obsession. Each of these fields houses an intrinsic force that Himes maximizes in the motions, tones, and subtones of word and phrase. Each field is the locale for the kind of sensorial engagement that implicates Himes within the tropics of modernism and the surreal, and in exile from the flat realism with which he is still customarily associated. His terrain is the figural, which as Lyotard reminds us, "is a denial of the position of discourse."[14] The plasticity of the figural improvises and highlights difference, finding its home in paradox and confusion, playing in an aphasic state marginalized by orders of knowledge and imperatives of proper designation.

Stumbling into a new mode of hearing and being during a marijuana stupor at the Blue Note in St. Germain Des Pres, one autumn night in 1961, he awakens to a revelation. "I suddenly realized my slang was ancient; I was inventing a language no one spoke anymore. What makes my books popular was not that they were hip; they were popular because they were absurd."[15] Like Walter Benjamin on hash, Himes realizes that language is not "his" to manipulate but that language "*happens to him* like an outward event."[16] He finds himself within its grip and not the other way around. Like Benjamin also, he recognizes this private truth of "self" only through ingestion of something exterior and inhuman.

Where he is lost during drinks at Les Deux Magots in 1953 and again at the Blue Note in 1961 is exactly at the boundary of the inhuman and the representational. For by thinking not in dogma or advocacy, but in sound and texture, not in discourses but in discontinuities and intervals, not in positionality but in energies and speeds, he abandons every mapping of the reassuringly human, of the uncomplicatedly "black" and crosses into the poetic nonidentical. In this zone, he relinquishes the notion that the ongoing mutilation of the American racialized can be converted either into an ideological referent or an object of aesthetic manipulation. Himes works within a more profoundly negative zone of art in which the redemptive tendency to try to equalize or protest the silencing of the abjected via the logic of representation is trashed by the unpresentable reality that haunts it. He realizes that to make the living history of that abjection the object of a cognition, a mere representation by concept is to once again callously "drown out the screams of its victims."[17] Himes's literature is concerned instead to create worlds of movement, sound, texture, line, and breakage that interact directly with bodies, institutions, laws, and cultures, amplifying the singularity of each by addressing not its powers of instrumental language but of affective furor, of each field's individual idiom of pure expressivity, its abilities to convey meanings that operate in excess of language. It is work that emphasizes less the presumed content of a discourse than the inscriptive cuts that modes of thinking such as affect and idiom enact on discourse.

The Open Secret of Time

Even in what he thought of as his "serious" novels, as "opposed" to the detective series he produced in Paris from 1957–1969, Himesian "authenticity" unfolds not at the levels of the sociological but always within the exquisitely *temporal* core of the affective; within his refusal to arrogate to a function of identity or "race" thinking the aphasic and suspenseful compulsions of thought, desire, and question that identificatory habituation stops cold; and that also cut art loose from any idea of its fixed comprehensibility. Unlike most writers occupying the genre spaces of naturalism or social realism, which allow the image of a more or less stoic subject to stand, racialized, sexualized,

gendered, flattened within the political grids of capitalistic modernity's classifications, the proliferation in Himes's work of disjunctive
energies and intensities scatters the notion of a self-coherent, unitary
protagonist who judges and organizes from without an equally freestanding, external world of meaning. In Himes, thinking is something that calls the thinker from the outside, again, something that
takes possession of him from a distance, transfiguring his being,
splintering him from an organized unit of coherence and autonomy
into a highly volatilized swarm of disjointed affects, impressions, sensations, memories, and constructs. In other words, for Himes, the social reality of reified, racialized life in the States is always already
beyond surrealism, and the movement of thinking, like that of literature, or music, or the sermon, exposes our actual experience of the
passage of time, presenting what Deleuze terms "the pane" through
which time is split and "presents pass, replacing one by the next while
going towards the future, but also of preserving all the past, dropping
it into an obscure depth."[18] In the following passage from Himes's
1938 short story "Pork Chop Paradise," the voice of the preacher performs the function of the interconnective pane:

> He rocked his congregations, he scared them, he startled them if
> by nothing else except his colossal ignorance, he browbeat
> them, he lulled them, he caressed them. He made hardened
> convicts want to shout, he made gambling addicts repent and
> give away their ill-gotten gains and stay away from the games
> for two or three whole days. He played upon people's emotions.
> His voice was like a throbbing tom-tom, creeping into a per-
> son's mind like an insidious drug, blasting the wits out of the
> witty, and filling the hearts of the witless with visions of ever-
> lasting beauty.
>   It had an indescribable range, sliding through octaves with
> the ease of a master organ. It was like a journey on a scenic rail-
> way, dropping from notes as clear and high as Satchmo ever hit
> on his golden trumpet, like the sudden startling dive of a pur-
> suit plane, to the reverberating roar of heavy artillery. You could
> see hell, in all its lurid fury, following in its wake, and then, with
> as abrupt a change, the voice took you to green pastures lush
> with manna.[19]

This voice is the mechanism by which opening fuses itself to opening; by which present disappears itself into a past now gone, displaced by another present now present. The immobility that is the scene of listening is at the same time the scene of this visual pageant's procession—a procession itself borne by the ongoing movement and changing of the voice's sonority. It is a literary playing out of what Eleanor Kaufman describes in a provocative discussion of time, image and *posed* immobility, as "a solecism of time, in which past and present inflect one another with a contradictory yet nonetheless sustainable tension."[20] We observe that the friction, or resistance between the fixity of the listening ear and the nonending fluctuation of crescendo and diminuendo projecting from the voice produces a continual (re)opening of the abundant internal life of visual/sonic forms themselves; the experience of changing images and sounds, which is only the exchange of different presents, is not determined by the organizing narrative of descriptions by the speaker, but is motored entirely by the vocative intensity or force of his explorations in the dimension of sonority itself.

Invited by Marcel Duhamel, editor of Gallimard's detective novel series, La Serie Noire, to start working in this genre in 1956, Himes initially balks, uncomfortable with what he considers his ignorance of the noir novel's conventions. Duhamel appeals to him with an ocular/auralization of literature in which the emphasis is relocated from plot and discovery of meaning or value to the movement of cut and paste; from writing in pathos to thinking in images of a psycho-visual and acoustic dream space of endless labyrinths and passages, in which colors, energies, and textures appear and shift without warning—writerly effects that are made more forceful by way of a certain immobility. Himes describes it thusly in his memoirs.

"Get an idea," Marcel said. "Start with action, somebody does something—a man reaches out a hand and opens a door, light shines in his eyes, a body lies on the floor, he turns, looks up and down the hall. . . . Always action in detail. Make pictures. Like motion pictures. Always the scenes are visible. No stream of consciousness at all. We don't give a damn who's thinking what—only what they're *doing*. Always doing something. From one scene to another. *Don't worry about it making sense. That's*

for the end. Give me 220 typed pages. . . . Keep the suspense
going. Don't let your people talk too much. Use the dialogue for
narration, like Hammett. Have your people use the description.
You stay out of it.[21]

The apparent refutation of thought argued by Duhamel is in truth
only the articulation of thought now unbinding itself from its presumptive obligation to the metaphysical *image* of thought. That dead
image is replaced with an emphasis on exteriority that necessitates a
new orientation toward time, in which time is no longer that which
connects, in the illusion of a linear unity, movements, ideas, and bodies, but is instead that which allows each of these to open up and unfold with power, independently of one another, according to the
inner logic and intensity of each. His indifference is not at all to the
motion of thinking, but only to the idea that this question is subordinate to that of *who* does the thinking. What Deleuze says of Kleist can
be thought equally productively of the Himes who produces worlds
of such indifference: that in his work, "feelings become uprooted
from the interiority of a subject to be projected violently outward
into a milieu of pure exteriority that lends them an incredible veloc-
ity, a catapulting force: love or hate, they are no longer feelings but affects. . . . Even dreams are externalized, by a system of relays and
plug-ins, extrinsic linkages."[22]

At work in Himes is a sensorial labor by which impression is reprojected not simply as "expression" but more like what Tom Cohen
calls ex-scription, in which the inscriptive cut made on us by the impressions we absorb from the outside creatively marks itself as the
trigger of a now-transfigured thinking.[23] The cut of the impression
that we attempt to narrate or represent necessarily reconfigures the
mechanics by which we narrate, thereby guaranteeing the virtual and
differential character of the former impression now rendered in another form. Here is an example of Himes energizing and surpassing
Duhamel's formation, in which the presumably descriptive actually
opens up an alternative of speed as a way of seeing and thinking matter, in which the value of an image seems to depends on its relation to
other images in the surface of the text and is therefore dependent on
the figuration of that text. By maximizing isolated faculties of de-

scription (darkness, speed, uncertainty) Himes forces the relinquishment of this habit of comparison, and makes available to us the invasion of nuance or timbre.

The second shot creased the back of his neck, burned through his fury like a red-hot iron and lighted a fuse of panic in his enraged brain. He was in an awkward position, his left leg crossed over his right onto the stair below, left arm raised in reflexive defense, right arm groping forward, and his body doubled over in a downward slant like an acrobat beginning a twisting somersault. But his corded muscles moved as fast as a striking snake. His taut legs propelled him in a burst of power across the landing and his right side slammed into the wall, bruising him from shoulder to hip.

Mother-raper! He cursed, gasping through gritted teeth and came of the wall turning, pushing with his right leg and right arm and right hip . . . moving so fast he was around the corner and out of range before Walker's third shot dug a hole in the white plaster wall where a fraction of an instant before, the shadow of his head had been.

He went down the bottom stairs in a somersault. It was started and he couldn't stop it . . . so he took it, catching the third stair with the palms of both hands. . . .

Walker chased him, charged down the top stairs teetering as though half blind. He missed the last stair before the landing, slammed sidewise into the wall and fell to his hands and knees.

"Wait a minute, you black son of a bitch!" he screamed unthinkingly.

Jimmy heard him and came up from his squatting position with a mighty push.

The minds of both were sealed, each in its compelling urge, one to kill and one to live, so that neither registered the humor in Walker calling to Jimmy to wait and get himself killed.

The differential force of the scene's speed emerges by way of its interspersed stoppages, as the very thinking necessary to movement articulates itself by way of a metaphorical vocabulary of action's necessary breaks. Metaphors of movement and intensity disguise the *arresting, cessational* function they actually perform; the "red-hot iron" that underscores the speed of the bullet that creases Jimmy's neck is itself a rigid solidity possessed of an internal force that leaves the permanent mark of a singe; the "striking snake" that makes visible the danger, speed, and rage that becomes threatening only within the suspended, poised coil of his taut, ready musculature; it is at the same time, however, a solidity, a firm body that while capable of murderously rapid motion, is also there, available to be captured and struck itself by a movement faster than its own. It is the "sealed" quality of each man's thinking—its inflexible indifference to the density of any physical obstacle to the surging of their movements—an unusually and powerfully enabling closure—that separates them hopelessly from any extraphysical dimension of abstraction, such as humor, honor, or justice.

In another passage, from *Yesterday Will Make You Cry* (1950), the customary freneticism of Himes's fiction is shifted from the fissured, entropic cityscape of Harlem tenements, canyons, and unlit streets to the claustrophobic interior of an American penitentiary in the 1930s. Within the immobility of the imprisoned consciousness giving spring to itself, the motion of the unannounced intervals between images articulates the facticity of thinking's weaving and unweaving of its own limits, which is only to say that what we observe in the passage *is* the conversion of matter's event into matter's reflection by way of an enforced fixity. This conversion provides the means of a certain transport out of lockdown's stasis (state lockdown) into the fluidity of what Deleuze calls "recollection-images," individuated, multiple images that trigger within us the past in which they are preserved. What emerges in the passage, however, is not simply the life of the boundary at which past collides with the present of its reanimation, but also what one sees/hears as an outward movement borne by the very gesture of thinking's rush, and the dissolving or collapsing of each of its images into the next—a jumble of movements and shifts whose friction eventuates in the production of images that live, and are yet unseen. This materiality of movement within the space of immobility is the historical writing of an utterance unable to assemble itself into a positive statement.

Those were the days; the moving, living, endless days with legs that dragged but yet kept marching through the stone and steel and five-foot thicknesses of concrete walls. The days with bloody guts filled with the gory slime of degeneracy, enclosed with the gray stone blankness of walls, lashed with bars falling in steady monotonous blows—the bleeding, living, peopled days of convicts doing time. . . .

But there were the nights, which were not nights at all but were the moments alone when he escaped the days. The moments when no one was with him, neither the convicts nor the guards, nor the discipline nor the rooted, immovable prison.

The nights of loneliness of which no one knew, which had no past, no future, no hope or perspective or foundations in respectability or beliefs or faith or love or hate, but which were only the times immediately present with thoughts which grew out of nothing and conclusions which grew out of them. . . .

All of those confused and not very clear and not very old and too touching thoughts and emotions which grew out of those nights out of hackneyed, tear-squeezing stories, out of lying awake when he should have been asleep, or from an old tune in clear notes on some distant convict's mandolin—a sudden lilt of melody across a moment's mood like an eccentric artist's fingers upon the chords of chaotic groping, weaving into romantic confusion or violent rebellion the new and jumbled and not very clear and too touching thoughts and emotions of those nights alone. . . .

And those thoughts, like angels' words, like the sidewalks trying to speak, like the mute prayers of the black scared night, weaving fantastic, unsleeping dreams into patterns of girls who were never born, and muted tones that were never played, and poems that were never written; into tense emotional situations wherein he always acted in a brave and noble manner; into horses breaking the barrier at Saratoga while he leaned against the railing, cigaret curling a nonchalant ribbon of smoke into the blue, sunny sky, with fifty thousand dollars on Red Rosebud. . . .

Only in his thoughts. The lovely stimulating bittersweet sensations—so utterly unreal. Like something from another world.

And the next day, ashamed of them. Ashamed as if they were the clap or syphilis or cancer.[24]

Memory's motion, as it slams against the thick concrete walls and lashing bars of the present, links imprisoned thought to the exterior surfaces and shapes of images and sounds that themselves *live*, embodying an unchecked freedom whose evidence is shown by their very disconnectedness to each other in (their) time and teleology—but not in space—the concretely rigidified space within which they collide without end. This is the scene of radical freedom heard in Mackey's remarkable distillation of the experimental/improvisational in his phrasing of a somehow "postexpectant" futurity, in which the imagining of an elsewhere of unborn girls, speaking sidewalks, unwritten poems and unperformed music finds the reality of these sounds and their contours, unbound from any purposiveness beyond their own expressivity or articulation. It is a freedom whose first emancipation is from the very hope of its foundation within language or culture. Himes meditates on the abyss of radical isolation in which thinking *becomes* thinking. The space of nothingness is by necessity one of contingency and purest experimentality in that nothing is returned to its occupant, no correction, no validation, no recognition, no refutation, no discourse of legitimation or even rejection. The materiality of its psychic and linguistic fabric is forced into an obsession with finding and moving beyond its own limits, its boundaries discovering and rediscovering themselves *only* in the exercise of their own gestures.

Such writing crumples the censoring schemas of genre that would divide surrealism from hyperrealism, "modern" from "postmodern," dismissing the despotic tendencies of those laws of canonicity and racialism that would neutralize into tone-deaf positionalities of either affirmation or repudiation the bodily shudders of horror and guttural cracks of laughter provoked by the laconic athleticism of Himes's expression. Hardly any plunge into a violently nihilistic pool of relativism, Himes's novels are rather an improvisational rethinking of time and event that, in their irreverent defusing of the definitional and in their cinematic poetics of discontinuity, expose and eviscerate the American culture industry that produces "race," "gender," and other categories of cultural identity solely to exploit them. In so doing, his work unfolds a strange and darkly impressionistic language in which those closely related dimensions of abjection, the niggered, the noncanonical, and the nonidentical, can converse openly, demanding an absolutely irreducible form that makes no pretense of strict representationality. This work foregrounds the figural materiality of language in which its accidental, unmotivated timbre or nuance touches that telic, ideologically programmed dimension, a meeting in which the ongoing mutual inscription of these two dimensions clamors for recognition as an event in itself.

What Is Left

Baldwin's informal notion of there being "nothing left" to introduce or to explore for black writing after *Native Son* automatically implies its opposite: that there exists a something to be left out. In this way he unintentionally announces his subscription to an analytic of propriety and exclusivity that he attacks and dismantles elsewhere throughout his life and career. As he and Wright skirmish on the ideological question of "what is left" for black writing after *Native Son*, Himes checks out, witness once again to the fact that *his* peculiar field of writerly interest—American absurdity—has just now proven itself as fertile as ever. The very articulation of the "nothing left" is enabled by its belonging to a strictly identitarian principle regulating a constellation of issues and pressures unique and proper to "the" project of African American writing. The negatively charged remainder that is everything outside that constellation or whatever might be "left" in the aftermath of the absolute truth apparently delivered/captured by *Native Son* is, for Baldwin (at least in this youthful, tense, challenged instance), a marker of impoverishment. But for Himes, the very enunciation of this "nothing left" functions as the invitation into an outward excursion. "What is left" has everything to do with how to play the membrane dividing and connecting what Himes hears as excess and what Baldwin hears as scarcity in the literary imagining of African American subjectivity in the 1940s and 1950s.

The vicious procedure by which the spectral figure of "blackness" is forced to internalize the rhetoric of otherness that literalizes its subjective distance from its "white" double, unfolds somewhat more subtly but no less fatally in *The End of a Primitive* (1955) than in *If He Hollers*. Himes again plays on the "white" egoism that creates the phantasmagorical myth of the bestial black Other who is materially conditioned to eventually become exactly the nightmare that "race" ideology has already ordained him to be. The protagonist, Jesse Robinson, is acutely aware (and more cynically so than Bob Jones before him) of the transformation and denuding of his chaotic "inside" of possibility, at the hands of an ideologically constricted and racialist "outside."

The terms by which Jesse attempts repeatedly to assert his completeness as a writer and an intellectual in racialist culture are not distant from those by which the novel must assert itself formally and aesthetically. It stands not only against its immediate precursors in African American literature such as Ellison's *Invisible Man* (1952) and Wright's *The Outsider* (1953), but also against the grand narrative of literary history itself, as Robinson's habits of quotation and reference from Rabelais to Gorki to Proust represent the tapestry of narratives into which Himes belatedly weaves himself. Jesse's Manhattan is interpretable only in its self-stratification into ontological categories of its own construction. It is a product of presumably stable determinations and oppositions such as "black" and "white," "high" and "low," "masculine" and "feminine," that create for it a readily accessible catalog of rubrics by which to illusorily define and comprehend itself.

The narratives of textual code and sign that the characters must assemble if they are to decipher culture are the same by which they are to assemble themselves into discrete beings. Wresting himself from the last in a series of nightmares structured by the thematic constant of his complete social invisibility, Jesse takes lonely survey of his Harlem rented room. He blearily recomposes himself amid the accumulation of temporal waste that metaphorically underscores his simultaneous superfluousness and fragmentation: dirty ashtray, half-emptied package of cigarettes, half-eaten candy bar, half-emptied milk carton, an alarm clock with a cracked crystal face. Then his eyes meet an ancient mahogany cabinet situated in a corner:

> Inside the cabinet, behind the closed doors, were his stacks of unpublished manuscripts, carbon copies, old papers and letters

which he always kept nearby, carting them from place to place, hanging on to them year after year, to remind himself that—no matter what he did for a living—he was a writer by profession.[25]

The only avenue into self-actualization for Jesse is textuality, as he has literally written himself into personal subjectivity, staging a rhetorical "identity" by which to insert himself into the grand narrative of abstracted humanity. Summoning himself into a suddenly coherent "self" by means of discarded, rejected writing, Jesse inscribes the supposedly "secondary" function of writing as something else, something *generative* that doesn't merely document his difference but also produces it. Himes narrates this function not only as a necessary precondition of the writer but also of subjectivity itself. This is not merely to undermine any presumed dichotomy between subject and object, but to demonstrate that anxiety and uncertainty compel the tissues of social narrative and signification that function above all as strategies of resolution, in the forms of codes, traditions and identities by which culture defines itself to itself.

The cost of such an existence for Jesse is the near absolute indifference of a postliterate culture, or what he terms "all the processed American idiocy." To comfortably situate himself at a remove from the culture of television and waste he so caustically dismisses, he must ignore his own participation within it, discounting the psychedelic possibilities at his immediate disposal in favor of the "higher" responsibilities of a serious writer:

He was still too drunk for a hangover but his head felt unset and his body unjointed and everything had a double-edged, distorted look like a four-color advertisement with each color slightly out of line.

However his brain was sharp. For the past five years it had never let him down. It was packed with some definite emotion, defined in intellectual terms; futile rages, tearing frustrations, moods of black despair, fits of suicidal depressions—all in terms of cause and effect, of racial impact, and "sociological import"— intellectual horseshit—but nagging as an unsolved problem, slugging it out in his mind, like desperate warriors . . . whatever he did to deaden his thoughts, there was this part of his mind that never became numb, never relaxed. It was always tense, hy-persensitive, uncertain, probing—*there must be some god-damned reason for this, for that.* (*End of a Primitive,* 33)

The deadpan absurdity of the second paragraph's reversal of the first nearly renders the scene comic. Jesse's logological anxiety even pene-trates and undercuts the inebriation by which he presumably at-tempts to obliterate it. But what is actually negated by the admittedly "desperate war" of telos, of "meaningfulness" and the primacy of fixed literary and intellectual conventions, even as they are recog-nized as the cheapest clichés, is the possibility of self-discovery or invention via actual experience, represented here by the state of drunkenness. Abandonment to radical ambiguity, to the aporetic wonder of "four color," "double-edged" distortion is finally forsaken in the name of "definite emotion" rendered in "intellectual terms" that can access nothing but a heavily commodified, popularly manu-factured, and conventional representation of "blackness," a politically soberized version of "black exotica." This commodity is bereft even of the charm of kitsch, for unlike kitsch, this kind of cultural reification takes itself dead seriously. The shattering racism that dictates the vi-cious reduction of life to what Jesse views as such one-dimensional "intellectual horseshit" is made possible only by an absolute nega-tion of irony and "tense," "hypersensitive" "uncertainty," all of which might undermine the "sociological import" of good "protest writ-ing." This genre, true to Himesian fatalism, goes out of style while Robinson is in midcareer—and its demise might seem to create an opening in which he might forge a finer art. But no such opportunity exists; one clichéd fad must be replaced on its death with another.

> Pope laughed. "You're a hell of a good writer Jesse. Why don't you write a black success novel? An inspirational story? The public is tired of the plight of the poor downtrodden Negro."
>   "I don't have that much imagination."
>   "How about yourself? You're certainly a success story. You've published twelve novels that were very well received."
>   "That's what I mean."
>   "I don't understand you."

"Damn right you don't," Jesse thought. He didn't care to remind Pope that a moment or so back he'd termed the rejected
novel as autobiographical. (124)

Himes's wicked burlesque directed at the racialist banality of American publishing and indeed, at the numerous authors who produce
such writing, reaches its most penetrating as he permits Jesse to per-
ceive the stupidity of his professional conditions, but also forces him
to internalize and accept them. The customary impressionism by
which Jesse is able to decipher at the level of the perceptual is brutally
repressed at the level of the professional. Sacrificed in his careerist capitulation is the recalcitrant inclination to intertextual distortion and
ironic revision that so marks his personality elsewhere. The differential character of his analysis, burdened and burnished as it is by material and political concern, is outlawed by the conventions of a literary
market that cannot allow the miscegenation of "black" writing and
modernist, impressionistic sensibility.

From where he stood at the corner of Eighth Avenue—a pest-
hole of petty thugs where a man could buy a gun, hot or cold,
for fifteen dollars up—down to the tricornered, old stone *Times*
building in the narrow angle were Broadway crossed Seventh
Avenue, was a block of infinite change. Once in the lives of very
old men it had been a mudhole; then had come an era of fashion, of furred and diamonded women with their potbellied es-
corts alighting from lacquered carriages beneath the glittering
marquees of plush modern playhouses. Now it was descending
into a mudhole again, but of a different kind. The once famous
playhouses, lumped together on both sides of the street, were
now crummy second- and third-run movie theaters, contesting
with the cheap appeal of a penny arcade with its shooting gal-
leries, mechanical games, flea circus, thimble arena where Jack
Johnson had done a daily stint of boxing in his waning years.
And in between there were the numerous jewelry stores with
fake auctions every night, beer joints, cafeterias, sporting goods
stores . . . book stores that dealt principally in pornography,
second-class hotels and filthy rooming houses.

"Poor man's Broadway," Jesse thought sourly, as his searching gaze flitted from the lighted movie signs to the passing faces: then his mind began improving on the commonplace phrase, "Melting pot . . . already melted—rusting now . . . last chance . . . I can get it for you hot—hotter than you think, bud . . . this side of paradise—way this side." (61)

Jesse fades into the loose narrative of images that he imposes on the urban landscape, finally disappearing behind the Fitzgerald reference that maintains its status as forebear only momentarily before it is corrupted by the street suggestion of the leering coda, "*way* this side." Rather than a mournful elegy to the block's bygone "era of fashion," the passage elucidates Jesse's vision of the inevitability of temporality's rush, of "infinite change," and of the perpetual improvisation made necessary by ongoing impoverishment. Even the deserted past is rendered in imagery of fleeting light and transient beauty, of "diamonded women" passing in "lacquered carriages beneath glittering marquees." The evident waste of the now "crummy" movie houses, "lumped together" into an undifferentiated mass still presents the opportunity of "Otherness" suggested by the "*way* this side" of paradise, clearly a "cheap appeal" but still an open invitation into an infinite, anarchic zone of differentiality rather than into a self-evident, solid "state" of ruin.

Himes's identification for the articulation of temporalized sensibilities in writers from Proust to Joyce translates into a precondition for the narrative structure of *Primitive,* in which the language of the interior is identical to that of the social, and in which the horrors of urban reality are staged in the unconscious. *Primitive* is not so much a naturalistic expression of the futility of relationships, "interracial" or otherwise, as it is an ironic catalog of the signifying procedures that expose the oxymoronic status of such positive terms as "interracial," that firstly presume a proper "racial" category to be engaged. In the figure of a "white woman" who is devalued and shunned by "her own," because she indulges in sex with "black men," and in the figure of a literary "black man" who privileges his own eccentricity above any collective implication or allegiance, Himes addresses a more comprehensive problem in modernism itself. This problem is the dismantling of the antagonisms of purity and contamination, home and homelessness, origin and absence that continually reproduce themselves as idealizations or abominations and that atrophy into social law.

What enraptures Jesse as he stands on the corner are writerly re-visualizations, by which to rediscover the animation of the images that swarm around him without freezing them into the stasis of defini-tion. These gestures—contradictory, unstable, dispersive—constitute the pure point of affect at which articulation itself is revealed as the tissue that substantiates the notion of a "self," the point at which ex-pressivity alone materializes the body of thinking. It is a space that, in other words, is hopelessly divorced from every discursive principle by which it would organize itself into a recognizable "positionality." Its occupant's thinking can determine itself only against the nothingness of its boundaries, can measure itself only against the absence of its re-turn or response from without. For Himes, the square cell of impris-onment in *Yesterday* and the Harlem corner of *Primitive* are exactly analogous to the philosophical zone of experiential/experimental *freedom* suggested in Paris by Duhamel and worked out exhaustively in each of the seventeen novels he produced. It is a freedom, follow-ing thinkers from Nathaniel Mackey to Jean-Luc Nancy, that is not addressed by any logic of rights or even knowability, but more by a post-Idealist/postexpectant conception of freedom, which abandons every notion of denotation, every claim of truth and propriety, find-ing itself only in constant confrontation with its utter inability to sta-bilize the foundations of a solid state calling itself an "I." It is the freedom of writing and of speech, to split from itself and propel itself toward its outside, in the very instant that its sounding opens it to it-self forever.

Notes

Introduction

1. For an important philosophical consideration of how experience and experiment are by necessity mutually constitutive, see Nancy, *The Experience of Freedom.*

2. Commenting on the poetry and thought of a young Eliot, Miller discusses this entropic zone in terms of what Eliot calls "immediate experience," a sphere in which "there may be distinguished neither mind nor selfhood . . . nor language to name them by, nor time, nor space, nor positions in space as 'points of view' on the whole. This is 'an undistinguished unity,' a 'sort of confusion.'" He quotes Eliot's 1916 dissertation on F. H. Bradley, describing this zone as "the general condition before distinctions and relations have been developed." This "unity," as Miller terms it, is not to be confused with any flattening, explanatory wholeness, but rather as a profound totality of incommensurable particularities, "the dark night of immediate experience" in which "though neither subject nor object nor any of their usual qualities can be distinguished . . . they are all there, in an inextricable confusion of 'many in one.'" Miller, *Poets of Reality: Six Twentieth Century Writers,* 130–33.

3. Hamacher, *Premises: Essays on Philosophy and Literature from Kant to Celan,* 10.

4. Benjamin, "Modernism," in his *Charles Baudelaire,* 67–101. Benjamin gives body to this enigmatically existential notion, writing that, "The hero is the subject of modernism. In other words, it takes a heroic constitution to live modernism" (74). Such is the manner in which, following Baudelaire, Benjamin imagines life that assembles itself, all but imperceptibly, from what the official worlds of politics, commerce, and action trash, ignore, and/or prohibit. But also implicit in this formulation is the idea that the heroic suicide is always something other than the strictly inward, solipsistic decision of a subject in possession of itself, something other than the pathos-saturated choice it is customarily thought to be; that it is rather, as Ronell writes in *Crack Wars: Literature, Addiction, Psychoanalysis* directed elsewhere, always connected to "another agency" (94). For Maurice Blanchot, this other agency is the zone of "disaster," the ever-present, if ever-refused, dimension of every assertive discourse, the realm of the chaos, nothingness and abyss that language calls on itself to fight, in other words, that is language's negative space of origin. This is the entropic zone into which the modernists of whom Baudelaire and later Benjamin speak are attracted.

221

5. Lacan, *Ecrits: A Selection*, 86.

6. Ronell, *Crack Wars*, 32.

7. Baudelaire, quoted in Benjamin, *Charles Baudelaire*, 78.

8. Ibid., 79

9. For a consideration of this difficult question of preinscriptive tension within "pre-subjective" space, see Lyotard, "Can Thought Go on without a Body," in his *The Inhuman*. His sharply redoubled distinctions between "the human" and "inhuman" play out on the battlefield of "development" or inscription, information, or accumulated language skill—what he considers "adult" or "human" knowledge as distinguished from the innocence, wonder, or a-linguistic inscriptedness (the "inhumanness") of the child.

10. Pater, "The Child in the House," in *Selected Writings*, 1–17.

11. See Pessoa's sublime *The Book of Disquiet*, throughout which the idea of a life of purely impressionistic experience is idealized to the exclusion of propriety, visibility, and usefulness. See also Vaneigem, *The Revolution of Everyday Life*, an incendiary book customarily discussed as a poetic companion to Debord's *The Society of the Spectacle*, which appeared in the same year in which *Revolution* was first published in France, 1967.

12. See Borch-Jacobsen, *The Freudian Subject*, 86–95. The discussions of the violence at the heart of the identificatory encounter typify much of Borch-Jacobsen's most penetrating analysis from this period in his work. See also Kojève's influential *Introduction to the Reading of Hegel*.

13. Blanchot, "The Paradox of Aytre," in his *The Work of Fire*, 63. Following Pascal, Blanchot asks that we be disabused of the notion of any purity properly unique to silence and that we acknowledge the range of its singular expressivity both as an internal property of language and as a force that precedes and outlives language, and is therefore not subject to speech's regulatory protocols.

14. Lyotard, *The Differend*, 13.

15. See Jameson's Afterword in *Aesthetics and Politics*, 201.

See also Lukács, "The Ideology of Modernism" (originally published in *The Meaning of Contemporary Realism*), in *Marxist Literary Theory* (141–63), which contains such observations as the following: "With Musil—and with many other modernist writers—psychopathology became the goal . . . of their artistic intention. But there is a double difficulty inherent in their intention, which follows from its underlying ideology. There is, first, a lack of definition. The protest expressed by this flight into psychopathology is an abstract gesture; its rejection of reality is wholesale and summary, containing no concrete criticism. It is a gesture, moreover, that is destined to lead nowhere; it is an escape into nothingness. Thus the propagators of this ideology are mistaken in thinking that such a protest could ever be fruitful in literature. In any protest against particular social conditions, these conditions themselves must have the central place." Or, ". . . we must consider for a moment the question of allegory. Allegory is that aesthetic genre which lends itself par excellence to a description of man's alienation from objective reality. Allegory is a problematic genre because it rejects that assumption of an immanent meaning to human existence which—however unconscious, however combined with religious concepts of transcendence—is the basis of traditional art." And finally, "Kafka is not able, in spite of his extraordinary evocative power, in spite of his unique sensibility, to achieve that fusion of the particular and the general which is the essence of realistic art. His aim is to raise the individual detail in its immediate particularity (without generalizing its content) to the level of abstraction. Kafka's method is typical, here, of modernism's allegorical approach. . . . The particularity we find in Beckett and Joyce, in Musil and Benn, various as the treatment of it may be, is essentially of the same kind. . . . We see that modernism leads not only to the destruction of traditional literary forms; it leads to the destruction of literature as such. . . . We have here a practical demonstration that—as Benjamin showed in another context—modernism means not the enrichment, but the negation of art." In his reference to Benjamin's thinking on modernism, already cited in this introduction as indeed being fundamentally situated within "another context," Lukács demonstrates a rare inclination toward understatement. For such art as would be "negated" by the writings of Kafka, Beckett, Joyce, Musil, and Benn would be the received ideological conception of "art" as a category of pure objects or things, exhausted of whatever dynamism may have triggered them and that are constituted by accepted realist or representational formulae—an art, in other words, opposed to practice, transfigurality or futuristic orientation.

See also Hartley, "Realism and Reification: The Poetics and Politics of Three Language Poets." Hartley situates the question of consistency between Lukács's theory of reification and his subsequent antifigurality as played out in his work on realism and modernism in literature. The culmination of cultural reification in which the proletarian subject, absolutely objectified by the alienating procedures of mass production, is converted into yet another commodity or thing within an economy of manufactured desires and pure subsistence, is offered no resistance or exit via any art that fails to faithfully reanimate narratively the conditions of the material scene. Modernism reanimates only what Lukács imagines as the angst and alienation that results from capitalist domination. Hartley's text, via arguments from the community of L=A=N=G=U=A=G=E poets, extends the question of language's materiality into dialogue with a Lukácsian equation that respects only a transparency of writing and verbal performance.

Finally, see Adorno, "Extorted Reconciliations," in his *Notes to Literature*, 215–40.

16. The following passage from de Man ("Conclusions: Walter Benjamin's The Task of the Translator," in de Man's *Resistance to Theory*, 92) may help make more plain the fluid concept of history to which Jameson is so intensely resistant. "Now it is this motion, this errancy of language which never reaches the mark, which is always displaced in relation to what it meant to reach, it is this errancy of language, this illusion of a life that is only an afterlife, that Benjamin calls history. As such, history is not human, because it pertains strictly to the order of language; it is not natural, for the same reason; it is not phenomenal, in the sense that no cognition, no knowledge about man, can be derived from a history which as such is purely a linguistic complication . . ."

17. Jameson, *A Singular Modernity: Essay on the Ontology of the Present*, 173.

18. Ibid., 5.

19. Lyotard, "Gesture and Commentary."

20. Jameson, *Postmodernism or, The Cultural Logic of Late Capitalism*, 61.

21. Lyotard, *The Postmodern Condition: A Report on Knowledge*, 81.

22. Ibid., 73.

23. Readings, *Introducing Lyotard: Art and Politics,* 72.

24. Adorno, *Aesthetic Theory,* 153–54.

25. See Jameson's Afterword to *Aesthetics and Politics,* 196–214.

26. See Pizer, "Jameson's Adorno, or, the Persistence of the Utopian," 127–51.See also Hullot-Kentor, "Suggested Reading: Jameson's Adorno," 166–77; and Geulen, "A Matter of Tradition," 155–66.

27. Another interesting "snapshot" is provided by the following moment in Lunn, *Marxism and Modernism: An Historical Study of Lukács, Brecht, Benjamin and Adorno,* 34–35. "Modern artists, writers, and composers often draw attention to the media or materials with which they are working, the very processes of creation in their own craft . . . In doing so, modernists escape from the timeworn attempt, given new scientific pretensions in naturalist aesthetics, to make of art a transparent mere 'reflection' or 'representation' of what is alleged to be outer reality. They also depart from the more direct expression of feeling favored by the romantics. The modernist work often willfully reveals its own reality as a construction or artifice, which may take the form of an hermetic and aristocratic mystique of creativity (as in much early symbolism); visual or linguistic distortion to convey intense subjective states of mind (strongest in expressionism); or suggestions that the wider social world is built and rebuilt by human beings and not 'given' and unalterable (as in Bauhaus architecture or constructivist theatre)."

28. Jameson, *Fables of Aggression: Wyndham Lewis, the Modernist as Fascist,* 2.

29. Carby, "The Body and Soul of Modernism," in her *Race Men,* 45–87.

30. Ibid., 83

31. Glissant, *Caribbean Discourse,* 142.

32. For a more sustained analysis of this kind of present-day academic provincialism, see Cohen's brilliant and iconoclastic study, *Ideology and Inscription: "Cultural Studies" after Bakhtin, Benjamin and De Man.*

33. Benjamin, *Charles Baudelaire,* 77.

34. Levinas, *Alterity and Transcendence,* 95.

35. Adorno, *Aesthetic Theory,* 40. Whatever value Jameson finds in the work of Adorno appears largely due to the negative dialectics that structure passages like this one. The social reality that Adorno designates as integral to the thinking and formation of art is customarily what Jameson fastens on, and not so much the subsequent flight of that art into another zone that, in Adorno anyway, balances, (or explodes) the equation against—or out of—all dialectics.

36. Ellison, *Invisible Man,* 7.

37. Lyotard, *The Postmodern Condition: A Report on Knowledge,* 33–37.

38. For a full-blown discussion of the necessity of the concept of "the Negro" to the idea of "the human" from which the figure of this Negro is then excluded, see, in addition to Robinson's seminal book, Judy's incisive and pivotal meditation, "Kant and the Negro." This essay is revised in his book, *(Dis)Forming the American Canon: African-Arabic Slave Narratives and the Vernacular,* 107–61.

39. Hegel, *The Philosophy of History,* 90–99.

40. Robinson, *Black Marxism: The Making of the Black Radical Tradition,* 81.

41. Butler, *Bodies That Matter: On the Discursive Limits of "Sex,"* 31.

42. Vaneigem, *The Revolution of Everyday Life,* 56.

43. Woolf, "Modern Fiction," in her *Common Reader,* 151.

44. Deleuze, *Essays Critical and Clinical*, 77. Deleuze considers the "formula" by which Melville's Bartleby disconnects himself from any logic of expectation by means of the celebrated phrase, "I prefer not to." The phrase constitutes, in Deleuze's thought, "a trait of expression that contaminates everything, escaping linguistic form," and initiating "an infinitely proliferating patchwork."

1. Holographic Ensemble

1. Pater, *Selected Writings*, 57.

2. Freud, "The Moses of Michelangelo," 122–23. Freud writes, "Some rationalistic, or perhaps analytic turn of mind in me rebels against being moved by a thing without knowing why I am thus affected."

3. The critical stakes of a serious analysis of the concept of "race," or more exactly, of racialism in literature, tend to emerge quickly in recent Conrad studies. Even within many thoughtful critical explorations of Conrad's work, this specific question of racialism is often either elided completely—and thereby immediately conspicuous in its silence—or it is submerged in favor of a direct engagement with the presumed "reality" of "race"—thus re-inscribing the very problem that Conrad's work deconstructs. Michael North deftly exposes the scholarly consequences of the former tendency in his commentary on a moment in Michael Levenson's work on this same novella. In *The Dialect of Modernism: Race, Language and Twentieth Century Literature* (37–58), North writes, "Though most critics would agree with Michael Levenson's levelheaded judgment, 'If we are to consider the preface, we must consider that to which it is prefatory,' very few actually attempt to connect the preface to the subject of the novel, as announced in its title. Levenson himself hardly mentions James Wait and does not discuss his race. For all the rivers of ink that have flowed over the tortuous racial politics of *Heart of Darkness,* it is hard to find a critique of *The Nigger of the "Narcissus"* that takes seriously the race of its title character."

At the same time, however, there may be a certain slippage at the level of rhetoric in North's lucid and timely intervention. For we are left to presume that by "his race," North means "taking seriously" the fact that "race" is only the sustained ideological imposition of necessarily racialist expectations upon Wait's character by others in the novel. Part of what is argued in my essay is that the essentialistic "seek-and-find" racial logic so completely exploded by Conrad in *Heart of Darkness,* is theorized reflexively and extensively (if less overtly) in the body and, as North notes, in the title of *The Nigger of the "Narcissus."* It is exactly within this context that Levenson's silence on racialism in his discussion of the text is so unthinkable; for if there is any single "subject" of the novel, it is certainly *not* Wait himself—if anything, he is more of an "anti"-subject. At issue in the novella is the radical dissolution of a social body kept illusorily whole by a self-legislated discourse of identitarian "race" thinking, situated against what it imagines, and therefore experiences, as utter incomprehension in its confrontation with a racialized being who fails to identify in terms of "race," and thus shatters the entire nexus of cultural fictions into which he is inserted.

4. Ray, "Language and Silence in the Novels of Joseph Conrad," 32.

5. See Miller's study in which he discerns that in Conrad's work, "Civilization is at once a social ideal and an ideal of personal life. The ideal society is imaged in the relation among men on board a well-ordered ship: a hierarchical structure, with

those at the bottom owing obeisance to those above, and the whole forming a perfect organism. As a personal ideal, submission to civilization may mean being one of the stolid, unimaginative people, like Captain MacWhirr in *Typhoon*. It may also mean setting up for oneself an ideal of glory, the winning of power and fame for the accomplishment of some difficult project." In *Poets of Reality*, 16.

Throughout his work, particularly in this novella as well as in *Heart of Darkness*, and in short fiction such as "Amy Foster," Conrad stages severe tensions between these conceptions of civilization and the nonvisible, utterly passive withdrawal from the "power" and "glory" of such civilization as embodied by those affirmative, "stolid" characters of "action" and decision. This withdrawal from the visible has much to do with what Conrad concentrates on as those mysteries of being and art in which it is only within work that we sense our most intensely personal moments of radical subjectivity or "true self," finding our strongest realization at the moment in which we are dissolved in the complete otherness of mental or physical labor.

6. Žižek, *Enjoy Your Symptom*, 56.

7. Consider Levenson's observation in *A Genealogy of Modernism* that "we can see in *Nigger of the 'Narcissus'* an alternation between the values of consciousness (which secure meaning and are exemplified by the narrator) and the values of unconsciousness (which facilitate work and solidarity and are exemplified by Singleton)" (35).

8. The question here is one of forging some sharedness, some sphere of dialogue, between human and inhuman, between unregulatable ruptures of and by life and the regulatory injunctions that organize and limit the expanse of that life. "As Joyce will say, paternity does not exist, it is an emptiness, a nothingness—or rather, a zone of uncertainty haunted by brothers." Deleuze, "Bartleby; or, the Formula," 84.

9. Some of this discussion's concerns are suggested more generally in DeMille, "Cruel Illusions," 697–714.

10. See Glissant, *Caribbean Discourse*, 124. "From the outset (that is, from the moment Creole is forged as a medium of communication between slave and master), the spoken imposes on the slave its particular syntax. For Caribbean man, the word is first and foremost sound. Noise is essential to speech. Din is discourse."

11. For another consideration of Conradian "murmurs," "gibberish," and other "asignifying" noises and sounds, again see North's *The Dialect of Modernism*, 40.

12. Said, "Conrad: The Presentation of Narrative," 28–46.

13. In a passage from *Nietzsche and Metaphor*, Kofman writes: "Since pleasure and pain are manifestations of a unique 'substratum' which is the same for all, the language of sounds, beyond the diversity of languages, is a universal language. The plurality of languages must be seen as 'the strophic text of this primordial melody of pleasure and pain.' The consonant and vowel systems in language are part of the symbolism of the gesture, for, without the fundamental tone, vowels and consonants are just positions of the organs, i.e. gestures: it is tonality, the echo of pleasure and pain, that serves as a foundation for the symbolism of the gesture" (7).

14. Hegel, *The Philosophy of History*, 91–99.

15. See Fuss, *Identification Papers*, 142.

16. Consider seriously the opposition traced by Harris ("The Frontier on Which *Heart of Darkness* Stands") between the idea of "the intuitive self" and "the historical ego" in the following passage from an essay on Conrad's *Heart of Darkness*. While the

phrasing of an "intuitive self" may suggest the idea of a self-sovereignty that is at odds with the primary thrusts of this study, Harris, with customary originality and subtle beauty, is actually talking about something like an essential dynamism and experimentality. In so doing, he opens what I hear as a philosophical dialogue with Blanchot on the material meaning and implications of totality; on the coexistence of the forces of visibility and action which only realize their power in the submerging of what they conspire to make invisible—but what remains, nevertheless, still there. "The capacity of the intuitive self to breach the historical ego is the life-giving and terrifying objectivity of imaginative art that makes a painting or a poem or a piece of sculpture or a fiction endure long beyond the artist's short lifetime and gives it the strangest beauty or coherence in depth. . . . The critical hurdle in the path of community, if community is to create a living future, lies in a radical aesthetic in which distortions of sovereign ego may lead into confessions of partiality within sovereign institutions that, therefore, may begin to penetrate and unravel their biases, in some degree, in order to bring into play a complex wholeness inhabited by other confessing parts that may have once masqueraded themselves as monolithic absolutes or monolithic codes of behavior in the old worlds from which they emigrated by choice or by force."

17. The "mist" that in this passage simultaneously obscures and creates oscillating registers of truth (with one trying to cut through the fog and gain access to some presumptive clarity or meaning, the other calmly unable to distinguish that fog from whatever truth it supposedly hides) is only another articulation of a recurrent philosophical motif that appears throughout Conrad's fiction. In the opening pages of *Heart of Darkness* is found perhaps the best known of these formulations: "But Marlow was not typical (if his propensity to spin yarns be excepted) and to him the meaning of an episode was not inside like a kernel but outside, enveloping the tale which brought it out only as a glow brings out a haze, in the likeness of one of these misty halos that, sometimes, are made visible by the spectral illumination of moonshine." Not only is this yet another direct instance of what Meisel or Bloom would identify as a Paterian indebtedness, in this case to the "wall of personality" from Pater's "Conclusion" to *The Renaissance* ("Experience, already reduced to a group of impressions, is ringed round for each one of us by that thick wall of personality through which no real voice has ever pierced on its way to us, or from us to that which we can only conjecture to be without."), but more crucially for the situating of this study, it demands an attunement to what is at stake for Conrad in the artwork's necessarily philosophical reorientation of the reading and writing of history—an attunement to those events that cut or inscribe themselves on such procedures of recording and composing but which at the same time must go completely undocumented because they belong to a dominion outside instrumental language. In one of the very few works of recent Conrad scholarship that has engaged the work on philosophico-aesthetic bases more immediately than on more explicitly historical ones, John G. Peters discerns in Conrad an impressionism that respects that "knowledge always comes [processed] through the medium of human subjectivity" (14). In Mallios's terms, as he writes of the Conrad considered in Peters's study, "*Perception* became the key object of raw, rigorous, and unrelenting impressionist attention— but not, *qua* science, in the interest of generating objective, universal, or systemic laws. Rather it became an occasion to explore all the arbitrary cognitive operations

through which 'knowledge' asserts itself as a kind of law: i.e., to probe all the operations of mind and all the local, mediating, contextual, and ideological factors that enable individuals to produce a world they do not know as 'known.'" See Conrad, *Heart
of Darkness*, 9. See Peters, *Conrad and Impressionism*, 14. See Mallios's review of Peters's book in *Modernism/Modernity*, 767–70.

18. See Lacan, *Ecrits*, 305.

19. Žižek, *The Metastases of Enjoyment*, 72.

20. Marcuse, *Eros and Civilization*, 113.

21. For a superb comparative analysis of Conrad's philosophical inquiries in literature, see Arac, "Romanticism, the Self, and the City." Arac writes: "Our 'study of
the orders of language' may date back only to Marx, Nietzsche, and Freud, but the
'duplicity of language' itself has no such recent beginning. Wordsworth shares much
not only with Conrad but also with Baudelaire; and their common strategies define a
major strand in the literary history of the period from the French Revolution to the
Great War. Against [Ian] Watt's emphasis on a 'central tradition,' I find that
Wordsworth and Conrad practice what Walter Benjamin called, apropos of Baudelaire, 'the art of being off center' (die Kunst des Exzentriks)."

22. Blanchot, *The Space of Literature*, 95.

23. Agamben, *Language and Death*, vi.

24. Bataille, *Erotism*, 46–47

25. Again, for other treatments of silence in the text, see both Said's "The Presentation of Narrative" and Ray's "Language and Silence in the Novels of Joseph
Conrad."

26. Blanchot, *The Writing of the Disaster*, 29.

2. Something Savage, Something Pedantic

1. For a reading of similar questions in Woolf's fiction, see Jackson's reading of
Woolf's *The Waves* in "Writing and the Disembodiment of Language." See also Laurence, *The Reading of Silence: Virginia Woolf in the English Tradition*.

2. Kracauer, *Theory of Film: The Redemption of Physical Reality*, 136–37.

3. Woolf, "Modern Fiction," in her *Common Reader*, 150.

4. Kracauer, *Theory of Film*, 31. See also Bishop's "The Subject in Jacob's Room,"
which draws heavily on important critical work on cinema. My observation above
seems to connect well with a quote from Benjamin that Bishop uses to his own advantage: "The film is the art form that is in keeping with the increase threat to his life
which modern man has to face. Man's need to expose himself to shock effects is his
adjustment to the dangers threatening him. The film corresponds to profound
changes in the apperceptive apparatus—changes that are experienced on an individual scale by the man in the street in big-city traffic." Bishop himself adds that it is
"not simply a question of optics, the multiple perspectives of Cubism, but a felt
rhythm, *the beat of modernization within modernism*" (my emphasis).

5. Nietzsche, *The Birth to Tragedy*, 170

6. Consider a passage below from Leaska, *The Novels of Virginia Woolf: From Beginning to End*, 64. In rather un-ironic fashion, Leaska traces the spatiality by which
Woolf detonates time in this novel, his own rhetoric demonstrating the radical limits
of presumable oppositions of externality to internality in the referencing and distin-

guishing of such notions as "control," "head," "heart," and "complete . . . full light."
The anthropomorphic logic of Leaska's imagery is undone by the inhumanity of the
act of writing itself. He writes: "The sequence of the various threads—those concentrated moments of feeling—determines the sequence of the reader's emotional evo-
cations. But the way in which those moments are laid side by side determines the
quality and intensity of the feelings evoked. Thus, it is in Virginia Woolf's ordering
and juxtapositioning of the stimuli that she controls the reader's range of response,
both in his head and in his heart; that she models her meaning with an infinite variety of image and accent, angle and outline; until all the strands are seen in one majes-
tic picture, complete and in full light." While the humanistic thrust of such criticism
may appear to corral Woolf's work back into a narcissistic economy of sentiment and
readerly reassurance, the distinct modes of techne that Leaska identifies as significant
(image, accent, angle, outline) are those by which those ideas are made recognizable.
They should be seen as pivot points out of humanist preservation and into the experimental realm of writing that, paradoxically, is the actual birthplace of technique,
where experience is not some pathway by which to reach some hidden, unseen
"heart" or core, nor to some intellectual center of "control" that is unraveled and re-
versed in the mute fascination of either writing or reading—but only to the combi-
nations of instruments that make experience palpable, audible, textu(r)al.

7. Again, it is necessary to see Bishop's "The Subject in Jacob's Room," in which
he writes that "Woolf, far from creating character, seems to be going out of her way to
un-create character . . . Woolf is showing the action of ideology in constructing
human character, revealing the process and effect of subjectivity . . . the book is
about society and the individual's relationship to it, about ideology, in Althusser's
sense of the word

Also, for a more concentrated analysis of plotlessness throughout Woolf's fiction, see Rosenthal, "The Problem of the Fiction." "Woolf is not the sole practitioner
of the twentieth century novel to have abandoned established notions of plot and
character . . . but in many ways her work is the most radical" 189.

8. Scott, *Refiguring Modernism, Vol. 2: Postmodern Feminist Readings of Woolf,
West and Barnes*, 30.

9. For a critical/hagiographic accounting of these issues as played out not only
in *The Voyage Out* but also in Woolf's own life, see Swanson, "'My Boldness Terrifies
Me': Sexual Abuse and Female Subjectivity in *The Voyage Out.*"

10. For another variation on connected themes, see Moore, *The Short Season
Between Two Silences: The Mystical and the Political in the Novels of Virginia Woolf.*

11. See Scott, *Refiguring Modernism*, 2, where she writes of Woolf: "She refused
the authoritarian tradition of *logos* that was the cultural inheritance of James Joyce,"
and consider its sharpness alongside what I find a more problematic passage later, in
which Scott seems hesitant to see Woolf's art as mobilized by what Scott terms "the
imagery of French deconstruction," and Julia Kristeva in particular, writing that such
authors as Woolf undermine the phallogocentrism of cultures in which "speaking
subjects are conceived of as masters of their speech." Scott says that "Kristeva's depic-
tion of woman's sense of self in relation to language is only partially adequate . . .
given Woolf's accomplishments and recent feminist renegotiations of the postmodern and the self. Woman's creation of 'an imaginary story through which she constitutes an identity' could serve to describe Woolf's repeated creation of fantasy

illustrations of creative women in process. . . ." This seems at least mildly at odds with the refutation of logocentricity she had just ascribed to Woolf—if the "imaginary story" by which new identity is inaugurated and grounded has such establishment as its aim, rather than realization of the movement by which its own materiality mode creates effects.

12. See Meisel, *The Absent Father: Virginia Woolf and Walter Pater,* 129. Here, Meisel considers Pater's *Marius the Epicurean* and that work's literary reanimation of the Heraclitean deconstruction of the relations between the presumed oppositions of reflection and perception, contemplation and feeling, matter and intelligence.

13. Lyotard, *The Postmodern Condition,* 80

14. In addition to the crucial readings of Hegel's *Phenomenology of Spirit* cited earlier from Kojève and Lacan, crucial commentary on this dynamic is offered by numerous thinkers, including notably Althusser and Butler, both in Butler, *Subjects of Desire: Hegelian Reflections in Twentieth-Century France* (New York: Columbia UP, 1999), and in Butler, *The Psychic Life of Power: Theories in Subjection.* See also Blanchot in *The Writing of the Disaster,* 14. "If there is a relation between writing and passivity, it is because both presuppose the effacement, the extenuation of the subject: both presuppose a change in time, and that between being and non-being. . . . Passivity: we can evoke it only in a language that reverses itself."

15. This question of the necessary separation of speaker from spoken, and spoken from intended connects well with Banfield's reflections on Woolfian time in "Time Passes: Virginia Woolf, Post-Impressionism and Cambridge Time." Banfield writes, "Given the discontinuity of experience, one must get a distance from it, just as one must step back from the Impressionist canvas to grasp its formal continuity, to recognize that 'the moment of importance came not here but there' (Woolf 1966–67, 1:107). 'Distance had an extraordinary power; they had been swallowed up in it, she felt, they were gone for ever, they had become part of the nature of things,' (Woolf [1927] 1955: 279). The aesthetic becomes dualist. The moment is contained and given a form in order to be placed in the series of immobilized moments. From this threshold position the moment 'of being' is created out of a present. For the impressions that make up the moment and the random configuration they assume can only be seized with the clarity required from a position outside experienced time. It requires what Woolf calls 'dissociating herself from the moment' (ibid.: 157), the arrested contemplation of Fry's (1926: 191) 'single ecstatic moment.' After having been recorded as on a blank plate, a kind of Proustian involuntary memory, the moment can then return as a remembered moment to make 'those moments of being' (Woolf 1985 [1976]: 78). The 'extreme distinctness' of childhood vision guarantees its retention, its engraved permanence: 'I still see the air-balls, blue and purple' (ibid.). So does the fact that 'something happened so violently that I have remembered it all my life' (ibid.: 71). The receptive organ's pristine nature is, however, only a precondition for the sharp engraving of momentary impressions. Something given in the event is also required to transform the ordinary moment. Its extraordinariness is thus discovered, not created. The discovery is a sudden exposure to the real, an eruption of the contingent, the feeling 'that I have had a blow' (ibid.: 72), as when color floods the visible world—'something happened so violently' (ibid.: 71). The future explodes into the present: 'suddenly one hears a clock tick. We who had been immersed in this world became aware of another. It is painful' (Woolf [1931] 1959: 273). An

event cracks open the 'oyster of perceptiveness' (Woolf 1966–67, 4:156), for the sense organs are 'sealed vessels afloat on what it is convenient to call reality; and at some moments, the sealing matter cracks; in floods reality; that is, these scenes' (Woolf 1985 [1976]: 142). The moment of being becomes 'more real than the present moment' (ibid.: 66–67). We can recognize here as well a theory of history, one which conceives of significant historical breaks occurring at various points, a revolutionary view of history."

16. Scott, *Refiguring Modernism*, 16.

17. Borch-Jacobsen, *The Freudian Subject*, 94.

18. See Snaith, *Virginia Woolf: Public and Private Negotiations.* "It is not enough that women make themselves public, but the variety of modes of expression (that) is important for Woolf. . . . Women must not be written into the public arena as types, as political tools: they must refuse to be 'stamped and stereotyped'" (46–47).

19. See Lackey's "Atheism and Sadism: Nietzsche and Woolf on Post-God Discourse," in which he writes: "In *Twilight of the Idols,* Nietzsche discusses the process whereby the 'inner world' is populated with 'phantoms and false lights,' suggesting in fact that consciousness and the ego are nothing more than a 'fable, a fiction, a play on words.' To understand verbal projections as the thing in itself is to mistake beliefs for reality, and since Nietzsche considers belief '*slavery* in a higher sense,' the 'seduction by grammar' becomes exactly that which enables the lordly rulers of language to take possession of individuals. This explains why Nietzsche thought knowledge of self a naive and unrealizable project—from the moment we enter into the community of language and values, we become physiologically false because we adopt, unconsciously, involuntarily, the words and moralities of the community. . . . While Woolf, like most writers, had a pathological relationship with words throughout her career, it was only from 1928 to 1931 that she finally began to abandon, in whole, the correspondence theory of truth and to see that life is no argument. Consequently, instead of seeing language as a tool for giving us access to or at best reflecting the 'reality' of the world, the Woolf of the late 1920s claims that 'discourse produces the effects that it names,' to quote Judith Butler. The character, Neville, from *The Waves,* best expresses this understanding of language when he claims: 'Nothing should be named lest by so doing we change it' (p. 81). For Woolf, to be is to be named; so when humans verbally interact with one another, there is always the danger of taking conceptual possession of the other, of subjecting the other into grammatical being through one's own verbal will to power."

20. Bishop, "The Subject in Jacob's Room," 164.

21. For a more psychologistic account of Betty Flanders, see Leaska's consideration of *Jacob's Room* in his Woolf study.

3. Maladjusted Phantasms

1. Glissant, *Faulkner, Mississippi,* 22.

2. Ladd, "William Faulkner, Edouard Glissant, and a Creole Poetics of History and Body in *Absalom, Absalom!* and *A Fable,*" 31–50.

3. Lacan, *The Four Fundamental Concepts of Psychoanalysis,* 106–107. For discussions of similar or closely related issues of psychoanalysis, recognition, and modern philosophy in the reading of Faulkner, see Irwin, *Doubling and Incest/Repetition*

and Revenge: A Speculative Reading of Faulkner. See also Fowler, *Faulkner: The Return of the Repressed.* Yet another crucial inquiry is made by Porter in "Symbolic Fathers and Dead Mothers: A Feminist Approach to Faulkner."

4. Snead was among the first to note that prior Faulkner scholars were every bit as anxious to authoritatively racialize Christmas and in so doing, thereby "explain" away certain of the ambiguities or contradictions initiated by his very arrival in Jefferson. Snead writes in *Figures of Division: William Faulkner's Major Novels* (88–89), "It is as revealing as it is embarrassing to consider how many readers fall into the same racist mentality as Jefferson, even despite Faulkner's own admonition that Christmas 'himself didn't know who he was—didn't know whether he was part Negro or not and would never know.' Early critics, especially insisted on calling Christmas a 'harried mulatto' or a 'white Negro.' Some credited Gavin Stevens's intentionally ludicrous 'blood' theory, discussing 'a sinister figure haunted by knowledge of his negro blood.' Cleanth Brooks is correct to say 'we are never given any firm proof that Joe Christmas possesses Negro blood'—indeed, at one point Joanna asks Joe how he knows one of his parents is 'part nigger.' Joe answers, 'I don't know it.' The simple basis of 'not knowing' about Joe's race (onto which others project would-be knowledge) is the chief rhetorical prerequisite for interpreting the novel . . . He symbolizes the frustration and resistance that knowledge encounters whenever it wants to become permanent, or 'written.' In the context of the town, he is above all a matter of 'rumor'. . . ."

5. Butler, *The Psychic Life of Power,* 102

6. This stepping out of recognition and into the possibilities of nonlegislated space exposes the mimeticism at the heart of the social and what it accepts/repeats as knowledge. The opportunity Christmas presents for actual, transformative understanding inheres in the very differentiality that is so unnerving in the context of Jefferson. As Nietzsche writes in "The Philosopher: Reflections on the Struggle Between Art and Knowledge" (131), again in a manner that brings to mind his contemporary, Pater, "Like recalls like and compares itself to it. That is what knowing consists in: the rapid classification of things that are similar to each other. Only like perceives like: a physiological process. The perception of something new is also the same as memory."

7. Moreland, "Faulkner and Modernism." Though it does not contain a sustained treatment of *Light in August,* see also Moreland, *Faulkner and Modernism,* as it extends a similarly aggressive approach into criticism other of Faulkner's novels.

4. The Business of Dreams

1. Bloom, ed., *Nathanael West's Miss Lonelyhearts,* 1.

2. For an extended and lively consideration of the character of Shrike, see Jones, "Shrike as the Modernist Anti-Hero in Nathanael West's *Miss Lonelyhearts.*" Jones writes, "With the gleam of polished parody, Shrike blocks every conceivable retreat from pain. . . . Shrike's flamboyant oratory delineates a modernist epistemology proclaiming the wisdom of a chilling contempt which mocks Camus' pronouncement that 'There is no fate that cannot be surmounted by scorn. "I sneer therefore I am." ' "

3. An interesting, if brief, even abortive gloss on the text's obsession with futility and false identification is found in Wexelblatt's "Nathanael West, Paul Valery and the Detonated Society." Taking up the thrust of a book outline from West's rejected 1934

Guggenheim application, Wexelblatt seizes on images that he argues are central to the unfolding of West's career. These include, in addition to the ideas of Spengler and Valery, "the necessity for violence," and "the composition of a suicide note *as an exercise in rhetoric*" (my emphasis).

4. For a reading concentrating particularly on the imagery of the cross in West, see Crowe's "The Desert, The Lamb, The Cross: Debased Iconography in Nathanael West's *Miss Lonelyhearts.*"

5. For different orientations in discussions of Christianity and religious tension/identification in *Miss Lonelyhearts,* see Smith, "Religious Experience in *Miss Lonelyhearts,*" and Abrahams, "Androgynes Bound: Nathanael West's *Miss Lonelyhearts.*"

6. Bollas, *Hysteria,* 107

7. Most West scholars weigh in, with varying degrees of interest, on the critique of capital that thematically helps to distinguish his four short novels. Distinguished among these scholarly efforts is Veitch's *American Superrealism: Nathanael West and the Politics of Representation in the 1930s.*

8. Considering Lonelyhearts's continually frustrated desire to spur or galvanize his readership around a core of transcendent values and behaviors, I want to return to Nancy's meditations on community and singularity. I find it productive to remember *his* remembering, in the essay "Myth Interrupted" in his *The Inoperative Community* (64) that "Blanchot has insisted that 'community,' in its very failure remains linked in some way to writing,' and has referred to the ideal community of literary communication.' This can always make for one more myth . . . the myth of the literary community was outlined for the first time . . . by the Jena romantics and it has filtered down to us in various different ways through everything resembling the idea of a 'republic of artists' or again, the idea of communism . . . and revolution inherent, *tels quels,* in writing itself. . . . It is as difficult to describe the structure of sharing as it is to assign an essence to it. Sharing divides and shares itself: this is what it is to be in common."

While Lonelyhearts is clearly not thinking about engendering a community in any way "literary," he is obsessed with the idea of a writing before (and in some way shaping or manipulating) a collective that has become such only in its reading of his work. What he fails to grasp are the connective interstices of endless exposure to otherness and self-loss that actually organize true collectives—interstices that form in the moments of reading and those of writing; in the giving over of self to textuality, in the dissolution of culturally petrified "self-images" while engaging the images and energies of textual movement, discovering dimensions of being not available within the logic of an already self-accountable "I." Lost for him is the trauma involved in actual sharing, in the deconstruction of a binary separating "the one" from "the other," the understanding that the experience of the irreducible otherness of the other is the only actual bonding mechanism enabling communion. Lonelyhearts keeps himself bound to the binary.

9. Wisker, *The Writing of Nathanael West,* 60.

10. See Lyotard, "The Inarticulate, or the Differend Itself." See also *The Differend,* 138–39.

11. For alternate considerations of Lonelyhearts in contexts of relationships and sexuality, see Fuchs, "Nathanael West's *Miss Lonelyhearts: The Wasteland* Rescripted."

See also Lynch, "Saints and Lovers: Miss Lonelyhearts in the Tradition." In this vein, also see Hickey, "Freudian Criticism and *Miss Lonelyhearts.*"

12. Kermode, *The Sense of an Ending.*

13. One of relatively few interpretive efforts to consider this textual "wasteland" of West's through prisms of modern philosophy is found in Hoeveler's "This Cosmic Pawnshop We Call Life: Nathanael West, Bergson, Capitalism and Schizophrenia."

14. See Hoeveler again for a different reading of Shrike's deadpan, which she interprets as the expression of a robotic machine.

15. Agamben, *Language and Death,* 46.

16. In addition to the Jones's "Shrike as the Modernist Anti-Hero in Nathanael West's *Miss Lonelyhearts,*" see also Madden, "The Shrike Voice Dominates *Miss Lonelyhearts.*"

17. Adorno, *Minima Moralia,* 75.

5. Chaos and Surface in *Invisible Man*

1. Fuss, *Identification Papers,* 144.

2. Žižek, *The Sublime Object of Ideology,* 48.

3. Fanon, *Black Skin White Masks,* 211.

4. Hortense J. Spillers, by way of introducing the reappearance of her 1977 essay "Ellison's 'Usable Past:' Toward a Theory of Myth," in her *Black White and in Color,* renders Ellisonian "blackness" this way (4–5): "Ellison . . . had few models before him in overturning the discursive decisions that had arrested notions of 'blackness' in retrograde rhetorical behaviors. Another way to put it is to say that the examples before him were endless. *His* problem was to slay them. By revising and correcting 'blackness' into a *critical* posture, into a preeminent site of the 'multicultural,' long before the latter defined a new politics and polemic, and by distinguishing it from a sign called the "American Negro" . . . Ellison harnessed 'blackness' to a symbolic program of philosophical 'disobedience' . . . that would make the former available to *anyone,* or more pointedly, *any* posture, that was willing to take on the formidable task of *thinking* as a willful act of imagination and invention.

5. For an excellent concentration upon the simultaneously contradictory/tautological/paradoxical governance of oxymoron in the novel, see Schaub, "Ellison's Masks and the Novel of Reality."

6. See Di Prima and Baraka, *The Floating Bear: A Newsletter,* 272.

7. De Man, *Allegories of Reading,* 112–13.

8. A scintillating and succinct analysis of deception and guile in the text is found in Smith's "The Meaning of Narration in *Invisible Man.*"

9. Hamacher, *Premises,* 17–18.

10. De Man, *Blindness and Insight,* 219–20 (my emphasis).

11. For another critical consideration of the narrative "boomerang" in Ellison, see O'Meally "The Rules of Magic: Hemingway as Ellison's 'Ancestor.'"

12. It is around the figure of Washington that Stepto formulates an orbit of influence connecting Du Bois and Ellison directly in his classic *From Behind the Veil: A Study of Afro American Narrative.* "When Du Bois, for example, urges that a true self-consciousness must replace the Afro-American's seemingly innate double-consciousness, and when Ralph Ellison implies in *Invisible Man* that an artist must

step outside the boundaries of what others call reality (an imposed fiction of history) in order to create, each is, I believe, championing an authorial posture beyond that which mistakenly attempts to control two texts—the author's and the one imposed" (45–46).

13. Fanon, *Black Skin, White Masks,* 220–21

14. On the question of "fighting" for the other's eye in Ellison, with a historicist glossing of the Hegelian paradigm in relation to both Ellison and Richard Wright, see Fabre's "From *Native Son* to *Invisible Man*: Some Notes on Ralph Ellison's Evolution in the 1950s."

15. For a theoretical engagement with the thinking involved in the "plunge," see Neighbors, "Plunging Outside of History: Naming and Self-Possession in *Invisible Man.*"

6. Assuming the Position

1. Himes, *The Quality of Hurt: The Autobiography of Chester Himes,* 199–200.

2. Consider the following passages from Jackson, "The Birth of the Critic: The Literary Friendship of Ralph Ellison and Richard Wright," which I quote at length. Jackson, who has since authored the first serious biographical study of Ralph Ellison, describes lucidly another transgression of the one-vision-at-a time rules of engagement that all but completely dominate the literature at the moment. What the passages expose are not merely the deeper implication of a nearly fatal myopia in the imagination of African American life and thought on the part of our culture industry, resulting in the calcification of an aesthetically narrowed "canon"; more important, they briefly throw light on pivotal moments of philosophical and artistic becoming, or discovery/intensifying of vision—divergent and even mutually hostile though these may have been—in the writing lives of Ellison and Himes. While not especially concerned with issues of Himes's stylistic endeavors, and indeed hurling Himes back into the premodernist schema that my essay attempts to dispel, Jackson is one of remarkably few critics to note the historical significance of Himes's novels in the *thematic* expansion of African American writing. Again, the structure of exchanges is triadic, this time involving Himes, Wright, and Ellison:

"When, for example, Wright asked about the value of Chester Himes's latest novel, *Lonely Crusade* (1947), Ellison was harsh in his criticism. He thought the book 'dishonest' and 'false,' and, most severely, not a work of artistic craftsmanship. Instead of well-digested political and social theories functioning implicitly within a novel that expertly maneuvered the reader toward a dramatic climax, Ellison saw Lenin's political terms from *Materialism in Empirio-Criticism* haphazardly strewn about: 'If a writer is serious about his politics and its relationship to man, then he should at least attempt to master the ideas (artistic, technical, philosophical, metaphysical) which that political position embodies explicitly.'

"While Ellison made no public attack on the novel, his feelings about the work had grave implications, in part because he and Himes were good friends. Ellison had helped Himes work out the ideas for the novel, and a conversation he had had with Himes was included verbatim in *The Lonely Crusade.* Himes's snippet of his conversation with Ellison further reveals Ellison's growing intellectual autonomy. His distance from his comrades increased as his opinions became more vigorous. Other black writers thought Ellison intelligent to a fault. Himes considered Ellison, called 'Ellsworth' in the novel, the epitome of 'the Negro scholar who not only was convinced, himself, of his own inferiority, but [who] went to great scholastic lengths to do so. . . .'

"Ellison's attitudes toward his colleagues were changing. He now needed the nurturing relationships of an intellectual fraternity less than he needed the high moral ground of his own intellectual truth. His pursuit of unflinching honesty had further ramifications. In the main, Ellison's judgments of Himes could be applied to Wright's past work. Ellison's negative estimate of Himes's application of philosophical theory became the overriding criticism of Wright's work in the future, especially of *The Outsider* (1953). In some ways Ellison's February 1948 letter marks the break between the formerly close friends and their artistic projects. Wright (and Himes who would soon join him as an expatriate) evidently felt the international domination of blacks by white imperialism demanded urgent action, and he chose to present his complex ideas as accessibly as possible. Wright also liked *The Lonely Crusade* and wrote an introduction to the French edition of the novel. He likened its power to Gunnar Myrdal's *An American Dilemma* (a study that Ellison found dangerous) and applauded Himes's use of 'rich images and sensual prose' to explore 'the schism between America's ideals and her practices.' Further eroding the artistic intimacy between Wright and Ellison was the fact that Himes's book, relative to what had preceded it, was very clearly an achievement. Himes had gone further than previous black writers in representing the struggle of the 'conscious' black agent to establish identity and integrity in a chaotic, adult political scene (as opposed to the youthful landscape of Bigger Thomas). Himes was the first black male writer to treat seriously the relationship between a black husband and wife, the complex gender relationships of black lovers, and the peculiar attraction between white women and black men. And Himes devoted serious attention to black rage in the working class in a manner very different from that of Wright's *Native Son*. Himes had produced a unique and valuable book that met several of Ellison's main artistic criteria: a conscious protagonist; awareness and understanding of political and philosophical debates of international importance; and recognition of the symbols and images of Negro folk forms. Ellison's assertion that Himes had improperly assimilated his thematic materials into an unobtrusive artistic frame probably threatened Wright. It is quite possible that Richard Wright thought of Ellison's criticisms of Himes as a gloved slap at his own work."

3. Als, "In Black and White," 93.

4. Adorno, *Aesthetic Theory*, 39–40.

5. Lyotard, "Gesture and Commentary."

6. De Certeau, *The Practice of Everyday Life*, 2.

7. Such an approach finds its most perfectly crystallized expression in Bone, *The Negro Novel in America*. Bone includes Himes's work in what he designates as the "Wright School" of African American writing, a naturalistic arc in which "literature is an emotional catharsis—a means of dispelling the inner tensions of race. Their novels often amount to a prolonged cry of anguish and despair. Too close to their material, feeling it too intensely, these novelists lack a sense of form and of thematic line. With rare exceptions, their style consists of a brutal realism, devoid of any love, or even respect, for words. Their characterization is essentially sociological. . . . The

white audience, on perceiving its responsibility for the plight of the protagonist, is expected to alter its attitude toward race. . . ." (157).

While most contemporary Himes criticism pushes recognition of the work's tonal dimension beyond Bone's rigidities, Denning is among the very few who appear to see in Himes's figurality at least the possibility of a radical literary politics. Restricting his analysis to the detective series, he concludes by writing of one of its later installments, *Blind Man with a Pistol,* that "Here the original comic absurdity is joined to his social vision, and the detective genre is twisted to a postmodernist experimentation that makes this a just contemporary of Ishmael Reed. Here nothing is solved . . . the Harlem of his topography assaults the imaginary Harlems of white America." See Denning, "Topographies of Violence: Chester Himes' Harlem Domestic Novels."

8. Als, "In Black and White," 90–91.

9. Blanchot, *The Writing of the Disaster,* 61.

10. Himes, *If He Hollers Let Him Go,* 2.

11. Ronell, *Crack Wars: Literature Addiction Mania,* 93.

12. Himes, *If He Hollers, Let Him Go,* 4.

13. Mackey, *Atet A.D.,* 50–51.

14. Lyotard, "Gesture and Commentary," 9.

15. Himes, *My Life of Absurdity: The Autobiography of Chester Himes,* 241.

16. See Ronell, *Crack Wars,* 30.

17. Adorno, *Negative Dialectics,* 67.

18. Deleuze, *Cinema 2: The Time-Image,* 87.

19. Himes, The Collected Short Fiction of Chester Himes, 261.

20. Eleanor Kaufman "Deleuze, Klossowski, Cinema, Immobility: A Response to Stephen Arnott," Film-Philosophy, Deleuze Special Issue, vol. 5 no. 33, November 2001. Online at www.film-philosophy.com/vol5-2001/n33kaufman.

21. Himes, *The Quality of Hurt,* 136.

22. Deleuze and Guattari, *A Thousand Plateaus: Capitalism and Schizophrenia,* 356.

23. Cohen, *Ideology and Inscription: Cultural Studies After Bakhtin, Benjamin and De Man,* 17.

24. Himes, *Yesterday Will Make You Cry,* 225–28.

25. Himes, *The End of a Primitive,* 36.

Bibliography

Abrahams, Roger D. "Androgynes Bound: Nathanael West's *Miss Lonelyhearts*," in *Nathanael West's Miss Lonelyhearts,* 21–37. Ed. Harold Bloom. New York: Chelsea House, 1987.

Adorno, Theodor W. *Negative Dialectics.* Trans. E. B. Ashton. New York: Continuum, 1983.

———. *Notes to Literature,* vol. 2. Ed. Rolf Tiedemann. Trans. Shierry Weber Nicholsen. New York: Columbia University Press, 1991.

———. *Minima Moralia: Reflections from Damaged Life.* Trans. E. F. N. Jephcott. London, New York: Verso, 1996.

———. *Aesthetic Theory.* Trans. Robert Hullot-Kentor. Ed. Gretel Adorno and R. Tiedemann. Minneapolis: University of Minnesota Press, 1997.

Agamben, Giorgio. *Language and Death: The Place of Negativity.* Trans. Karen E. Pinkus with Michael Hardt. Minneapolis: University of Minnesota Press, 1991.

Als, Hilton. "In Black and White: Chester Himes Takes a Walk on the Noir Side." *The New Yorker,* June 4, 2001, 90–96.

Althusser, Louis. *Writings on Psychoanalysis: Freud and Lacan.* Trans. Jeffery Mehlman. Ed. Olivier Corpet and Francois Matheron. New York: Columbia University Press, 1996.

Arac, Jonathan. "Romanticism, the Self, and the City: The Secret Agent in Literary History." *boundary 2,* vol. 9, no. 1, a supplement on irony (Autumn 1980):75–90.

Banfield, Ann. "Time Passes: Virginia Woolf, Post-Impressionism and Cambridge Time." *Poetics Today* 24, no. 3 (2003):471–516.

Bataille, Georges. *Erotism: Death and Sensuality.* Trans. Mary Dalwood. San Francisco: City Lights Books, 1986.

Benjamin, Walter. "Theses on the Philosophy of History," in *Illuminations,* 253–64. Ed. Hannah Arendt. Trans. Harry Zohn. New York: Schocken, 1969.

———. "Modernism," in *Charles Baudelaire: A Lyric Poet in the Era of High Capitalism,* 67–101. Trans. Harry Zohn. London, New York: Verso, 1997.

———. *Charles Baudelaire: A Lyric Poet in the Era of High Capitalism.* Trans. Harry Zohn. London, New York: Verso, 1997.

Bishop, Edward. "The Subject in Jacob's Room." *Modern Fiction Studies* 38, no. 1 (Spring 1992):147–75.

Blanchot, Maurice, *The Space of Literature*. Trans. Ann Smock. London, Lincoln: University of Nebraska Press, 1982.

———. *The Work of Fire*. Trans. Charlotte Mandell. Stanford, Calif.: Stanford University Press, 1995.

———. *The Writing of the Disaster*. Trans. Ann Smock. London, Lincoln: University of Nebraska Press, 1995.

Bloom, Harold, ed. *Nathanael West's Miss Lonelyhearts: Modern Critical Interpretations*. New York, New Haven, Philadelphia: Chelsea House Publishers, 1987.

Bollas, Christopher. *The Shadow of the Object: Psychoanalysis of the Unthought Known*. New York: Columbia University Press, 1987.

———. *Hysteria*. London, New York: Routledge, 2000.

Bone, Robert. *The Negro Novel in America*. New Haven, Conn.: Yale University Press, 1965.

Borch-Jacobsen, Mikkel. *The Freudian Subject*. Trans. Catherine Porter. Stanford, Calif.: Stanford University Press, 1988.

———. *The Emotional Tie: Psychoanalysis, Mimesis and Affect*. Trans. Douglas Brick. Stanford, Calif.: Stanford University Press, 1992.

Butler, Judith. *Bodies That Matter: On the Discursive Limits of "Sex."* London, New York: Routledge, 1993.

———. *The Psychic Life of Power: Theories in Subjection*. Stanford, Calif.: Stanford University Press, 1997.

———. *Subjects of Desire: Hegelian Reflections in Twentieth-Century France*. New York: Columbia University Press, 1999.

Carby, Hazel V. *Race Men*. London, Cambridge, Mass.: Harvard University Press, 1998.

Cohen, Tom. *Ideology and Inscription: "Cultural Studies" after Bakhtin, Benjamin and de Man*. Cambridge: Cambridge University Press, 1995.

Conrad, Joseph. *The Nigger of the "Narcissus,"* in *The Portable Conrad*. Ed. Morton Zabel. New York: Viking, 1969.

———. *Heart of Darkness*. Ed. R. Kimbrough. New York, London: Norton, 1988.

Crowe, Marian E. "The Desert, The Lamb, The Cross: Debased Iconography in Nathanael West's *Miss Lonelyhearts*." *Christianity and Literature* 45, nos. 3–4 (Spring–Summer 1996):345–58.

Debord, Guy. *The Society of the Spectacle*. Trans. D. N. Smith. New York: Zone, 2001.

De Certeau, Michel. *The Practice of Everyday Life*. Trans. Steven Rendall. London, Berkeley: University of California Press, 1984.

Deleuze, Gilles. *Cinema 2: The Time-Image*. Trans. H. Tomlinson and R. Galeta. Minneapolis: University of Minnesota Press, 1989.

———. "Bartleby; or, the Formula" in *Essays Critical and Clinical*, 68–90. Trans. D. W. Smith and M. A. Greco. Minneapolis: University of Minnesota Press, 1997.

———. *Essays Critical and Clinical*. Trans. D. W. Smith and M.A. Greco. Minneapolis: University of Minnesota Press, 1997.

Deleuze, Gilles, and F. Guattari. *A Thousand Plateaus: Capitalism and Schizophrenia*. Trans. B. Massumi. London: Athlone, 1988

DeMille, Barbara. "Cruel Illusions: Nietzsche, Conrad, Hardy, and the 'Shadowy Ideal'" in *Studies in English Literature, 1500–1900* 30, no. 4 (Autumn 1990):697–714.

De Man, Paul. *Allegories of Reading: Figural Language in Rousseau, Nietzsche, Rilke, and Proust*. London, New Haven, Conn.: Yale University Press, 1979.

————. *Blindness and Insight: Essays in the Rhetoric of Contemporary Criticism.* *Theory and History of Literature,* vol. 7. Ed. Wlad Godzich and Jochen Schulte-Sasse. Minneapolis: University of Minnesota Press, 1983.

————. *The Resistance to Theory.* Minneapolis: University of Minnesota Press, 1986.

————. *Aesthetic Ideology.* Ed. Andrej Warminski. *Theory and History of Literature,* vol. 65. Ed. Wlad Godzich and Jurgen Schulte-Sasse. Minneapolis: University of Minnesota Press, 1996.

Denning, Michael "Topographies of Violence: Chester Himes' Harlem Domestic Novels." *Critical Texts* 5 (1986):10–18.

De Vries, Hent, and Samuel Weber, eds. *Violence, Identity and Self-Determination.* Stanford, Calif.: Stanford University Press, 1997.

Di Prima, Diane, and Amiri Baraka. *The Floating Bear: A Newsletter.* La Jolla, Calif.: Laurence McGilvery, 1973.

Du Bois, W. E. B. *The Souls of Black Folk.* Ed. David W. Blight and Robert Gooding-Williams. Boston, New York: Bedford Books, 1997.

Eagleton, T., and D. Milne, eds. *Marxist Literary Theory.* Cambridge: Blackwell, 1996.

Ellison, Ralph. *Invisible Man.* New York: Vintage International, Random House, 1952; 1995.

Fabre, Michel. "From *Native Son* to *Invisible Man*: Some Notes on Ralph Ellison's Evolution in the 1950s," in *Speaking for You: The Vision of Ralph Ellison,* 199–216. Ed. Kimberly W. Benston. Washington, D.C.: Howard University Press, 1987.

Fanon, Frantz. *Black Skin, White Masks.* Trans. C. L. Markham. New York: Grove Press, 1952; 1967.

Faulkner, William. *Light in August.* New York: Vintage International, Random House, 1932; 1990.

Fowler, Doreen. *Faulkner: The Return of the Repressed.* Charlottesville: University Press of Virginia, 1997.

Freud, Sigmund. "The Moses of Michelangelo," in *Writings on Art and Literature,* 122–54. Stanford, Calif.: Stanford University Press, 1997.

Fuchs, Miriam. "Nathanael West's *Miss Lonelyhearts: The Wasteland* Rescripted." *Studies in Short Fiction* 29 (1992):43–55.

Fuss, Diana. *Essentially Speaking: Feminism, Nature and Difference.* New York, London: Routledge, 1989.

————. *Identification Papers.* New York, London: Routledge, 1995.

Geulen, Eva. "A Matter of Tradition." *Telos* 89 (Fall 1991):155–66.

Glissant, Edouard. *Caribbean Discourse: Selected Essays.* Trans. J. Michael Dash. University Press of Virginia, 1989.

————. *Faulkner, Mississippi.* Trans. Barbara Lewis and Thomas C. Spear. Chicago: University of Chicago Press, 2000.

Hamacher, Werner. *Premises: Essays on Philosophy and Literature from Kant to Celan.* Trans. Peter Fenves. Cambridge, Mass.: Harvard University Press, 1996.

————. "One 2 Many Multiculturalisms," in *Violence, Identity, and Self-Determination,* 284–325. Trans. Dana Hollander. Ed. Hent De Vries and Samuel Weber. Stanford, Calif.: Stanford University Press, 1997.

Harris, Wilson. "The Frontier on Which *Heart of Darkness* Stands," in *Research on African Literatures* 12 (1981):86–92.

Hartley, George. "Realism and Reification: The Poetics and Politics of Three Language Poets." *boundary 2,* vol. 16, (Summer 1989):1,2.

Hegel, G. W. F. *The Philosophy of History.* Trans. J. Sibree. New York: Dover, 1956.
———. *The Phenomenology of Spirit.* Trans. A. V. Miller. Oxford: Oxford University Press, 1977.
Hickey, James W. "Freudian Criticism and *Miss Lonelyhearts*," in *Nathanael West: The Cheaters and the Cheated,* 111–150. Ed. David Madden. DeLand, Fla.: Everett/Edward Press, 1973.
Himes, Chester. *My Life of Absurdity: The Autobiography of Chester Himes,* vol. 2. New York: Thunder's Mouth Press, 1976.
———. The *Quality of Hurt: The Autobiography of Chester Himes,* vol. 2. New York: Thunder's Mouth Press, 1995.
———. *If He Hollers Let Him Go.* New York: Thunder's Mouth, 1995.
———. *The End of a Primitive.* New York, London: Norton, 1997
———. *Yesterday Will Make You Cry.* New York: Norton, 1999.
———. *The Collected Short Fiction of Chester Himes.* New York: Thunder's Mouth Press, 2000.
Hoeveler, Diane Long. "This Cosmic Pawnshop We Call Life: Nathanael West, Bergson, Capitalism and Schizophrenia." *Studies in Short Fiction* 33 (1996):411–22.
Horkheimer, Max, and Theodor W. Adorno. *Dialectic of Enlightenment.* Trans. John Cumming. New York: Continuum, 1972; 1997.
Hullot-Kentor, Robertt. "Suggested Reading: Jameson's Adorno." *Telos* 89 (Fall 1991):166–77.
Irwin, John. *Doubling and Incest/Repetition and Revenge: A Speculative Reading of Faulkner.* Baltimore: The Johns Hopkins University Press, 1975.
Jackson, Lawrence P. "The Birth of the Critic: The Literary Friendship of Ralph Ellison and Richard Wright." *American Literature* 72, no. 2 (2000):321–55.
Jackson, Tony E. *The Subject of Modernism: Narrative Alterations in the Fiction of Eliot, Conrad, Woolf and Joyce.* Ann Arbor: University of Michigan Press, 1994.
———. "Writing and the Disembodiment of Language." *Philosophy and Literature* 27, no. 1 (2003):116–33.
Jameson, Fredric, ed. *Aesthetics and Politics.* Trans. Ronald Taylor. London, New York: Verso, 1977.
———. *Fables of Aggression: Wyndham Lewis, the Modernist as Fascist.* Berkeley: University of California Press, 1979.
———. *The Political Unconscious: Narrative as a Socially Symbolic Act.* Ithaca, N.Y.: Cornell University Press, 1981.
———. *Late Marxism: Adorno, or, the Persistence of the Dialectic.* London, New York: Verso, 1990.
———. *Postmodernism or, The Cultural Logic of Late Capitalism.* Durham, N.C.: Duke University Press, 1991.
———. *A Singular Modernity: Essay on the Ontology of the Present.* London, New York: Verso, 2002.
Jones, Beverly J. "Shrike as the Modernist Anti-Hero in Nathanael West's *Miss Lonelyhearts.*" *Modern Fiction Studies* 36, no. 2 (Summer 1990):218–23.
Judy, Ronald A. T. "Kant and the Negro," *Surfaces* 1, 1991. Online: pum12.pum.umontreal.ca/revues/surfaces/vol1/vol1TdM.html.
———. *(Dis)Forming the American Canon: African-Arabic Slave Narratives and the Vernacular.* London, Minneapolis: University of Minnesota Press, 1993.

Kaufman, Eleanor. "Deleuze, Klossowski, Cinema, Immobility: A Response to
    Stephen Arnott." *Film-Philosophy*, Deleuze Special Issue, vol. 5 no. 33,
    November 2001. Online: www.film-philosophy.com/vol5-2001/n33kaufman.
Kermode, Frank. *The Sense of an Ending: Studies in the Theory of Fiction.* Oxford:
    Oxford University Press, 1966.
Kofman, Sarah. *Nietzsche and Metaphor.* Trans. Duncan Large. Stanford, Calif.:
    Stanford University Press, 1993.
Kojève, Alexandre. *Introduction to the Reading of Hegel: Lectures on the Phenomenol-
    ogy of Spirit.* Trans. J. N. Nichols with R. Queneau. Ed. A. Bloom. Ithaca, N.Y.:
    Cornell University Press, 1980.
Kracauer, Siegfried. *Theory of Film: The Redemption of Physical Reality.* Oxford:
    Oxford University Press, 1960.
Lacan, Jacques. *Ecrits: A Selection.* Trans. Alan Sheridan. New York, London: Norton,
    1977.
———. *The Four Fundamental Concepts of Psychoanalysis.* Trans. Alan Sheridan. Ed.
    J. A. Miller. New York, London: Norton, 1978.
Lackey, Michael. "Atheism and Sadism: Nietzsche and Woolf on Post-God
    Discourse." *Philosophy and Literature* 24, no. 2 (2000):346–63.
Ladd, Barbara. "William Faulkner, Edouard Glissant, and a Creole Poetics of History
    and Body in *Absalom, Absalom!* and *A Fable*," in *Faulkner in the Twenty-First
    Century: Faulkner and Yoknapatawpha, 2000,* 31–50. Ed. Robert W. Hamblin
    and Ann J. Abadie. Jackson: University Press of Mississippi, 2003.
Laurence, Patricia Ondek. *The Reading of Silence: Virginia Woolf in the English
    Tradition.* Stanford, Calif.: Stanford University Press, 1991.
Leaska, Mitchell. *The Novels of Virginia Woolf: From Beginning to End.* London:
    Weidenfeld and Nicolson, 1977.
Levenson, Michael. *A Genealogy of Modernism: A Study of English Literary Doctrine,
    1908–1922.* Cambridge: Cambridge University Press, 1984.
Levinas, Emmanuel. *Alterity and Transcendance.* Trans. M. Smith. New York:
    Columbia University Press, 1999.
Lukács, Georg. *The Meaning of Contemporary Realism.* Trans. John and Necke
    Mander. London: Merlin, 1963.
Lunn, Eugene. *Marxism and Modernism: An Historical Study of Lukács, Brecht, Benjamin
    and Adorno.* Berkeley, Los Angeles, London: University of California Press, 1982.
Lynch, Richard. "Saints and Lovers: Miss Lonelyhearts in the Tradition." *Studies in
    Short Fiction* 31, no. 2 (Spring 1994):225–35.
Lyotard, Jean-François. *The Postmodern Condition: A Report on Knowledge.* Trans.
    G. Bennington and B. Massumi. *Theory and History of Literature,* vol. 10. Ed.
    Wlad Godzich and Jochen Schulte-Sasse. Minneapolis: University of Minne-
    sota Press, 1984.
———. *The Differend: Phrases in Dispute.* Trans. G. Van Den Abeele. Minneapolis:
    University of Minnesota Press, 1988.
———. "Gesture and Commentary." Trans. S. Schwartz. Unpublished: *Inart.*
———. *The Inhuman: Reflections Upon Time.* Trans. Geoffrey Bennington and
    Rachel Bowlby. Stanford, Calif.: Stanford University Press, 1991.
Mackey, Nathaniel. *Atet A.D.* San Francisco: City Lights Books, 2001.
Madden, David. "The Shrike Voice Dominates *Miss Lonelyhearts,*" in *Critical Essays
    on Nathanael West,* 203–13. Ed. Ben Siegel. New York: GK Hall & Co., 1994.

Mallios, P. "Conrad and Impressionism." *Modernism/Modernity* 10, no. 4 (2003):767–70.

Marcuse, Herbert. *Eros and Civilization: A Philosophical Inquiry into Freud.* Boston: Beacon Press, 1966.

Meisel, Perry. *The Absent Father: Virginia Woolf and Walter Pater.*, London, New Haven, Conn.: Yale University Press, 1980.

———. *The Myth of the Modern: A Study in British Literature and Criticism after 1850.* London, New Haven, Conn.: Yale University Press, 1987.

Miller, Hillis, J. *Poets of Reality: Six Twentieth Century Writers.* Cambridge, Mass.: Harvard University Press, 1966.

Moore, Madeline. *The Short Season between Two Silences: The Mystical and the Political in the Novels of Virginia Woolf.* Boston: Allen & Unwin, 1984.

Moreland, Richard. *Faulkner and Modernism: Reading and Writing.* Madison: University of Wisconsin Press, 1990.

Moreland, Richard. "Faulkner and Modernism," in *The Cambridge Companion to William Faulkner,* 17–31. Ed. P. Weinstein. Cambridge: Cambridge University Press, 1995.

Nancy, Jean-Luc. *The Experience of Freedom.* Trans. Bridget McDonald, Stanford, Calif.: Stanford University Press, 1988.

———. *The Inoperative Community.* Ed. and trans. Peter Connor. Minneapolis: University of Minnesota Press, 1991.

Neighbors, Jim. "Plunging Outside of History: Naming and Self-Possession in *Invisible Man.*" *African American Review* 36 (Summer 2002): 227–242.

Nietzsche, Friedrich. *The Birth of Tragedy.* Trans. Walter Kaufmann. New York: Vintage, 1967.

———. "The Philosopher: Reflections on the Struggle Between Art and Knowledge," in *Philosophy and Truth: Selections from Nietzsche's Notebooks of the Early 1870s,* 131. Trans. and ed. D. Breazale. Atlantic Highlands, N.J.: Humanities Press, 1979.

North, Michael. *The Dialect of Modernism: Race, Language, and Twentieth-Century Literature.* New York: Oxford University Press, 1994.

O'Meally, Robert G. "The Rules of Magic: Hemingway as Ellison's 'Ancestor,'" in Speaking for You: The Vision of Ralph Ellison, 245–71. Ed. Kimberly W. Benston. Washington, D.C.: Howard University Press, 1987.

Pater, Walter. *Selected Writings of Walter Pater.* Ed. Harold Bloom. New York: Columbia University Press, 1974.

Pessoa, Fernando. *The Book of Disquiet.* Trans. Richard Zenith. New York: Penguin Books, 2000.

Peters, John G. *Conrad and Impressionism.* Cambridge: Cambridge University Press, 2001.

Pizer, John. "Jameson's Adorno, or, the Persistence of the Utopian." *New German Critique,* no. 58 (Winter 1993):127–51.

Porter, Carolyn. "Symbolic Fathers and Dead Mothers: A Feminist Approach to Faulkner," in *Faulkner and Psychology,* 78–123. Ed. Donald M. Kartiganer and Ann J. Abadie. Jackson: University Press of Mississippi, 1994.

Ray, Martin. "Language and Silence in the Novels of Joseph Conrad." In *Critical Essays on Joseph Conrad,* 19–40. Ed. Ted Billy. Boston: G.K. Hall, 1984.

Readings, Bill. *Introducing Lyotard: Art and Politics.* London, New York: Routledge, 1991.

Robinson, Cedric. *Black Marxism: The Making of the Black Radical Tradition.* Chapel Hill: University of North Carolina Press, 1983; 2000.

Ronell, Avital. *Crack Wars: Literature Addiction Mania.* London, Lincoln: University of Nebraska Press, 1992.

Rosenthal, Michael. "The Problem of the Fiction," in *Critical Essays on Virginia Woolf,* 87–199. Ed. Morris Beja. Boston: G. K. Hall, 1985.

Said, Edward W. "Conrad: The Presentation of Narrative," in *Critical Essays on Joseph Conrad,* 28–46. Ed. Ted Billy. Boston: G. K. Hall, 1985.

Schaub, Thomas. "Ellison's Masks and the Novel of Reality," in *New Essays on Invisible Man,* 123–56. Ed. Robert O'Meally. New York, Cambridge: Cambridge University Press, 1988.

Scott, Bonnie Kime. *Refiguring Modernism: Vol. 2: Postmodern Feminist Readings of Woolf, West and Barnes.* Bloomington: Indiana University Press, 1995.

Smith, Marcus. "Religious Experience in *Miss Lonelyhearts,*" in *Nathanael West's Miss Lonelyhearts,* 37–52. Ed. Harold Bloom. New York: Chelsea House, 1987.

Smith, Valerie. "The Meaning of Narration in *Invisible Man,*" in *New Essays on Invisible Man,* 25–54. Ed. Robert O'Meally. Cambridge: Cambridge University Press, 1988.

Snaith, Anna. *Virginia Woolf: Public and Private Negotiations.* New York: St. Martin's Press, 2000.

Snead, James. *Figures of Division: William Faulkner's Major Novels.* New York: Methuen, 1986.

Spillers, Hortense J. *Black, White and in Color: Essays on American Literature and Culture.* London, Chicago: University of Chicago Press, 2003.

Stepto, Robert. *From Behind the Veil: A Study of Afro American Narrative.* Urbana: University of Illinois Press, 1979.

Swanson, Diana. " 'My Boldness Terrifies Me': Sexual Abuse and Female Subjectivity in *The Voyage Out.*" in *Twentieth Century Literature,* 41 (Winter 1995):284–309.

Vaneigem, Raoul. *The Revolution of Everyday Life.* Trans. Donald Nicholson-Smith. London: Rebel Press, 1967; 2001.

Veitch, Jonathan. *American Superrealism: Nathanael West and the Politics of Representation in the 1930s.* Madison: University of Wisconsin Press, 1997.

West, Nathanael. *Miss Lonelyhearts.* New York: New Directions, 1933.

Wexelblatt, Robert. "Nathanael West, Paul Valery and the Detonated Society." *ELN* 25 (March 1988).

Wisker, Alistair. *The Writing of Nathanael West.* New York: St. Martin's Press, 1990.

Woolf, Virginia. *Jacob's Room.* New York: Harcourt Brace Jovanovich, 1922, 1997.

———. *The Common Reader. First Series.* Ed. Andrew McNeillie. New York: Harcourt Brace Jovanovich, 1925; 1984.

Žižek, Slavoj. *The Sublime Object of Ideology.* New York, London: Verso, 1989.

———. *Enjoy Your Symptom: Jacques Lacan in Hollywood and Out.* New York, London: Routledge, 1992.

———. *Tarrying with the Negative: Kant, Hegel, and the Critique of Ideology.* Durham, N.C.: Duke University Press, 1993.

Index

movement and intensity, metaphors
of, 210; negative zone of art, 205;
nonidentity, 194; nonsubjectivity,
200; nuance and timbre, 209;
Pinktoes, 200; "Pork Chop Paradise",
206–7; racialism, 202, 204;
racialization, 194, 196; style, 197;
thinking movement/motion,
expressivity of, 200, 206, 212; work
as "oppositional", 197; *Yesterday Will
Make You Cry*, 210–12, 219
Historical materialism, 25
Hume, David, 171–72

I

Identification Papers (Fuss), 161
"The Ideology of Modernism" (Lukás),
19, 222–23n
If He Hollers (Himes), 198, 200, 201–3
Invisible Man (Ellison): as African
American literature, 214; blackness,
29, 171–72, 173; Brother Jack, 166;
chaos versus order, 1–3; Clifton,
187–89; cultural expectation, 167;
cultural identity/designation,
169–71; death, 189; divergent
selfhood, 184–87; expressivity and
signification, distinction between,
165, 166; freedom bestowed, 182; the
glass eye, 190–91; grandfather, death
of, 176–78, 180–81; history, 184,
187–88; identity and the "I", 163–65,
191; irony, 179–80; Jack, 190;
language, chaotic origins of, 2–3;
modernist subjectivity, 26; Mr.
Norton and Trueblood, 171;
narrative strategy, 173–74;
nonrecognition, 173; oppositional
racial duality, confrontation with,
163; oratory calling, 165–66;
propriety and identity, liberation
from, 166–67; racist convention,
181–83; Rinehart, 167–69; social
void, 172, 173; voice/voicing,
164–65; white privilege, idealization
and identification with, 183–84

J

Jacob's Room (Woolf): academic
superficiality, 100–101; academy and
church, barring of women from,
90–91; Archer, 102–3; Cambridge,
93–94, 96–98; Charles Steele, 103–6;
Clara, 78; Cowan, 94–96; Mrs.
Durrant, 77, 78; Edward Bishop, 100;
elitism, 81; feminine fault, 78–86;
Mrs. Flanders, 102–3; Florinda,
81–86; foundationalism, 92–93;
identitarianism, 88–91; identity,
refusal to narrate, 74–75, 107–8;
identity formation and subjectivity,
88; institutionalized identities,
shattering of, 73; Jacob, 75–78, 79,
81–82, 83, 84–86, 101–2, 106–8; Julia
Hedge, 91–92; language, chaotic
origins of, 3; Mr. Letts, 78; Mrs.
Norman, 79; plotlessness of, 74–75;
Mrs. Plumer, 79–80; Richard
Bonamy, 98–99, 101–2; Umphelby,
95–96; youth, 77, 89–90
Jameson, Fredric, 5, 19–20, 22, 23–24
Joyce, James, 21, 87, 88–89

K

Kant, Immanuel, 30, 171–72
Kaufman, Eleanor, 207
Kelley, William M., 201
Kermode, Frank, 153–54
Kleist, Heinrich Von, 208
Kojève, Alexandre, 17, 62, 87, 111, 139
Kracauer, Siegfried, 72, 73

L

Lacan, Jacques, 44, 57, 62, 87, 90, 116–17
Ladd, Barbara, 115–16
Language: anterior incomprehension
of, 6; chaotic origins of, 2–3, 18;
cultural identity, 3, 10; evocation
versus information, 5–6; figural
dimension of, 87–88; *Invisible Man*
(Ellison), 2–3; of modernism, 10–11;

Kevin Bell is assistant professor of English and Comparative Literary Studies at Northwestern University.